NMARK

GERMANY

ITALY

SICILY

D0058335

LUCK AND CHUTZPAH

Against all odds

A Gift

H.G. Kahn &
Gefen Publishing House

Inviting your comments:
POB 36004 Jerusalem 91360
info@gefenpublishing.com

LUCK
AND
CHUTZPAH
Against all odds

H. G. KAHN
WITH HILLEL HALKIN

gefen גפן

publishing house בית הוצאה לאור

JERUSALEM ♦ NEW YORK

Partially based on the English translation by Henry and Ruth Nijk of the original Dutch *Mazzal en Lef.*

Typesetting: Marzel A.S. – Jerusalem

Cover Design: Studio Rami & Jaki / Osnat

Cover Photo: Don & Lisa King / The Image Bank

Edition 9 8 7 6 5 4 3 2 1

Gefen Publishing House Ltd.   Gefen Books
POB 36004, Jerusalem   12 New St., Hewlett
91360 Israel   N.Y., U.S.A. 11557
972-2-5380247   516-295-2805
E-mail: isragefen@netmedia.net.il

Printed in Israel

Send for our free catalogue

Library of Congress Cataloging-in-Publication Data

Kahn, H. G. (Hans G.), 1922-
Luck and chutzpah: against all odds / H.G. Kahn ; with Hillel Halkin.
p.   cm.
ISBN: 965-229-159-5

1. Kahn, Hans, 1922-. 2. Jews—Netherlands—Biography. 3. Holocaust, Jewish (1939-1945)—Netherlands—Personal narratives. 4. Holocaust survivors—Israel—Biography. 5. Netherlands—Ethnic relations. I. Halkin, Hillel, 1939-. II. Title.
DS135.N6K34 1997
940.53'18'092
[B] – DC20   96-32616
                                                     CIP

To my sons:

Raphael, Michael and Benjamin

Contents

לֹא הַמֵּתִים יְהַלְלוּ־יָהּ
וְלֹא כָּל־יֹרְדֵי דוּמָה

(תהילים קט"ו)

The dead do not praise God,
nor do those that descend
into the silent Abyss

(Psalms 715)

Introduction

Whenever I mentioned some episode, some fragment, concerning the fateful events that occured during my youth, or whenever I tried to use the example of my experiences and actions, intending to help them deal with their problems, my sons invariably wanted to hear more. They were eager to get the whole story. But that tale is not suitable for casual dinner conversation, it is too full of passion and suspense.

During many long years, most of my time and energy was devoted to the creation of a fleet of rather unconventional ships and to running a worldwide shipping enterprise. Such activity obviously did not leave the time that telling the full story merits. Now that I have mostly accomplished what I set out to do, it has become possible to review the path that brought me from dungeon to freedom and from ambition to realisation.

My youth is full of dark and frightening shadows: the Holocaust. But this book tells the story of a fight, my fight, and of victory. I hope it gives strength, not only to my sons, but to all human beings – Jews and gentiles alike – who with some luck and much chutzpah can turn the wheels of fortune around.

H.G. Kahn
Caesarea, Israel
June 1996

Chapter One

My name is Hans Kahn and I own ships. Except for a while when I was dodging the Nazis, that's always been my name and I've always wanted to own ships. And I've always done what I wanted.

I suppose you could call me a Holocaust survivor. But I didn't survive the Holocaust. I wasn't liberated from it. It liberated me.

Much of the time I live in Amsterdam, in an early seventeenth-century house at the corner of two main canals, the Keizersgracht and the Leidsegracht. It's a narrow old Dutch merchant's house with six floors and a single room on each. All I know about the man who built it is that he made his living from the sea like me. On the brick walls facing the canals are five gilded shields telling the world what he did. One has a picture of a scale, one of a ship, one of a hogshead, one of a sugar loaf, one of a gunnysack.

It's one of the oldest buildings on the canals, a sober dwelling built in an age when a man put his money into his business and not into the molding of his house. If you stand facing it across the Keizersgracht, you can see that it leans slightly to the right, toward the Leidsegracht, as if pushed by the weight of the long row of houses to its left. And if you stand facing it across the Leidsegracht, you can see that it leans slightly forward, toward the Keizersgracht.

A poet might call it a monument to tenacity, struggling to hold its ground against the pressure of an unrelenting world.

But I don't care much for poetry. And all the old houses in Amsterdam lean. Look up and you'll see a horizontal beam projecting from the top of the square coping that hides their pitched roofs. These beams are used to this day for hoisting bulky items like furniture that can't be carried up the winding stairs and have to brought in through the windows. The walls were built inclined toward the street to help such loads clear the bottom floors.

Very appropriate, too, because figuring out better ways to lift a heavy load is what has made me a rich man!

In the early morning, looking out of my bedroom window, I could be in a ship in port. The houses are in dark shadow and the yellow streetlights make bright puddles in the canals. Ducks paddle on the water and gulls fly over it. Sometimes herons. It's so quiet you can hear them plash.

That's not an hour I'm usually up at. Generally, I'm out of bed by nine and ready by ten to start the hour's drive to Rotterdam, where the offices of Kahn Scheepvaart are. That's the operational and technical arm of Jumbo Navigation, my shipping company, and it's where the real work is done.

I cross the Singelgracht, not far from the Amstel River that once marked the border of the Jodenbuurt, the old Jewish quarter in which I spent my teenage years; pass the grand buildings of the Rijksmuseum and the Concertgebouw; and head out of town on the ring road that is part of the A-10, the Amsterdam-Rotterdam highway – which in turn is part of the E-10, the trans-Europe thruway on which you can drive from Copenhagen to Naples without stopping for a red light. I think of myself in the same kind of concentric circles. The order is just slightly different. First I'm a Jew. Then a European. Then a Dutchman. I've never felt any contradiction between those things.

The road cuts through tulip fields and past canals, windmills, and dikes. The windmills pump the water from the lower canals to the higher ones. If they didn't, all of western Holland would be flooded, since it's several meters below sea level and must be continually reclaimed from the sea. "God made the world and the Dutch made Holland," the Dutch like to say, and at least the second half of that statement is true. Perhaps it's what makes the Dutch so independent. That's what I like about them.

I drive fast. I'm a good driver and no one is going to tell me what to do. Once I was stopped driving 100 miles an hour on my way back from Rotterdam, where I had been aboard a ship of mine and had a drink. The cop was wearing jackboots. I hate that. I refused to take an alcohol test. He took me to the station, where the sergeant wanted to lock me up. I looked at him and said, "Do that and I'll kill you." He saw I meant it and changed his mind.

Afterwards I realized the risk I had run. But at the moment I didn't give a damn. I would have done anything to get out of there. I felt like a caged animal.

I hate all authority. All governments, too. They're a bloody, stinking lie.

I drive into Rotterdam along the Maas, the main arm of the Rhine delta that runs through the city. Docks and shipyards line the whole length of it. It's the biggest port in Europe, Rotterdam, a city to work in, as Amsterdam is a city to live in. Before the Willem Bridge a small island divides the river into two channels. Down one of them, ships head for the North Sea. On the mainland side of the other is Kahn Scheepvaart.

We occupy two floors and a bit of a third in a four-story building at 100 Haringvliet. On the top floor is my and my son's office, the Engineering Department, the Bookkeeping & Administration

Department, and a conference room. The Operations, Commercial, Crewing, and Technical Departments are on the floor below, together with the command room or "aquarium" – a large space with big windows in which the department heads generally sit. One floor further down is Kahn Logistics, which helps move cargo to destinations that can't be directly reached by sea. We have nearly 60 employees in Rotterdam, plus 200 sailors on our ships and another 15 or so people working elsewhere.

Technically speaking, we are what is known in the trade as a "heavylift shipping company." This means that we have a fleet of specialized ships that, though not particularly large, are equipped with powerful cranes that can lift loads far beyond the capacity of bigger vessels. Because of this we can transport in one piece extremely large and heavy items that a normal cargo liner can't handle: huge generators, gas turbines, modules, pressure vessels, reactors, transformers, shiploaders, derricks, floating grab cranes, ammonia converters, and the like. And we not only move what others can't, we get it to where they can't get to. If you need a 300-ton turbine unloaded on a portless coast in Indonesia, we'll do it for you. If you're sending an entire power plant to the far end of a desert in Central Asia, we'll even assemble it for you upon delivery. Just give us the address.

It's precision work. Make a mistake and you'll have a disaster on your hands. Suppose you have to deliver three cranes to the Israeli port of Ashdod, each weighing 200 tons and thirty meters high. That's as tall as a ten-story building. We did it a few years ago. We had to calculate to a centimeter what lashing points to tie them to, to keep them from going over the side in bad weather; to design new lifting gear; to drop the wheels of those cranes directly on their tracks with no margin of error to speak of. And we had to do it while keeping the ship from listing more than one-quarter of one degree, which I assure you isn't simple.

We work for the big boys: ABB, General Electric, General Motors, Hyundai, Mitsubishi, Siemens, and so forth. That means we have to be highly flexible, because they make very technical stuff that must be tested before shipment but has to go the minute it's ready, since it costs huge sums and the interest on it is greater than the freight. They've been building this thing for three years, and now they don't want to wait another minute. And so little Hans says, "I'll look after it for you. Be a nice boy, and I'm a nice boy. Squeeze me, and I'll squeeze you. If anything goes wrong, you don't have to pay. But I'm going to charge you high prices."

And they say: "Okay."

Why?

Because their shipping costs are only 4% or so of their total overhead. It's not a significant amount for them to pay more and get the service they need. And if there's a delay – say a problem in the testing – they tell me: "Sorry, old boy. That ship of yours can wait."

This doesn't make me very happy, not when maintaining a ship costs many thousands of dollars a day. But I can't afford to lose my special relations. They're the big boys and I'm the little stinker.

You can afford to operate that way as long as the balance is in your favor. We're now moving a liquid gas plant from Korea to Malaysia in several voyages. It's in hundreds of sections that have to be brought to a port called Kemaman and towed up the Paka River on barges. The Koreans don't usually pay well, but this time they did. For such a project you have to organize deep loaders and all sorts of other things in advance. The Koreans aren't going to do that. Neither are the Malaysians. They know we're better at it than they are. It's a hell of a good proposition.

You have to keep an ear out. We have offices in Singapore, Tokyo, New York, and London, and agents in many other places.

It's their job to know what's going on, what's being ordered, what's happening politically.

But the politics aren't always nice. Let's leave them out of this.

There's no fuss when I enter the office. No "Hello, Mr. Kahn," "How are you, Mr. Kahn," "Good morning, Mr. Kahn." One or two hand waves is all.

I like it that way. I've tried to build the company to work without me. By now, except for emergencies, I should be background music. What I look for in hiring a man is not just ability – that goes without saying – but character. I want individuals who can solve their own problems and make their own decisions. Of course, if they make the wrong ones, I might chop their bloody heads off... but no, I don't do that, really. I've rarely fired anyone after six months of working for me. And no one who has worked more than six months for me usually leaves. My employees know I'm loyal to them. I don't give them rules. I wouldn't dream of asking them to punch a clock. If there's work to do, they stay until it's done. If there's none, they go home. It's the same with our ships. I've never told any of our crews that they have to prepare to unload even if they come into port at one o'clock in the morning, but they know damn well without being told.

The first thing I do upon arriving in my office is study a currency chart. This is prepared for me each morning on the basis of the latest quotes from two banks in Geneva and Rotterdam.

While our clients pay mostly in dollars, we have to settle the majority of our accounts in gulden and Deutschmarks, so it's a matter of deciding what to keep our cash in. This Monday morning in March, the dollar is holding steady. I decide not to make any changes.

Next I turn to a map on the wall. On it are magnetic counters arranged by our office co-ordinator Ineke Quist to show the latest position of Jumbo's ships.

That dark blue counter off the coast of Georgia, for example. That's the *Jumbo Challenger*, on her way to the Gulf of Mexico. She's one of three ships in the world that can lift a thousand tons in one hoist. Another is her sister ship the *Fairmast*, and a third belongs to our competition.

The *Challenger* has just loaded part of a power station in Albany, destined for Dabhol, India, and is now headed for Houston to pick up five locomotives bound for Nouadhibou in Mauritania. From there she'll enter the Mediterranean, pass through the Suez Canal, and be at Dabhol by April 24. That's not a date to miss. Soon after that the summer monsoons begin and you don't want to be in an unprotected anchorage like Dabhol in bad weather.

There happens to be a little problem, though, because the superintendent sent by Operations to Nouadhibou has reported that the only barge available there for off-loading heavy cargo is so rusty that, if the locomotives don't slip through the holes in its bottom, they'll sink it together with themselves. Leave it to the Mauritanians! Of course, they squawked like chickens when we told them we'd have to charter a barge elsewhere at their expense, but no barge-ee, no locomotive-ee. We've ordered one brought down from Rotterdam and hope it will make Nouadhibou in time to keep the *Challenger* from being held up.

The lilac-colored counter is the *Fairlift*. She's docked in Dalian, China, where she's picking up a crane bound for Egypt. Near Brazil is the *Daniella*, which is sailing empty to Houston to load cargo the *Challenger* left for her.

The *Stellaprima* is the ship moving the gas plant to Malaysia from Mipu, Korea. And the yellow counter that looks misplaced by Mrs. Quist in the middle of South America is the *Fairload*. She's on her way up an upper branch of the Amazon to a Peruvian river port called Iquitos, carrying power station equipment from the U.S. She's got a pilot aboard and is a day ahead of schedule. That's good, because by April 10 she has to be turned over in Albany to a Japanese company that has time-chartered her.

Iquitos is some 1,500 miles as the crow flies from the mouth of the Amazon on the Atlantic and only 500 miles from the Pacific, but between it and the latter the Andes are standing in the way. Not even Kahn Logistics can move a power station on the backs of llamas. What we're trying to figure out at the moment – we've got an advance man working on it – is how to get upriver from Iquitos, where the water becomes quite shallow. The Peruvians have discovered a big natural gas field at a place called Camisea and some of the big American oil boys are going to develop it.

The problem is how to bring in the equipment. If it were up to the American engineers they'd build a second Panama Canal, but that's big-boy philosophy, not mine. The idea here is to think primitive; the more primitive, the better. Right now we're considering floating the stuff on enormous rafts roped to double tiers of oil drums. Thirty by twenty meters is about as long as a raft can be – any more and it won't get around the turns in the river.

I like jobs like these. They're a challenge.

Light blue is the *Fairmast*. She's in drydock in Rotterdam, undergoing massive repairs. I'll get to that.

The *Jumbo Spirit* is nearing Calcutta with a 415-ton ammonia converter, while that red counter in the North Sea is the *Stellamare*. She was slowed by a storm in the Bay of Biscay and is late for a 244-ton turbine scheduled for shipping from Vlissingen to Aqaba.

The green counter is the *Stellanova*, just finished loading a 480-ton generator in Hiroshima bound for Java. And there's the *Gajah Borneo*, which is waiting to load a large buoy and five heavy lifts in al-Musafah for Angra dos Reis in Brazil. The clients had paid to keep her waiting off the coast of India, because the cargo wasn't ready on time, but there's so much piracy on the Indian coast that we decided to move her to Abu Dhabi.

Yes, piracy. And governments do nothing to stop it. All they do is prevent ships like ours from carrying the weapons to defend themselves.

Finally, there's my private yacht, the *Ophira*. She's in Eilat right now with my Indonesian deckhand Jani, though as placed by Mrs. Quist she's hiding the whole state of Israel. But you can't blame Mrs. Quist, because Israel is a small country and the *Ophira* is a big yacht. She's 62 feet of sleek beauty, with a teak deck on an aluminum hull that I designed and had built in Holland. Last autumn Jani and I sailed her from Indonesia to Oman, with an unexpectedly long stopover in the Nicobar Islands, where we were arrested by the Indian police for diving in a restricted area. Naturally, the polite little notes sent by the Dutch embassy to inquire whether there might not perhaps be a mistake in the detention of Heer Kahn were of no help in freeing me. If it weren't for my contacts with the Israelis, who pulled strings in Delhi, Jani and I would still be there, covered with barnacles. In the winter we brought the *Ophira* to Eilat, and next spring we'll sail her through Suez.

I own three homes ashore, but the *Ophira* is my favorite. Once I get a mile out to sea on her, I'm a free man.

I go through the papers on my desk and step into the Engineering Department next door. Engineering is the section I like best. That's why I've put it next to my office. Making money isn't very interesting. It's not even something I ever particularly wanted to do. Building ships is. And in the shipping business you have to build all the time. You can't even speak of profits. That's a misconception. Whatever we make has to be reinvested, because otherwise we'll be stuck with a bunch of obsolete hulks.

The ship we're about to build now will be called the *Jumbo Vision* and we've ordered it from a yard in Turkey. This is the first time we've ever built outside of Holland and it's something of a gamble, since the Turks have never made heavy-lift carriers before. At 10 million gulden less than the Dutch bid, though, their offer was too good to turn down, especially since we have to come up with half of the purchase price up front, because Jumbo never takes a bank loan for more than fifty percent of the value of a ship. That's why we get better terms from the banks than do a lot of so-called countries.

There are blueprints of the *Jumbo Vision* on the walls of Engineering, and I spend several hours discussing them with our naval architect and fleet manager. We have to make up our minds, because at the last moment we've decided to build a faster ship and this calls for structural changes. The heavy-lift business itself has been changing. Since our ships need greater stability than ordinary cargo liners, which can make up to 20 knots, they're forced to be slower. Until now we've considered 13.5 a good average speed, but today there's more competition and customers are more insistent on quick delivery than ever.

The question is, how much faster can the *Jumbo Vision* go?

For every extra knot, you have to sharpen the hull to reduce friction in the water, and the sharper the hull the less stable the ship. It's a delicate trade-off, and as I look at the latest plans, which are calculated for 16.5 knots, there are lines in the hull I don't like. I say they're too sharp. The architect and fleet manager disagree. We debate for most of the morning and decide in the end to plump them out and come down to 15. Every ship is a compromise.

This isn't to say that it's now taken care of. I still have to deal with the Turks. They've promised me a delivery date by the end of 1998, with stiff penalties for not meeting it, and I've obtained a bank guarantee linked to this. If I come and tell them we've redesigned the *Jumbo Vision*, I know exactly what they'll answer. "Of course, Mr. Kahn, our pleasure, Mr. Kahn, but you realize this means that we can no longer meet our original obligations." Why keep to their side of the bargain when I haven't kept to mine?

I'll have to use all my powers of persuasion to hold them to schedule. I check my appointment book, call Mrs. Quist, and tell her to put me on a flight to Istanbul on Friday. Although I'd love to send someone else, I'm the only one who can handle this. It's not even for Michael, the only one of my three sons who has gone into the business with me – and anyway, he's in Bahrein, touting Jumbo at a trade fair.

It's time for lunch, but I'll skip it. I rarely eat at work. I light a cigar and go down to the third floor to look in on the Technical Department, whose head, Jan Berkhout, is standing at a drawing board with his assistant. They're bent over plans of the *Stellaprima*, moving about differently shaped paper cut-outs with labels like:

De-ethanizer

458 tons

48.10 × 6.00 × 6.05.

The Koreans keep changing the cargo for the next run from Mipu, and each time they do the stowage plan must be redone. Their latest change, Jan tells me, is removing a 118-ton flash drum, which is still on the production line, and adding four 122-ton dehydrators instead. Now, as though solving a children's puzzle, he's trying to figure out how to place them.

I move on to our Commercial head, Peter Bloch, who's in the "aquarium." He's worried about the *Fairmast*. She was supposed to be out of drydock by the end of April, in time to move a 950-ton petrochemical reactor from Rotterdam to Yanbu, Saudi Arabia. But it doesn't look as if she'll be ready by then, and the clients are making unhappy noises.

Our only other ship capable of hoisting the reactor is the *Jumbo Challenger*. She has no room for it on board, but Peter suggests putting the cargo on a gearless ship we can charter and diverting the *Challenger* to Yenbo on her way to Dabhol to offload there with her cranes.

I ask Jan if it can be done. "The *Challenger* won't be able to lift 950 tons with a full ship unless she has enough counterweight on the starboard side," he says. "We'll have to tell them in Houston to put as much weight as they can there."

"How much?" Peter asks.

"At least 500 tons more than port."

"Impossible," says our Operations chief, Hanno van Dyk, who is sitting nearby.

Hanno speaks by phone to our superintendent in Houston, who promises to check it out. Frankly, I'm not keen on the idea. It will get the *Challenger* to Dabhol in the monsoon season and it may not even be necessary. In shipping anything can happen. I don't believe in deciding before you have to. The reactor's manufacturer hasn't even given us the required notice that it will be ready on time. Maybe it won't be. Why do anything now?

I'll sleep on it tonight. Making decisions isn't just knowing the facts. You can know them all and still not know what to do. You need an instinct for sorting the facts out into what's important and what isn't. It's an automatic process with me. Sometimes I program it before going to bed and wake up in the morning with the answer. It's not me who has figured it out. It's 'it.'

Meanwhile, I'll go have a look at the *Fairmast*.

The *Fairmast* is what we call a D-class vessel, built in 1983 with 6350 tons deadweight and a cargo capacity of 15,000 cubic meters. A little over a year ago she did a job in China, delivering an atomic power station from France. One of the pieces weighed 1000 tons. It strained her to the limit and some steel plates in her double bottom torqued several centimeters. It was nothing serious, but we decided to bring her into the Manila Bay shipyard for repairs.

In Manila Bay they put her in a drydock with two other ships, both considerably larger than she was. You can't monkey around with a steel bottom under water. They began cutting the torqued plates out. And then, before they were replaced, the yard decided to refloat the dock in order to tow one of the bigger ships out of it. It was a crazy thing to do. Refloating the *Fairmast* without all her plates was like making you go for a walk without your vertebrae. And although she might have seemed smaller and less valuable than the other ship, she was worth $10,000 a day while that big boy made only $6,000. But the shipyard was too bloody stupid to think that way. "No," they said, "we're going to do it." "Not if we can stop you," we said, and we went to court and got a restraining order. They disobeyed it, boarded the *Fairmast* by force, and refloated it. It totally cracked the ship. The whole top plate of the double bottom was warped.

You wouldn't have believed it. You might not have noticed anything just by looking at it, but that whole ship was useless. The only solution was to put in a complete new middle section.

By now I trusted no one but the Dutch. There was nothing to do but get the *Fairmast* back to Rotterdam, where she had been built.

The insurance boys didn't like that. They went blah-blah-blah and insisted there were other ways to repair the ship. "All right," I said and I wrote out a statement and gave it to their lawyer to sign. It didn't say very much – just that his company was responsible to all eternity if lives were lost due to faulty repairs. He began to cough as though he had swallowed a mouthful of my cigar smoke. "Hogh! Hogh! Hogh! But is it the only way, Mr. Kahn? Perhaps there's a cheaper one."

"I'm sure there is," I agreed. "And it will land you in jail."

The insurance boys paid.

That's the *Fairmast* over there. That high yellow shape sticking up along the river among the jumble of derricks and warehouses is her mast crane. I'd know our ships anywhere, at any distance or angle.

It's always impressive to see a ship in drydock, even if it's not a very large one. Viewed from the bottom of her hull, the *Fairmast* towers 25 meters to her deck and another ten meters to her bridge. And since her deckhouse and mast crane are located on her starboard side to allow maximum deck space for large cargoes, she's propped up there by a series of huge hydraulic jacks that look like crutches. She's one big invalid.

A ship in drydock is like a patient in the hospital. And if you climb the metal stairs to the dock's upper rim and look down where the *Fairmast*'s hold used to be, you can see the operation in progress.

Of the 110 meters of her original length, 60 have been cut out of her midsection, leaving her fore and aft parts disconnected. But 30 meters of the new midship are already being placed in position. Welders are joining them together, fastening them with steel beams that look like sutures. Amid the flash of their acetylene torches the men seem to work in silence, drowned out by the roar of a ventilator pumping air to workers in the double bottom through a huge hose that resembles a giant vacuum cleaner's. Tools, wires, pipes, and cable spools lie scattered like surgical instruments.

In the new 30 meters, the water ballast compartments are exposed in naked cross-section. On each side of the *Fairmast* are rows of these, the contents of which are pumped back and forth to control the heel of the ship during cargo operations by computer-operated remote controls on the bridge. And facing inward are slotted columns that we call the *ritssluiting*, which is the Dutch word for "zipper." An original invention of ours, these serve to create an adjustable tweendeck that can accommodate different heights of cargo in a way no one thought of before us.

I board the ship and climb the stairs to its bridge, peering into the crane house with its great winches whose heavily greased cables are thicker than a muscular arm. It makes me unhappy to see a ship like this. She's so dead and dirty, such a hell of a mess. It will take weeks to get her back into shape, even after all the repairs are finished.

Returning to my car, I come by surprise across the cut-out old sections of the *Fairmast*, still sitting in the water. I had thought they had already been hauled away for scrap. And beyond them, waiting to be returned to its stowage place in the ship, is a rectangular yellow tank some 12 by 6 meters that looks like a big tub. This is the stabilizer, and while it may not seem like much, it's the secret of Jumbo's success.

It was an idea we hit upon back in the 1960s, when I was running a company called Hycar Line. We were turning over millions of dollars and raking in the money, but I was doing it with chartered ships and didn't regard myself as a real shipowner. Neither was I attracted to the idea of buying ordinary freighters. Following the advent of the container revolution, shipping was more and more turning into a mass-production, conveyor-belt operation. I wanted something special, an area I would have to myself.

And standardized containers couldn't carry everything. Locomotives, for example, or completely assembled ships' engines, could hardly be fitted in a box – and what to do with a 300-ton transformer that had to be transported from Hamburg to Bombay?

A concept was forming in my mind. One day I went to the Krupp Company, which was shipping cranes to Saudi Arabia the way it was done in those days, assembling them to see if they worked, then dismantling them into small pieces to pack them in crates, and sending crews to Saudi Arabia to reassemble them. "Suppose I could move those cranes for you in one piece?" I asked them. "Would you be interested?" "Of course," was the answer. "Where's your ship?"

I didn't have one. No one did. And the challenge wasn't just to build one that could carry large, heavy pieces. It was to build one that could lift them with its own cranes, so that it could load and unload them anywhere.

The problem, of course, was stability. When the boom of a crane swings out over the side of a ship with a load, the heavier the load and the higher and more outwardly angled the boom, the more likely the ship is to capsize. That's simple mechanics.

How do you increase stability in such a situation? According to the conventional wisdom, by widening the base of the ship or lowering its center of gravity – that is, by building absurdly broad or absurdly heavy vessels. I went through all the traditional stability equations: that was all they had to say.

Well, then, I thought, stability equations are nonsense. There must be another way.

And then it came to me. Outriggers! It wasn't my idea. It was the Polynesians'.

The canoes of the South Pacific carried, parallel to themselves, long, thin floats to keep them from capsizing. It's like the difference between balancing on a rope and standing on your two spread feet.

I even worked out a differential equation to express how this principle could be applied to heavy loads. You'll find it referred to as "the Kahn Rule" in the curriculum of Dutch nautical colleges.

What came of it all was the stabilizer. Every Jumbo ship has one, plus a specially engineered system to attach it to the ship after it has been lowered into the water. It seems too simple to be true, but it's the reason we can deliver a 620-ton self-elevating work platform to Nigeria and place a 120-ton template on a dime in an offshore oilfield in Zaire.

There's no need to return to the office. It's been a quiet day, without a single crisis. And single crises are the exception in my business. For some reason, they tend to come in groups.

For example, you're juggling three or four different cargoes, trying to decide which to take on a certain ship. If you take the first, you can't take the second; if you take the third, you can take the second but not the first; if you take the fourth... and you have to decide at once, because otherwise someone else may grab them.

Before you have time to think it over, though, you're told that a ship of yours is heading for a congested port and will have to anchor a week before she can take on her cargo. What do you do? Instruct her captain to change course immediately and proceed to his next loading port so as to avoid extra costs and fines for being delayed? But this means that you have to find another ship available to take the cargo that's been left behind....

You tell your Operations chief to look around – and there's a call from the Commercial Department. A Jumbo ship is arriving in Pakistan with a cargo from America, something from Amalgamated Whatsis. And though there's a $100,000 fine for late delivery, those bloody stupid Whatsis boys haven't paid the freight yet. Worse yet, when you tell Whatsis' head accountant on the phone that you want to talk to his boss, he tells you the fellow is playing golf in Florida and can't be reached. "Baloney," you say. "If you don't get him in an hour I'm dumping the cargo in Colombo!" But you can't do that before your Colombo agent tells you that the quay won't collapse beneath the load, and your agent is out for lunch. And meanwhile Whatsis' lawyer is on the phone, threatening to sue you for damages – well, you get the idea...

I'm getting hungry. Maybe I'll have a rijsttafel tonight at a little Indonesian restaurant that I know.

I leave Rotterdam on the A-10. Half way to Amsterdam I pass Scheveningen, where I lived as a boy, and Rijnsburg, where

Spinoza lived. Now there's a guy I love. I must have read his *Ethics* ten times.

Near Noordwijk there are some grassy sand dunes. Although they're really quite low, they seem like mountains after the flatness of the landscape. On top of them, overlooking the sea, I lived for twenty years with my second wife. To get to our house, I turned off on the A-4 and followed some country roads.

And once, coming home on a quiet day like this, I made the turn and suddenly slammed on the breaks and pulled over to the side of the road.

I was literally trembling with anger. I was shaking so hard that I couldn't drive. And it had come from nowhere. A second before it hadn't been there at all.

I was out of control. Furious. At the Germans. At the world. And most of all at the Jews. I was so goddam mad that I started to cry.

It lasted a couple of minutes. I just sat there and cried. After a while I started to shake my head. I shook it back and forth. Back and forth. That's my way of making it go away. And in the end it does. It's like waking from a dream.

Chapter Two

Religion and money were quite casually there from the start, as though ours by natural right. No one told me that both could be lost.

My father's father, Samuel Kahn, was a German Jew from Witten-an-der-Ruhr, a follower of the modern Orthodox leader Rabbi Samson Raphael Hirsch, who fought both the Reform Jews and the ultra-traditionalists. After the great split of 1876, when parliament passed the *Austrittgesetz*, the "Exit Law" allowing German citizens to organize in whatever religious frameworks they wanted, he followed Hirsch out of the official Jewish community and started a new congregation of his own.

My father, Isidor Kahn, practiced Orthodoxy with an easy nonchalance, as if it were a sign of good breeding like the expensive clothes that he wore. He was not a very serious person. When he was young, he studied law but I don't believe he ever practiced. He was charming, gallant, and impractical, a genial man with wavy hair, thick brows, and heavily lidded eyes that seemed to hide an amusing secret. In appearance he rather resembled Maurice Chevalier.

My mother was the wealthy daughter of a Berliner named Max Jaffa, the owner of the largest private bank in Germany. It was housed in a building like a Greek temple. There were no sons to inherit it, and when she married my father, Max Jaffa adopted him symbolically by having him change his name to Kahn-Jaffa. When Max Jaffa died young, the bank passed into my father's hands.

Although my father had no head for business and the bank was soon ruined by the great crash, we were very rich for a while. When we went to St. Moritz on vacation, he rented a whole Pullman car. He drove around in an American Packard – or rather, was chauffeured in it, since he never bothered to learn how to drive. When I was quite little he took my sister Ellen and myself on a trip to Holland. My sister, who was sitting in the Packard's back seat, kept shouting, *"Meine Mühle! Meine Mühle!"* – "My windmill! My windmill!" – as if she had a premonition that one day this would be our adopted country.

My father's greatest success, it would seem, was getting himself appointed Portuguese consul in Berlin. Although the title was purely honorific, he was very proud of it and went about with a pin on the lapel of his spiffy suits, a small, spoked wheel with a red-and-green rim striped yellow on the sides – the colors of the Portuguese flag.

I was born in 1922, two years after Ellen. In our childhood snapshots we are always together, looking identical in page-boy haircuts: Ellen and Hans in matching smocks, Ellen and Hans in matching sailor suits, Ellen and Hans in matching fur coats with matching sleds. Only the eyebrows are different. Ellen's are flat, accepting. Mine are arched, challenging.

We lived in Berlin, on Hohenzollern Street, near the Tiergarten. All I remember of the house is its red plush curtains that had bell-shaped copper toggles on their draw strings. I don't remember very much of my mother Lotte, either. In a photograph, her hair is fashionably bobbed and she gazes glamorously upward as if awaiting the results of a screen test. She went out every evening, generally not with my father, and slept until noon the next day. There was a great gloom in the house. My room was above hers and I was not allowed to disturb her. Once, after I had waited all morning and finally taken out my trains and begun to play, I was summoned downstairs and made to stand silently as a punishment in the corner of her darkened bedroom for what seemed like ages. I bridled at the injustice.

My mother walked out on my father when I was four. After that she disappeared from my childhood. When she died long afterwards in Brazil, I didn't shed any tears for her.

There were always governesses. The first was an English-woman, Miss Eide. She smelled bad.

Next came Fraulein von Selchof. She was the daughter of a down-and-out Prussian Junker. By now my father was alone and I think she hoped to marry him. She must have thought I was neglected, because I remember her telling him that she wanted to take me back with her to Prussia and his saying absolutely not. What ended her career with us, however, was something else. She was quite religious and one day she told me that Jesus had risen from the dead. Impressed, I told my father, who explained that Jesus' friends had come at night and taken his body from the grave. While that satisfied me, it did not satisfy him and he gave Fraulein von Selchof the sack.

Actually, I didn't mind not having a mother as long as I wasn't yelled at for doing things like shooting marbles in the house. Then I hid behind the plush curtains.

After Fraulein von Selchof was fired, I was packed off to my Uncle Moritz's house in Cologne. One day the Packard drove up with my father. Beside him was someone new. Her name was Bianca and my father called her "Bichen." I hated her at first sight.

She was a 40-year-old spinster who had met my father at a spa and fallen in love with his suave elegance, a horsey woman with small eyes, a large mouth, a high forehead, and a jaw like a pit bull terrier's. Her father, a nouveau riche who billed himself as "the cinema king of Hamburg," had a wooden leg. He had started out cranking a projector in a movie house in which his wife played the piano, and now he owned a whole chain of theaters. Yet another, the Capitol, he built for my father as a dowry.

My father didn't pretend to love Bichen back; that would have strained anyone's credulity. What he told me was that having been powerfully impressed by her devotion to her orphaned nephew Petichen, he was marrying her to give me a mother. But small though I was, I knew that was horse manure. He was doing it for her money. Who else would support him now that the bank had failed?

They were married in 1929, the year of the crash. Soon after we all moved to Holland, Petichen too. Getting away from his creditors may have had something to do with it, but in all fairness to my father, he saw Hitler coming before most people did. That same year SA men had marched down the street on which we lived, shouting anti-Jewish slogans. Although I was too young to know exactly what was going on, I could feel the tension in the air for days afterwards.

As much as I hated Bichen, I loved Holland from the first moment. It was the complete opposite of Germany. In Germany there had been nothing but rules: how to stand, how to sit, how to eat. ("Don't slump in your seat, Hans!" "Elbows off the table, Hans!") It was all so proper, so *spiessbürgerlich*. And there was a sense of doom everywhere. Holland was free, a country of individualists. I remember my first Dutch joke:

"Why do both Dutch and Germans cross the street when they see a policeman?"

"The Germans cross it because they're afraid the policeman will kick them in the rear. And the Dutch cross it because they're afraid they'll kick the policeman."

We settled in Scheveningen, near The Hague. That's where the Capitol was. My father's attempts to manage it were predictably unsuccessful and he turned it over in the end to two brothers named Hirschberg in return for a percentage of the profits. It was a triangular building, with a red carpet in the lobby and an orchestra with a *Kapellmeister*, which continued to play overtures and finales even after the introduction of talkies. I was sometimes allowed to bring friends and even to give them free ice cream. Once, when the Capitol premiered a Dutch film called 016, based on the true story of a Dutch submarine that had circled the earth, Queen Wilhelmina attended. Ellen and I presented her with flowers. I wore a white shirt, white shorts, white socks, and black patent-leather shoes and felt extremely important.

016 was my first sea story, but I don't recall it making much of an impression. My romance with the sea started later with a book I read about the legendary pirate Klaus Stortenbecker, "The Robin Hood of the Baltic." He became my hero, a man who lived by his courage and his wits. His boat was his kingdom. He did what he wanted and was free.

I wanted to be like him. Although I had no friends, I didn't feel sorry for myself. I didn't need anyone. I liked being alone.

I never suffered from it. There were always things for me to do. I made a skatebox and rode around on it for days. I biked down the country roads. I went for long walks in the woods and stole apples from the farmers' orchards. Sometimes I went to the shore and netted crabs and shrimp. And if I wasn't out in the open, I was reading: Doctor Doolittle, Karl Mai, the Grimm Brothers (I didn't like them), Hans Christian Andersen (I did). And Robinson Crusoe, of course.

And Boccaccio. I found a copy of him on my father's shelf and read it in bed at night with a flashlight. That's how I got my sex education. I was always interested in girls. I can still tell you some of those stories now.

Everything would have been fine if not for Bichen. She was so mean it was sick, a pathological miser when it came to everything but her nephew. If she made sandwiches for the three of us, she'd put tiny dabs of butter on Ellen's and mine and great gobs on Petichen's. When Petichen had a birthday, he was given a bicycle; for mine, I got a pair of gloves. My clothes were old and worn because Bichen never bought me new ones. And I lived in a tiny attic room while Petichen had the big bedroom beneath me.

My room had its advantages, though. Bichen kept chocolates in a cabinet, and the only way to get some was to steal them. And while I was at it, I stole for Ellen too, because she didn't dare do it herself. Once Bichen caught me and locked me in my room. I opened the window, climbed out on the roof, slid down the drainpipe, and was free. It was the first of many escapes in my life.

My father saw what was happening but did nothing. I had no respect for him. I understood even then that he was a weakling.

I learned to fight my own battles. One time Bichen gave me a piece of herring for my supper that was so rotten it was fluorescent. It actually glowed in the dark. I took it and nailed it to the wall above her pillow. She screamed so loudly when she entered her room to go to bed that I heard her all the way up in the attic.

Though no longer the banker and diplomat, my father had remained the same snob. Because the local Scheveningen school was not good enough for him, I had to bike every day through the woods to The Hague, where I attended a more prestigious institution. The only real difference was that in The Hague we studied French beginning with the fifth grade. I had no idea how useful it would prove to be.

Since Scheveningen had no Jewish school, my father hired a private tutor for Ellen's and my religious education, a Dr. Wertheimer. We mostly studied the prayerbook, which bored me stiff. After a while I was switched to a Mr. Goldman, who gave me bar-mitzvah lessons. My Torah reading was from Genesis, and I still remember the beginning of it by heart, complete with the chant notes: "And Jacob dwelt in the land of his father's sojournings, in the land of Canaan..." The entire orchestra of the Capitol, led by the *Kapellmeister*, came to play at the party in my honor.

At home there was pro forma observance: Bichen lit the Sabbath candles on Friday night and my father blessed me and Ellen, laying his crossed hands on our heads, and made the kiddush over the wine. And next to our house was a low structure, one room of which contained three Torah scrolls. Sometimes, on special days like *Jahrzeits*, anniversaries for the dead, my father assembled a *minyan* or prayer group there like a landed aristocrat with his own private chapel.

One of these Torah scrolls survived the war and I donated it to a synagogue in The Hague. I've kept its red velvet cover as a memento. Embroidered on it in frayed thread is a golden crown with what looks like a Greek amphora on each side. Between the amphorae is a Hebrew inscription, dated 1904 and dedicating the scroll to "my mother and teacher Idel, who has passed away." It bears the name of "Mikha'el the son of Yitzhak Jaffa" – in other words, Max Jaffa, my grandfather.

What I liked best about being Jewish was the fact that we were *kohanim*, priests from the lineage of Aaron. This meant that, once I was bar-mitzvahed, I stood in front of the congregation on holidays with my father to give the priestly blessing. Cloaked from head to foot in a white prayer shawl, my arms extending outward while I pivoted chanting from the waist, I felt a surge of mystical power as I performed the eerily ancient ceremony.

I felt special beneath that shawl. It made me proud. Not only did I belong to the Chosen People, I belonged to the chosen of the chosen. Why, Moses was practically my uncle! Before the blessing I would step out into the synagogue's anteroom with my father while the Levites in the congregation washed our hands, pouring water on them from a silver pitcher.

To this day I can spread my fingers the way (or so I was told as a child) only a real priest can, the forefinger and middle finger to one side and the ring finger and little finger to the other, as we did while reciting the blessing. I can remember the different melodies for it, too – the ordinary holiday chant, the special Passover chant that was sung to the tune of a Seder song, and the chillingly solemn chant of the High Holy Days. When I attend services today, which isn't often, I don't join the other priests, but neither do I stand with the congregation while it's blessed. I walk out and wait until it's over. Somewhere I recall having read that a priest who doesn't bless isn't allowed to be blessed either.

Another benefit of being Jewish was the extra days off from school. First came Rosh Hashanah. The year I started junior high school in The Hague, I went to the principal and asked for two days off. "All right, Kahn." Then came Yom Kippur: another day. "All right, Kahn." Then Sukkot. "How many days is it this time, Kahn, one or two?"

I decided to go for broke. "Eight."

He looked at me wearily. "Tell me, Kahn, is it going to go on like this all year?"

I wished it could have.

By now a constant stream of relatives fleeing from Germany was passing through our home, all hoping to get to the United States, Canada, or South Africa. Many were in a state of shock, with frightened looks on their faces.

There was my Uncle Bernard, my father's youngest brother and a fat and jolly character; a doctor of law, he had discovered that he was incapable of protecting his own rights. And there was my father's eldest brother Georg, a tiny, excitable fellow with a white goatee. With him came kind, sweet Aunt Rosa, as miniscule as her husband. They had been forced to leave a flourishing wholesale textile business in Cologne, and now Uncle Georg spent his days at the American consulate, begging for a visa. Their children were already in the United States, but America didn't need old people.

Bichen's sisters and brothers-in-law from Hamburg also turned up, accompanied by their families. They were beautifully dressed and still looked every bit the prosperous burghers that they had recently been, but they were totally destitute. Bald-headed Grandpa Henschel came too, stumping around on his wooden leg with his overblown and moronic wife. The deposed cinema king of Hamburg spent his days playing solitaire on our porch.

There was also a refugee named Rabinkoff, an unassuming-looking man who was, so it seemed, a *talmid chacham*, a Jew of great Talmudic learning. For some reason my father took him in and gave him a room next to the chapel. Perhaps he considered it a Jewish duty, to be performed with the same noblesse oblige as the rest of his religion.

This Rabinkoff was the reason that my family met the Neubauers, who were to play a major role in my life. Dr. Neubauer was a German Jew who had moved to Amsterdam to become rector of its Rabbinical Seminary, and he came one day to visit our new boarder, whom he had known from Germany. With him came his youngest son Yehoshua, whom I first nearly killed and then saved.

One of my favorite occupations at this time was sailing on a lake where boats could be rented for two-and-a-half guldens a day. I didn't bother taking lessons; I just started renting boats and making every mistake that I could – capsizing, breaking the mast, and what-not. I must still have been learning when I invited Yehoshua Neubauer to sail with me, because before I knew it I was in the water and he was nowhere in sight. Luckily, the lake was shallow at that point and I had the presence of mind to dive for him. I spotted him by the bubbles rising from the bottom and managed to get him, still breathing, back to shore.

But things were getting worse at home. Bichen was turning me into a little criminal. I stole everything I could lay my hands on. If she put twelve prunes on the table, for instance, it was pointless to ask for one. I simply waited until her back was turned and ate it – and when she turned around and said (she was sure to count them), "Hans, there's a prune missing," I made an innocent face, which was something I was good at (I still am), and exclaimed: "What, a prune? I'll help you look for it." And with that I got down on my hands and knees to search. Bichen knew I was mocking her, but there was nothing she could do about it.

I branched out further afield, too. At school we had a twelve-to-two recess when the children went home for lunch. One day I discovered where the examinations were kept and snuck in during the next recess and stole copies of them. My teachers were amazed by the sudden improvement in my marks.

I was also rebelling intellectually. There was a girl I knew named Betty Kanner who was a confirmed Communist, and through her I began reading Marx. For a while I was convinced by his theories, but then I turned against them, and Betty and I began to argue. Perhaps I was also reading Nietzsche by this time. In any case, I told her that I had no sympathy for the weak. Socialism, Christianity – they were all the same attempt to gang up on the strong and drag them down. They went against human nature by trying to make a norm of the ideal. Betty was always talking about "the oppressed masses." "Where are they?" I would ask. "If they're in Holland, I've yet to see them."

Still, I enjoyed our conversations. I've always preferred playing ping-pong with a good mind rather than with a weak one that can't return my serves.

In the end, my relations with Bichen came to a head. One of the many things I was not allowed to do was to slide down the banister from my room, and one day she caught me at it and began to yell at me. Worse yet, she grabbed me and tried to restrain me.

"Let me go!" I said.

"I will not! This is my house!" she shouted.

I punched her so hard that I gave her a black eye.

At last my father realized that one of us would have to go. The Neubauers, who needed the money, were willing to take me as a boarder, and it was arranged for me to go live with them in Amsterdam.

Amsterdam was a new world. Everything was more intense, more Jewish, more cosmopolitan than Scheveningen. If moving to Holland was the first revolution in my life, moving to Amsterdam was the second.

The Neubauers lived on the top two floors of a five-story walk-up on the Niuewe Prinsengracht, a street of nineteenth-century red and orange brick houses down the middle of which ran the "New Prince Canal." It was near the right bank of the Amstel River, at the very edge of the Jodenbuurt, but already so solidly Jewish that only a single non-Jew lived on it, a bicycle repairman who also worked as a *shabbes goy*, a Gentile allowed to perform tasks forbidden to Jews on the Sabbath.

The Neubauers didn't avail themselves of his services. This wasn't because they weren't observant enough to benefit from them, but because they were too principled to resort to such ruses. They were the most honest people I had ever met, and for someone like me who was in the habit of lying at the drop of a hat, they were a salutary shock.

I learned my lesson early on. The family always had many guests, especially on the Sabbath, for which Mrs. Neubauer baked pastries filled with poppy seeds that I was very fond of. After removing them from the oven she put them on top of the closet to cool, and as soon as she left the kitchen I would come in and filch some. This had not been going on for very long when she said:

"Hans, you don't have to steal. You can eat as many pastries as you like. Just tell me when you take any, so that I can bake more. Otherwise there won't be enough."

What a difference from what I was used to! It made an enormous impression on me.

I might have been even more awed had I realized, as I did later, that Razi Neubauer was constantly struggling to make ends meet. The Neubauers had six children, and although the three eldest were already living in Palestine, a tribute to the Zionist education they had received at home, Mrs. Neubauer's sister Edith had come to join them from Vienna and there was never enough money or room. Since there was nowhere else for it, the first room on the bottom floor was Dr. Neubauer's study, which one entered directly from the front door and was almost forced out of again by the sheer resistance of his books. There were books everywhere, up to the ceiling and all over the floor. You literally had to step over them to gain access to the rest of the apartment.

Dr. Yekutiel Neubauer was a kind of modern Hasid, half European intellectual and half other-worldly Jew. The grandson of a German-born diamond dealer who had acquired Turkish citizenship while living in Rumania, and the only son of the latter's eccentric son who had embraced Orthodoxy as an adult, he had received his doctorate from the University of Leipzig at the age of 22 with a dissertation on "The Criticism of Biblical Criticism." And yet his subsequent marriage to a young woman from Poland was a traditionally arranged match that was brokered by the famous

Rebbe of Belz. He had a short beard, thick glasses, and dreamy eyes, and his absent-mindedness was proverbial. Once, it was said, he was sighted at the tram stop near his house with one leg in and one leg out of his trousers. I can't vouch for that, but I do remember him opening the sliding doors of his study to see what the racket interrupting his reading was, looking at the noisy kids in the back room, removing his glasses, and running a hand over his tired eyes as if to ask: "My goodness, am I seeing double or are all those children really mine?"

He was the soul of innocence. One time, feeling obliged to act *in loco parentis*, he called me into his study for a man-to-man talk on the facts of life. He was then writing a book on ancient Jewish marriage laws, but it quickly became clear that, from Boccaccio alone, I knew more about the subject than he did.

I shared a room on the top floor with Yehoshua and we quickly became friends. Although he was two years younger than I, we both went to the Amsterdam Jewish High School, which was located in a handsome white building on the Herengracht, one of the wealthiest streets in town. It was an excellent school, many of whose teachers had doctorates.

Actually, Jewish studies were not emphasized strongly there: we had two hours of Jewish history and two of Bible a week, and only one of Hebrew. Although I was suspended every few months for disciplinary problems, I proved to be a good student. Mathematics, physics, and chemistry were subjects that I liked. I remember our physics teacher, Pukki, chalking Einstein's famous equation $E=mc^2$ on the blackboard and declaring: "If we should ever succeed in converting the mass of this chalk into energy, we would have enough of it to power every car, locomotive, ship, and airplane in the world for several years."

I didn't mind history, either. But literature left me cold – I thought Goethe a bore and Shakespeare a bloody horror – and I suffered through languages. Despite my background in French, I felt a positive aversion for French verbs, which was softened only by the big breasts of Madame Bouman-Franchimon, who sat massaging them in front of our class while she drilled us in the imperfect indicative. My classmate Joop Chazan and I would gamble on the color of her panties. "Pink," I would say. "White!" Joop would counter, placing his bet. Then one of us would drop a pencil and we both bent down to pick it up, glancing up Madame's skirt.

Sad to say, that was my most daring sexual exploit in those days.

Already then I liked to sleep late; rising hurriedly, I would bike to school along the canals and sneak into the second class of the day while hoping no one would notice. In nice weather I went sailing on the lakes, and after a few days of this I would telephone our principal, Mr. Jacobs, and negotiate my return. He always agreed because he wanted a class with high marks and I had them. And anyway, I deserved a vacation now and then, for after sitting all day in school I had to spend two more hours every evening studying Talmud with Yehoshua under the tutelage of an old-fashioned pedant hired by Dr. Neubauer.

Amsterdam was a wonderful city. Although its 80,000 Jews, over ten percent of the population, were so much part of its life that the local slang had dozens of Hebrew words in it, most maintained their Jewish identity. There were Jews everywhere, up, down, left, right – Dutch Jews, German Jews, East-European Jews, refugee Jews, Hasidic Jews, misnagdic Jews, and of course, the old Spanish-Portuguese Jews who were called "the *meshuggene* Portuguese" because they were supposedly addled from centuries of inbreeding. And unlike the bourgeois Jews of Germany, the Jews of Amsterdam had a genuine proletariat, with shoemakers, tailors, diamond workers, and other laborers who spoke Dutch with a distinct Jewish singsong. On Jewish holidays, the Jodenbuurt closed down.

In the Waterloplein, the Jewish market square where everything was peddled from herring to old clothes, boys stood around before Passover beside piles of burning bread, crying, "*Chometz! Chometz! Wie heeft chometz?*"

Though the Nazis bombarded Holland with their propaganda, there was little noticeable anti-Semitism – and the anti-Semites who existed didn't like Germans any better than they liked Jews. Even as Hitler's army marched into Czechoslovakia, the Dutch were confident that nothing would happen to them. After all, the Germans hadn't attacked Holland in World War I and everyone knew the country was impregnable. Its very flatness enabled it to be easily flooded against an invader, as it had been against the Spanish in the Eighty Years War. And certainly the Jews of Holland had no reason to be afraid. Hadn't Queen Wilhelmina demonstratively visited a synagogue in Amsterdam after the pogroms of *Kristallnacht* to show solidarity with her Jewish subjects? In a pinch she was sure to protect them.

At Friday night dinners at the Neubauers', a German invasion was but one subject discussed. Although Dr. Neubauer's salary at the Rabbinical Seminary left little scope for luxuries, there were always a half-dozen guests or more around the festively set table, heatedly debating the issues of the day in three or four different languages. Prominent Jewish professors from Berlin disputed the causes of anti-Semitism with Hasidic rabbis from Poland in a mixture of German and Yiddish; Hebrew-speaking emissaries from Palestine argued with anti-Zionist Dutch Jews.

At other times, stormy conversations erupted on fundamental questions of religion, until it seemed as if the world around us no longer existed. Dr. Neubauer would facilitate these exchanges, often sitting quietly while they went on and then intervening to ask a question or focus things. No one was ever put down with a reference to his or her age, status, or lack of experience; every argument was subjected to a critical review on the basis of its axiomatic foundation and the consistency of its conclusions. Euclid would have enjoyed it.

And just in case there were not enough guests, the three males in the family – Dr. Neubauer, Yehoshua, and myself – were instructed by Mrs. Neubauer to bring back any homeless souls found by us at the Sabbath service that we attended before the meal. This sometimes meant another mouth or two apiece, because the three of us rarely went to the same prayer house. Amsterdam was full of synagogues, each with its own flavor and style, and Yehoshua and I would sample them as though from an à la carte menu, going separately to different ones each week.

We avoided the grand ones, of course – the stately *Snoge* or Spanish-Portuguese Synagogue on the Daniel Meyerplein and the two large Ashkenazi synagogues that stood across from it, the Grote Schul and the Nieuwe Schul. All three were Orthodox but very formal. The Nieuwe Schul even had an all-male choir and the congregants arrived in tophats, which weren't any funnier than the elaborate headgear worn by the Sephardim who prayed in the *Snoge*.

The synagogues I went to were the little ones that dotted the streets of the Jodenbuurt, especially the Nieuwe Kerkstraat. There were Dutch ones and German ones, Polish *shuls*, Lithuanian *shtieblakh*, and Hasidic *kloyzn*. I liked the Hasidic ones best. In Scheveningen I had gone through the motions of praying, but now I began to pray with real feeling – and the motions had become those of the bearded Jews beside me, who rocked back and forth with religious fervor.

I must have been about sixteen years old. It was very mystical, kabbalistic. I believed that if I immersed myself in God, I could influence the course He took. I actually thought I could bring about a change in Him. In the month before the High Holy Days

I rose in the middle of the night to go to penitential prayers. Around the Friday night table I took the side of Dr. Neubauer against the skeptics – a group that included his daughter Hannah, who was the rebel in the family. I remember an argument about *torah mi'shamayim*, whether the Torah was man-made or God-revealed, and another about *hashgacha p'ratit*, whether God took an active role in human affairs. I said He did.

Basically, I liked systems. I still do. My mind was always trying to order things, to arrange them intellectually. And a system rising to an apex, where it was presided over by a divine Superjudge who cared enough about us Jews to give us His law and rule over us, seemed a very nice idea.

Hannah Neubauer was two years older than I. Although she was very quiet, whatever she said was original. More than anyone in the family, it was she who taught me to be true to myself and not to try being what I wasn't. To this day, if my wife tidies up our house for guests and I scold, "If it was good enough for us, it's good enough for them," I think: I learned that from Hannah.

The Neubauers also made a Zionist out of me. All their children were active in Zichron Ya'akov, the religious Zionist youth movement, and because of them I joined too. Mostly this meant attending lectures and courses on a variety of subjects, including Hebrew literature from the medieval Spanish poet Yehuda Halevi to modern Jewish authors such as Bialik and Ahad Ha'am. This was not something that many youngsters did. Most Dutch Jews felt too well-integrated to think they were living in exile. The chief rabbi refused to attend functions at which Hatikvah, the Zionist anthem, was played. Even at the Jewish High School, Zionist activities were frowned upon.

Of course, some Jews took a more pragmatic view of things – like my father. He wasn't a Zionist, but when he saw that the Jews in Palestine weren't doing so badly, he began to speak differently of them. He even began to tell stories about having been dandled as a child on the Zionist leader Max Nordau's knees. But that was a pure crock. He was a phony, just like Hannah Neubauer said.

There was one thing that I didn't agree with my fellow Zionists about. Zichron Ya'akov was very *halutzic* – that is, it expected us all to be pioneers in the land of Israel and to till its ancestral soil. But farming didn't attract me. Try as I might, I could discern no higher purpose in growing cabbages.

And ever since I had seen a Zionist pamphlet with photographs of Jewish naval cadets in white uniforms who were being trained in the Italian port of Civita Vecchia, I knew exactly what I wanted to be: a Jewish sailor. I wasn't about to spend my life bent over a hoe.

Sometimes, on Saturday mornings, after dropping in on one of my Hasidic prayer groups, I would walk down the Jodenbreestraat to the port. I liked to look at the old steamships and African traders. On the way back I would pass the Amsterdam Nautical College, in front of which a few cadets might be standing, and imagine myself walking into a *kloyz* with a uniform like theirs. What would the Hasidim think? I wanted to bring the two worlds together – or at least to witness the shock when they collided.

I spent the summer of 1939 cycling through Belgium and the Netherlands with my best friend Joop Citroen, who also studied at the Jewish High School. We biked through Brabant to Brussels, where the World Fair was being held, spending the nights in youth hostels or with hospitable farmers and doing our own cooking along the way. We hardly had a penny in our pockets, and there was no school, no radio, and no newspapers to worry or distract us. Sometimes we rode high along the dikes, looking down on the little cows and houses. There were endless vistas of meadows, unknown villages, and long, tree-lined roads, and over our heads, the big Dutch sky with its boundless horizon like the sea's. At night we lay on our backs and watched the stars. I was interested in astronomy and knew the names of many of them.

One night we arrived at the Frisian side of the Afsluitdijk, the long barrier dike connecting Holland and Friesland, built to reclaim the Zwiderzee. From the distance we saw piles of sandbags, and coming closer we were surprised to see soldiers, wearing helmets and heavily armed. I had never seen real-life soldiers before. What on earth were they doing?

They themselves hardly seemed to know. "The Afsluitdijk has to be protected," was as much as they were able to tell us. Leaning back unconcernedly against the sandbags, they seemed more on holiday than mobilized to fight the enemy.

"Do you really think there'll be a war?" I asked the sergeant.

He dismissed the question with a wave of his hand, the casual arc of his cigarette leaving a cloud of smoke suspended in front of me. "If I were you, I wouldn't worry."

In September the Germans invaded Poland. Soon after, my father came to visit me at the Neubauers'. He looked extremely worried and told me that we were leaving Holland for England. Petichen was already there. I had been registered at a Jewish boarding school in Brighton and should be ready to leave at a moment's notice.

My reaction was immediate. "Absolutely not!"

It made no sense. I had only one more year until my matriculation exams and this was no time to change schools, much less countries. I didn't want to leave the Neubauers, either. For the first time in my life I was living with people in an atmosphere of trust and respect.

There was another reason, too. I was in love. The emotion was as suppressed as it was intense, for even if my feelings were acknowledged, Hannah Neubauer failed to reciprocate them. Still, my obsession with the slim, blond girl who now spent long hours painting in the attic for the art course she was taking made the prospect of a dull existence in some gray and foggy English coastal town even more abhorrent. I didn't want to be tucked away in a stupid British boarding school. I was not going to England.

Chapter Three

Hannah was a sphinx. You never knew what she was thinking. But when early on the morning of May 10th, 1940, the radio told us that the Germans had invaded Holland, all the faces in the Neubauers' living room had the same impenetrable expression. Everyone was thinking his own thoughts. Or perhaps it was the same thought: that we were now in Fate's deadly grip.

During the war's first few days we swung back and forth between hope and despair. Were we trapped like rats, or could we count on our soldiers, like the ones I had seen behind their sandbags the summer before? The radio tried to sound encouraging: the IJssel defences, the much-touted barrier created by flooding large areas of low-lying land, were sure to block the enemy advance... Vigorous resistance was being put up in the hilly Grebbe region... The Dutch troops at the Afsluitdijk were fighting courageously... Calls went out for civilian volunteers to help the war effort.

Yehoshua Neubauer and I offered our services. I was given an armlet to wear and set out on my errands biking around Amsterdam, proud to have refused a decadent life at a British boarding school. I almost felt sorry for my sister Ellen, who was vacationing on the Riviera with Bichen.

After a few days of this, my father suddenly reappeared in Amsterdam. Having thought he was in England, I was astounded to see him. There was no time for him to explain how he had returned.

"Hans," he said, "pack a bag, quick. We're going to IJmuiden. There's a fishing boat there that will take us to England."

"I'm not going anywhere," I told him. "This is where I belong."

But for once he was resolute. Or perhaps I had simply never seen him so desperate. I gave in and agreed to accompany him. Even now he had his chauffeured car, although it was no longer the Packard.

The port of IJmuiden was in chaos, packed with people like us, all trying to escape at the last minute. We pushed through the frantic crowd, looking for our fisherman. Suddenly, like a wheat field flattened by the wind, the crowd threw itself on the ground as a German Stuka dive-bomber hurtled over the wharfs, screeching down at a British warship still in port.

We found our fisherman – but his mind had been changed by the Stuka. Not even offering to double the handsome sum he had already been paid could now convince him to risk the hundred-mile voyage across the North Sea under threat of German air attack. Others had the same bad luck. We spent the night in a park, surrounded by hundreds of dejected adults and bawling children. Rumors abounded: the Stuka had sunk a boat full of refugees... The British warships would take aboard whoever succeeded in getting one of the passes to be handed out at the city hall in the morning... When morning came, however, it turned out that, although the warships were still there, they were waiting exclusively for some Very Important Persons from The Hague.

In the pitiless daylight it was clear we had no chance. The realization completely took the wind out of my father and he began to cry like a child. I tried soothing him and for a moment it seemed that he was about to pull himself together. All at once he put a hand in his trouser pocket, pulled out a handful of pills, and tried stuffing them into his mouth. I grabbed his wrist and twisted it. The pills fell to the ground. I didn't bend down to see what they were.

The return trip to Amsterdam was a nightmare. When we reached Haarlem we were held up by a long column of German soldiers and equipment. So near the coast, they were proof that the war was over. Holland was occupied.

The column was seemingly endless, yet its soldiers moved through the streets as naturally as if they had always been there. I was fascinated by the motorcycle scouts who rode in front of it. Each time they reached an intersection, they got off their cycles and directed traffic with the calm precision of a local policeman. It sent shivers down my spine. How could we ever have believed that our Dutch soldiers on bicycles would be a match for such a juggernaut?

Fascinating, too, were the passers-by with their stolid faces, too stunned by the ease with which this well-oiled war machine had rolled into their city to express emotion. Most were silent – except, I remember, for a German servant girl (thousands of such girls were employed as household help in Holland during those years) who stood brazenly waving at the German soldiers.

I felt guilty about my father, who was now trapped because of me. We returned together to the Neubauers'. When I opened the front door of the building, he halted on the steps and stared blankly ahead. Then he began to cry again.

I stood looking at the helpless man who had raised me. At exactly that moment I became an adult. Unlike him, I would never bend or surrender.

★ ★ ★

My father returned to our old house in Scheveningen and I went back to the Neubauers'.

That first summer of the occupation, it almost seemed as if nothing had happened. Although a German military regime replaced the Dutch government, which had fled to England with the queen, life went on as always. The Germans took no anti-Jewish measures and within a few days my high school resumed its old routine. And since our matriculation exams were scheduled for June, there was intensive studying to be done.

I was good at cramming for exams. Late one June evening after midnight, though, I shut the organic chemistry texts on the table and decided that I had had enough. My mind was beginning to wander. I was seventeen-and-a-half years old, I had never been to bed with a woman, and I was painfully in heat.

My real passion was for Hannah Neubauer, but however badly I wanted her, she had never encouraged my advances and clearly wasn't going to. That left Sis.

This was a young woman several years older than I who attended a Hebrew grammar class that I taught for Zichron Ya'akov. Her name was so dumb-sounding that I had renamed her Shifra after a Hebrew midwife mentioned in the Bible. Although she wasn't especially pretty, I could sense from the eyes she made at me that she was available.

I stole out of the house, jumped on my bicycle, and headed for the Amstel, the street along the river on which she lived. Once beneath her window, I whistled. There was no answer. I waited for a while and threw some pebbles against her window. Still no answer. Well, there was always my organic chemistry to go back to... but just as I was remounting my bike, the front door opened and Sis let me in. Seconds later she was back in bed with me lying beside her.

The experience, to tell the truth, was disappointing; I must have been far too excited. Sis didn't seem to mind, though, because I was given further visiting rights, of which I made extensive use.

★   ★   ★

I passed my exams and received my high school diploma. What next? Making up my mind was no problem: I wanted to go to nautical college. The problem was finding the money for it. When I told my father of my plans, he looked at me as if I were demented. "Is this what you've been given an education for?" he asked. "To end up swabbing decks?" He wouldn't even discuss the subject.

I decided to try my uncle Nehemiah de Lieme, the husband of my father's sister Rebecca, who had moved to Holland when she married him. A tall, stooped man partial to large, floppy black hats, Uncle Nehemiah was the one real Zionist in our family and had considerable influence with his brother-in-law. "My father just doesn't understand," I told him. "I'm going to be a Jewish ship owner. When we have our independence in Palestine, people like me will be needed."

But my Uncle Nehemiah was a highly practical man. "What exactly will there be to ship from Palestine on those boats of yours?" he scoffed. "Jaffa oranges? Nine months of the year they're not even in season!"

In the end, with the help of the Neubauers, who knew the Jewish director of the Rotterdam port, I was enrolled in the nautical college there. I found a room with a Jewish family and spent the summer earning my tuition fees by tutoring not very bright girls who had failed their matriculation exams in mathematics. Words like "function" and "logarithm" made them turn pale with fright. It was depressing work, but two-and-a-half gulden an hour was good money in those days. In September 1940 I started the college.

Unfortunately, I didn't stay in it past the winter. That same month the Germans started tightening the noose. They began mildly enough, stamping *Jood* in Jewish identity cards. This was a simple matter, since in Holland everyone was traditionally registered by religion at birth, and with the government exiled in England there was no one to hide or remove the town registries. In neighboring Belgium, where the king and his ministers remained, the Germans had a harder time.

This was just the beginning. Now that they had identified the Jews, the Germans could move against them. In the following months, they disconnected all Jewish telephones; then expelled the Jews from the universities; then from all other schools; then forbade them to employ Gentiles; then forced them to leave all coastal areas; and then, in May 1941, required them to wear the yellow star.

There was a method to this step-by-step approach, so different from the Germans' behavior in Eastern Europe. The Dutch were not Poles or Ukrainians. Before shipping the Jews off to the death camps, it was necessary to isolate them and to get the Dutch public to think of them as pariahs. And too unimaginative to see what was happening, Holland's Jews went on believing that each measure was the last and that the worst was now over with. The Germans were clever psychologists. They knew exactly how to create a feeling of helplessness while leaving just enough hope to keep one from striking out in desperation.

I had to leave the nautical college, while my father was evicted from Scheveningen and moved to the small town of Bussum. Seeing my chagrin, two of my teachers, as disgusted by developments as I was, offered to instruct me privately during the evening hours. Besides giving me lessons in spherical trigonometry, celestial navigation, and seamanship, they found me a job as an apprentice in the Piet Smit shipyard. A fine example of Holland at its best!

The job at the shipyard, which mostly involved bringing tools from the storeroom, paid the nominal sum of ten Dutch cents an hour, but it gave me practical experience with shipbuilding and marine engines. It also enabled me to contribute in a modest way to the anti-Nazi resistance. The workers at the shipyard, which was now producing vessels for the German navy, tried fouling things up as best they could, and one day, standing atop the scaffolding of an eight meter high diesel engine to which I had fetched a heavy valve, I saw an opportunity to join in. Some German officers with leather caps and boots had come to tour the yard, and as they passed beneath me, the valve "accidentally" slipped from my hands and narrowly missed braining one of them. With *Jood* stamped in my identity card, I was probably as lucky as the officer that it did.

Although I had dirty blond hair that let me pass as a Christian and I kept the fact of my Jewishness to myself, word of it somehow got out. Some of the younger workers took to making remarks and playing practical jokes on me, such as hiding my lunch box. Sooner or later I would find it, but the search wasted a large part of the lunch break. Once, when after looking in vain I saw one of my tormentors grin, I snapped at him:

"You bloody bastard!"

"You rotten little Jew!" he shot back. "Don't you dare talk to me like that!"

I swung and knocked him to the ground. He was too stunned to try to hit me back.

Not that people like him wouldn't gladly have dropped a whole tool chest on some German. On the whole, their attitude was, "We may not like our Jews, but they're *our* bloody Jews, and the Germans had better keep their damn hands off them!"

There were more serious incidents of sabotage too. In the shipyard was a submarine that had been commissioned for the Dutch navy. When it was finished at last, after everything had been done to delay its completion, some workers strung underwater cables across the slipway. As the sub was launched, these broke the blades of its propellor.

The Germans started searching for saboteurs. Since the shipyard was no longer a safe place for me, I left it and went back to the Neubauers'.

In Rotterdam I hadn't lived among Jews, and it was a shock to return to the Jodenbuurt in the spring of 1942 and see the yellow stars sewn prominently on everyone's clothing. I myself refused to wear one and took my chances going where I pleased without it, but it infuriated me to see how most Jews submitted. By now the Germans had organized a *Joodse Raad*, a "Jewish council" that had the job of registering Jews, issuing them special passes for leaving the Jewish Quarter, and so on. One Friday night I started an argument at the Neubauers' by telling a guest who was a member of it:

"You people are lousy collaborators."

"That's not so," the man protested. "If we didn't do it, the Germans would – and then it would be far worse."

"You're deluding yourself," I replied.

Yehoshua Neubauer agreed with me. "We should be doing something instead of waiting like sitting ducks!"

"But what?" asked his father. "We have no other options."

"We have the option of not cooperating," I said. "Why make the Germans' job easier by doing their work for them?"

In fact, in 1943 the Dutch resistance destroyed all the central archives in Amsterdam. Had that happened a year earlier, many Jewish lives might have been saved.

But the Jews lacked fighting spirit. It wasn't in their character. Not long before the deportations began, the Germans, who had already decreed that all Jewish deposits be transferred to a central bank, issued an order requiring Jews to turn in their household silver and other valuables. Most people, my father too, obeyed. It made me so mad I could have screamed. How could anyone be so stupid as to hand over everything he owned to Herr Hitler, who must have been having a good laugh?

Speaking of laughs, I was now a rabbinical student. Thinking that the Nazis might show me greater consideration if I were preparing myself for such an august position, Dr. Neubauer had registered me in his Seminary. Of course, I never went to classes. By now I had stopped going to synagogue too, although I still prayed every morning at home, winding my *tefillin*, my leather phylactery straps, around my arm.

The Neubauers were less worried than other Jews. They had their Turkish papers and thought that these would protect them.

The deportations started in the summer of 1942. *Freiwilliger Arbeitscinsatz in der Ostzone*, they were called at first – Volunteer Employment in the Eastern Territories. The "volunteers," the official story went, were going to perform labor there, for which they would be rewarded with good conditions. Incredibly, many Jews assumed this to be true. Although I was as ignorant as they were of the mass killings that had been going on for over a year in Eastern Europe, I didn't believe a word of it. It was clear to me that those going "abroad" would never come back.

The deportations took place in the middle of the night, an hour preferred by the Germans because most people were asleep then and didn't see the ghastly scenes. But who could sleep on such nights? From the top floor of the Neubauers' Nieuwe Prinsengracht apartment, by sticking my head out the window and looking to the right, I could see the processions of Jews with their suitcases moving slowly down the Weesperstraat on their way to the railroad station. Since the city was blacked out against air raids, they had to light their way by flashlights covered by blue gels. It gave them a ghostlike appearance, like columns of the dead being marched off to Hades.

For a moment I pitied them. Then I exploded with anger. Why, they were signing their own death warrants! The pathetic sight only strengthened my resolve. If the Germans wanted me, they would have to come and get me.

Some Jews began "diving," as going into hiding was called. It wasn't that difficult to find someone to take you in. There were plenty of good Christians around, like the ones who sheltered the family of Anne Frank at the far end of the Prinsengracht, the long street that ran into the Nieuwe Prinsengracht at the Amstel. But that wasn't for me. It gave me the shivers just to think of it, playing possum in some back room or attic while waiting for fists to pound on the door. I wasn't going to be shut up like that. And meanwhile, since the deportees were being asked to "volunteer" in alphabetical order, I had a few days to think it over.

Another possibility was to go underground by joining the Dutch resistance. Not many Dutch Jews did that, however, and I had no contacts to help me. And I didn't want to be underground. I wanted to be in the most open place there was. I wanted to be on the sea.

Via Radio Orange, the exiled Dutch government's broadcasts from London, I knew that the remnant of the Dutch East Indies fleet that hadn't been sunk by the Japanese was now in England. Suddenly it was clear to me: I would join it. It would be a way not only of becoming a sailor, but of fighting the Germans as well.

And so, having once refused and once been refused a trip to England, I would become an *Engelandvaarder*, "an Englandbounder," as those who sought to join the free Dutch forces were known. But how?

There were two ways.

One was by crossing the North Sea, either directly or via neutral Sweden. But the direct route was impossible because of German sea and air patrols, while getting to Sweden meant either finding a place on a Dutch coastal trader, for which I lacked the necessary connections, or cutting overland through Germany. And even I didn't have the nerve for that.

The other way was crossing the length of Belgium and France to neutral Spain and continuing to Gibraltar.

As the Talmud says, there is a short way that is the long way and a long way that is the short way. I decided to choose the latter. Although the sea was a ten minute walk from where I lived, I would head for it in the opposite direction.

Before I could do anything practical about setting out, a letter addressed to Hans Kahn was delivered to the Neubauers' address, requesting me to report for voluntary employment at two o'clock the next morning to Amsterdam's Central Railway Station.

While I sat thinking of my next move, I was told that I had a visitor. It was Hannah Kahn, who was not a relative but an ex-classmate of mine. She too had received the same letter and was debating what to do. "How bad can it be, this work that they want us to do in the East?" she asked me.

Although I didn't answer, my look of contempt answered for me.

She glanced around the room, as if looking for a packed suitcase. "You're not going, then?"

"Of course not."

"But if I don't go," she wailed forlornly, "they'll take my parents in my place. I have to choose between myself and them, don't you understand?"

I understood only too well. "Listen," I said. "Get this into your head. Sooner or later the Germans will take your parents anyway. The whole purpose of their creating this kind of moral dilemma is to make them help you with their dirty work."

"Then you're not going?" she asked again, as if hoping she had heard wrong the first time.

There was nothing I could do to convince her. In her mind she was already on her way. I never saw her again.

★   ★   ★

That night I stood at the window again, looking down at the flickering lights on the Weesperstraat. For a moment I imagined myself holding one of them. Then I turned away.

I could no longer stay with the Neubauers. My address was known and I would have to move quickly before the Germans came and took me.

I found temporary lodgings on the Rijnstraat, in the southern part of Amsterdam, with a young Jewish couple that had two small children. It wasn't the safest place, but for a few days it would be all right.

The next thing was to get hold of false papers certifying that I was a good Aryan. I had been told that a certain Mr. Hillesum, a prominent member of the Jewish community, was able to provide them. Such a document would get me as far as Belgium.

Hillesum was not at home when I called, but as soon as I mentioned the code word I had been given, his wife realized why I had come.

"Come back with two passport photographs," she told me.

How stupid not to have thought of that myself!

That same day I returned with the photographs. She took them, wrote my name and address on a slip of paper, led me into the living room, removed a book from a shelf, stuck the photographs and address inside it, and returned it to its place. "You'll hear from us," she said. "It may take two or three weeks, but we'll see to it."

I couldn't believe it. You didn't have to read many detective novels to know that a bookcase was just about the most obvious place to hide anything. And what I had realized, the Gestapo would realize too.

Besides, two or three weeks was an eternity. I had no intention of hanging around that long. And from Mrs. Neubauer I had two addresses in Antwerp, one of a relative of hers who could put me up and one of a Jewish pharmacist who could get me a forged Belgian identity card. What difference did it make if I was a Belgian goy or a Dutch one? I could pass as either, since Flemish and Dutch were practically the same language. Mrs. Hillesum must have thought me a queer customer when I said, "You know, I think I've just changed my mind. I'll take those photographs and my address back. I need a little more time to consider it."

I returned to my lodgings.

"Well," anxiously asked my young landlady, who knew the errand I had gone on, "were you succccessful?"

"Not exactly," I said.

Her face fell. "You mean those people can't get you papers?"

I knew that she and her husband were desperate to escape too. They were thinking of trying to get to Sweden or Switzerland but had no chance of making it without forged documents.

"It's complicated," I said.

I didn't want to tell her about the Hillesums. It was by then a general rule to trust no one. We lived like hunted animals. Anyone could give you away if caught, even your best friend. As a matter of fact, I had run into my best friend Joop in the streets of the Jodebuurt a few days before, and while each of us had told the other that he had decided to make a run for it, neither of us had even asked what the other's plans were.

And besides, if it wasn't safe enough for me, it wasn't safe enough for her either.

"Please," she begged. "You have to help us." All she wanted was the Hillesums' address. She would take care of the rest.

Now I was sorry that I had told them anything. And yet why not give her the address? They were trapped anyway. The Hillesums were their only chance. What did they stand to lose?

On the other hand, you never knew. Perhaps they could go on living where they were. If the Hillesums were raided, the Germans would be on their doorstep in no time.

"Please," she said.

The younger of her two children was a lovely three-year-old boy.

I gave her the Hillesums' address and the code word and explained why I thought them too risky. Then I set about arranging my departure.

It was neither as easy nor as immediate as I had hoped.

There were two things left to do: say my goodbyes and get hold of some money. The money part was difficult enough, but saying goodbye to the Neubauers, my father, my uncles and my aunts was far more daunting. The thought of a parting handshake with people who might no longer be alive when I returned – if I returned – was like the thought of visiting a deathbed. How could you say *tot ziens*, "See you again," when the odds were that there would be no again?

First I went to see Uncle Georg and Aunt Rosi. They had already "dived" and were hiding in an attic in the Jodenbuurt. Yet though the darlings didn't say anything, it was clear that they knew the score. Those two sweet, once so sprightly people sat staring at me with dull, lifeless eyes. They were completely finished, simply waiting for the moment when they, too, would be taken away.

I would have liked to breathe some fire into them, but it was useless. They wished me luck, and I them, even though I knew that my wishes would make no difference.

My father, by now, had left Bussum and was living in a third-rate boarding house in The Hague. I put my yellow star in my pocket and set out on the several hours' bike ride to see him.

I arrived in the nick of time. He had just finished making arrangements to be hidden in a lunatic asylum, where he thought he would be safe. Although I suspected this of proving that he belonged in one, I wasn't going to argue about it.

In any case, he was happy to see me and agreed that I should try to get away. Bichen and Ellen were now in Lisbon, thanks to his Portuguese connections, and perhaps I should try to join them there. Unfortunately, he had no money left to give me. The only thing he had not surrendered to the Germans was some fairly valuable Persian rugs, which Uncle Georg and he had hidden with the neighbor in Bussum by dragging them out of the house through the back garden at night. This neighbor was a director of the Dubec cigarette factory in Amsterdam and lived there most of the time. My father gave me a letter to him, deeding him the carpets on the condition that he let me have as much money as he could.

We didn't have much to say to each other. What could we have talked about? I spent the night with him and before we parted the next day he placed his hands on my head and blessed me, the way he had done on Sabbath eves when I was little. Then he turned around, entered his little boarding-house room, and closed the door behind him.

★ ★ ★

Back in Amsterdam, I first went to see the Dubec man. He was a tall, heavyset fellow, quite a jolly type, who received me hospitably in his private office. I showed him my father's letter. Fortunately, he grasped the matter at once, saving me the trouble of going into details. Without further ado, he began to look for all the cash he had available. All in all he managed to collect some five thousand gulden, quite a large sum by any account. No doubt we could have gotten more by selling the carpets on the open market, but he also could have fobbed me off with a bit of small change, and I felt grateful that he hadn't done so.

My farewell call on the Neubauers, who had already given me a number of addresses that would prove most helpful in the months to come, was almost my undoing. On my way from the friendly Dubec man, my pockets bulging with money, I found the Waterloplein teeming with German military cars and the *Grüne Polizei*, the special police force of the Gestapo, busily sealing off the area. No sooner did I reach my old room on the Nieuwe Prinsengracht than Hannah Neubauer arrived, out-of-breath, with the news that the Germans were going from house to house, arresting every single Jewish resident. We were caught, so it seemed, in the middle of one of the first *razzias* – the total neighborhood round-ups instituted by the Germans as a result of their disappointment with the turnout for their *Freiwilliger Arbeitseinsatz* campaign. Those caught in these dragnets were sent to a transit camp in Westerbork, and from there to camps in Eastern Europe.

The Neubauers' Turkish papers would hopefully see them through, but I had no protection whatsoever. Suddenly Hannah had an idea. "Come, Hans," she said, climbing the stairs to the attic. I followed her and she pointed at the large coal bin that stood with its padlock in the corner. Without another word I lifted the lid and scrambled in among the coal lumps and the grit. Hannah banged the lid back down and clicked the lock shut. I heard her steps as she ran back down the stairs.

The next hours were the worst of my whole life. At times there was utter silence, as if I were the last person on earth, and at others shouts and shrieks quite close to me. As much as I tried to orient myself, it was impossible inside the blackness of the closed bin to tell exactly where these were coming from. The people I heard could have been the Neubauers or the neighbors in the adjoining apartments.

More and more I felt sure that Hannah and her family had been arrested. I felt sick. Then furious. Then panicky. If the Germans had taken the Neubauers and the whole house was empty, I was a dead man. I might as well be buried in a coffin deep in the ground. In fact, a coffin would be more comfortable than this bin in which I would die semi-crouched, choking on coal dust and my own bile.

I heard loud footsteps tramping up the stairs. Someone waved a flashlight, and through a crack in the wood I caught a glimpse of a pair of heavy leather boots. Should I cry out and join the Jews at the railroad station? But I also might be shot on the spot. Ready a few seconds previously to give anything to be heard, I was now praying to go unnoticed. And as luck would have it, there was so much dust in my nostrils that I was dying to sneeze.

The narrow beam circled the attic and the boots passed in front of the coal bin. For a moment they stopped there. Then, just when I believed myself to be lost, their owner turned and left the attic. The entire episode must have lasted several minutes, but it seemed to me like hours.

★ ★ ★

Hannah could not help laughing when she removed the padlock and I crept out, black as pitch. Although the Neubauers had passed a few anxious moments, their Turkish papers had been honored.

Giddy with relief, I began to laugh too, but as soon as we looked out the attic window, our laughter stopped abruptly.

The Jews below were indeed no longer "volunteers." Massed together in the Nieuwe Prinsengracht with their hands held at the backs of their necks, they resembled frightened prisoners-of-war. Beside them, in one big heap, as if waiting to be torched into a bonfire, were piled the belongings they had been allowed to take with them. Every few minutes, an army truck drove up. The flap was let down and a human cargo was shoved inside to the snarls, jeers, and laughter of the soldiers and police.

Something snapped inside me. "*Chayes!*" I cried out, much louder than I should have. The animals!

Hannah quickly pulled me away from the window. It was a good thing I hadn't been heard.

"I can't stay in Amsterdam one more day," I said. "I'm leaving tomorrow."

"How?" she asked. "Where?"

"I'll head for the Belgian border and try to get across."

She thought for a moment. "I have a non-Jewish girlfriend who has cousins in Brabant, farmers who live close to the border. Maybe she can help."

She sewed my five thousand gulden into the waistband of my pants. When we looked back out the window, the Nieuwe Prinsengracht was quiet and deserted. Hannah slipped downstairs, taking her papers, and biked off to talk to her friend Babette. After a while, she returned. Her friend would escort me to the farm.

★ ★ ★

It was my last night in Amsterdam. Hannah and I lay side by side but apart, whispering. At long last we fell asleep. Just before closing my eyes I rolled onto my side, looked at her, and asked her to promise to try to escape to England. She did and gave me a photograph that I have kept to this day.

The next morning her friend and I cycled to the railroad station. We had already wheeled our bikes into it when I said:

"Just a second. I forgot something."

I walked back out, took the yellow star from my pocket, and dropped it in a nearby mailbox.

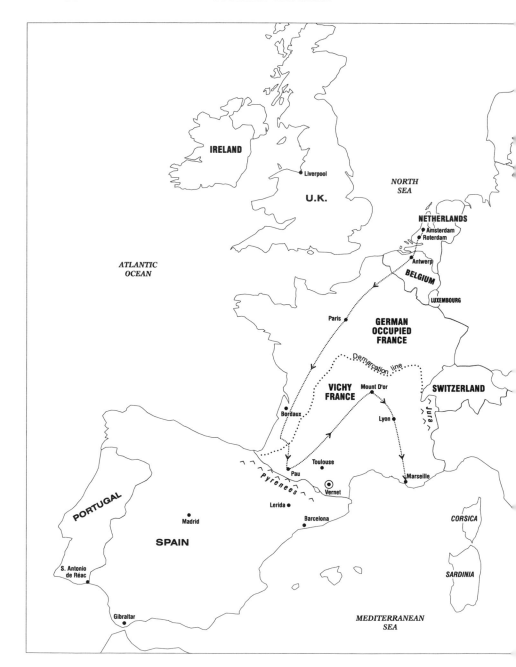

The Flight

Chapter Four

My plan, as I explained it to Babette, was simple:

"We'll put our bikes on the train. That way we're most likely to look like two young people going on a hike. You buy the tickets – youth fares with bicycles."

Even though the station was crawling with German military policemen and Babette looked a bit shaky, it worked. As I had thought, no one challenged us when we walked along the platform, smiling and talking while pushing our bikes. We were even allowed to use the freight elevator to get to the platform. We put the bikes inside the freight car and took our seats next to the window. In no time we left Amsterdam behind us and the Dutch countryside was rolling by. Although I had always loved its broad expansiveness, I wasn't touched by it today. The years in Holland had been good ones for me, but now they had been taken away as abruptly as they had begun.

Mainly I was concerned with the possibility of an identity check. The train was a local that stopped at every town, and each time we halted I was afraid German soldiers would enter our compartment to ask for our papers. But our luck held, and after what seemed ages we were cycling through Brabant, the southern-most district of Holland.

Babette wanted to return to Amsterdam that same day, and soon after arriving at our destination she headed back. She didn't even bother telling her cousin what my plans were, and thinking I wished to hide on his farm, he promptly suggested that I go to work in the cowshed. Even after I told him that I meant to proceed at once to the Belgian border, he tried talking me out of it. "It's a risky business," he said. "A Jew like you would do better to stay here with me."

"That's very kind of you," I answered. "But I'm an *Engelandvaarder*. I have to push on."

I didn't add that I had decided long ago that farming was not for me.

That same evening he showed me a path through the woods that would lead me across the border.

I departed the next day, leaving my bicycle as a gift for him. To lessen the danger of being spotted by a passing patrol he had advised me to wait until dark, but long before the summer sun had set I impatiently swung my small bundle of food and clothing over my shoulder and set out into the woods.

It was a hot July day and soon I was sweating heavily. Fat horse-flies swarmed over me, a new one settling on my face for every one I brushed off. Before long I realized I was in trouble. In my haste I had not listened carefully to the farmer's directions, and while at first I was sure that I was walking straight ahead, I now began to fear that I was going in circles. Was I already in Belgium or still in Holland?

I had learned my first lesson as a fugitive: never let your concentration slip.

My whereabouts were soon made clear by two Belgian gendarmes who appeared through the trees. Burly fellows, they had a daunting look. "Good day," they said in the bumpkinish

Flemish accent that the Flemings resented us Dutch making fun of. "Where are you bound for?"

"No place special," I answered, trying to sound like them. "I was just out for a walk."

"With that pack?"

I should have thought of that! "Well, actually, I'm on my way to Brasschaat." That was the first town on the Belgian side.

"Through these woods? Your papers, please."

At this point it struck me that wholesale lying was getting me nowhere. And although their tone was intimidating, they didn't strike me as types who would relish turning me in to the Germans. "Look," I said. "I have no papers. I'm from Holland and I didn't take them with me. I can't stand the damn Dutch any more and I'm going to my aunt in Antwerp. And it looks like I've lost my way."

That succeeded beyond all expectations. The two of them broke out laughing so hard that they actually began to totter. "You're walking to... to..." They had to calm down before they could finish the sentence. "Antwerp?" That started them off again. "To visit your *aunt*?" Another wave of hilarity. "And then you'll mosey along to your uncle in London? You've still got quite a way to go."

They poked each other in the ribs. By now it was clear that they had a pretty good idea of who I was. Suddenly they grew serious. "You see that path? Follow it and it will take you to Brasschaat. And make sure you find a roof over your head before dark, because this place gets lousy with German patrols then!"

I started walking as fast as I could in the direction they pointed to, having learned two more things. One was that, although I was already a good liar from childhood, I must from now stick to lies with enough truth in them to be credible. The other was to trust my intuitions. When faced with a split-second decision, that was all I would have to go by.

Though the days were long, it was getting dark when I reached the outskirts of Brasschaat. There weren't many houses along the road, but they made up in size for what they lacked in number. Every few hundred yards stood a huge villa, surrounded by an even bigger garden. I was clearly in a wealthy suburb.

I halted in front of a large house that stood partially hidden by some neglected-looking shrubbery. It seemed empty. I decided to give it a closer look, approached the back door, and gave it a gentle push. It almost fell off its hinges.

I stepped inside. Except for the mice whose turds I could smell, the place was obviously deserted. It was so dark that I had to grope my way to the top floor. Too exhausted to look for a mattress or a blanket, I lay down on the bare floor and was fast asleep at once.

Only when I awoke the next morning did I realize the condition of the house. The entire floor around me was littered with empty bottles, cigarette butts, and left-over food. In the hallway, in front of the open door of a broken toilet, lay a copy of the *Völkischer Beobachter*, the Nazi newspaper. It was only a few days old and a German soldier had used it to wipe his behind with. Those weren't mouse turds I had smelled.

I left in a hurry.

Lesson four: inspect your surroundings more carefully before plunking yourself down in them.

By now I was beginning to understand that if I went on being stupid, I wasn't going to get very far. But realizations were one thing and thinking ahead was another. Seeing a tram that said "Antwerp," I jumped aboard it, congratulating myself on my luck. I even had the foresight to stand up front next to the driver, where I could keep an eye out for danger. A moment later, however, as I saw the conductor making his way up the aisle, I realized that I had done it again. Here I was with five thousand gulden sewn into my trousers and not a sou of Belgian money to buy a ticket with! And there was not even a stop ahead to get off at.

I put a hand in my pocket, jiggled it there as if searching for some coins, pulled it out empty, and gave the conductor the same baffled look I once had given Bichen when there was a prune missing from the table. "Honestly, I don't know what happened to me this morning," I said... in perfect Amsterdam Dutch.

Luck was with me again. The conductor put his mouth close to my ear and asked where I was going.

I told him the address and he instructed me where to get off the tram and how to walk from there.

So far I had every reason to be favorably impressed by the Belgians.

My reception by Mrs. Neubauer's cousin, a single parent with several small children, was most cordial. I could stay, she told me, as long as I wanted – or at least until I had done everything necessary for continuing my journey.

The first thing was changing some money, which she did for me with the help of friends. Besides being able to pay my way around Antwerp, I could now make a financial contribution to her household. It wasn't much in return for the risk she was taking, but it was the best I could do.

Next I headed for the pharmacy. A bell tinkled as I entered, summoning a shrunken old man in a white coat from a back room. I came to the point straightaway:

"My name is Kahn and I'm from Amsterdam. I'm a good friend of the Neubauers. They told me you could get me a Belgian identity card."

The man stared at me as if I were speaking Chinese. "Your prescription, please," he said.

Had I walked into the wrong place? I pulled out the piece of paper with the address the Neubauers had given me. No, there was no mistake. "Here, look," I said. "I wrote down exactly what Mrs. Neubauer told me."

The old pharmacist studied the paper. "Neubauer, Neubauer," he mumbled as if repeating the name of a new drug he hadn't heard of. He shook his head, waited another moment to see if there was anything else I wanted, and turned his back on me to continue with some job.

I was dumbstruck. I might as well have ceased to exist for him. Just as I was about to head for the door, a young woman stepped out of the back room.

"Betty!"

I couldn't believe my eyes. It was Betty Kanner, my old friend from Scheveningen.

Had she heard me and recognized my voice? I didn't know, but she pulled me into the back room and began giving me a different dose of medicine. "Hans, where are your brains? Do you think you can just walk into a place like this and ask for false papers as if they were nose drops? How was the owner supposed to know you weren't a German informer? And how did you know he was the owner? He could have been an assistant who knew nothing about what goes on here. You could have cooked not only your own goose, but ours too!" After such a tonguelashing, I didn't dare ask Betty what she was doing there. With her political views she was very likely in the underground, but I never found out. And I was too happy to care. Without her miraculously turning up, I would have been worse off than in Amsterdam.

Even then the old pharmacist was not easy to appease. Betty had to give me her warmest personal recommendation before he forgave my rashness and gruffly promised to see what he could do.

He asked me to write down a few personal details, and I gave him the passport photos I had taken in Amsterdam.

A few days later the forged papers were in my hand. Hans Kahn from Amsterdam was now Hendrik de Groot, a naval cadet from Louvain. I had even been given my first choice of occupation!

There was no point in my hanging around Antwerp any longer.

My next stop would be Paris, where I had yet another address from the Neubauers, that of a Mrs. Weissglass. I intended to get the lay of the land there and decide how to get to the Spanish border in the south.

There were still express trains running from Brussels to Paris, but even with my new identity this seemed too risky a route. If I were in the Germans' shoes and looking for runaway Jews, I thought, I would concentrate precisely on such main arteries rather than on slow, local trains. And so even though I felt nervous on the latter, which took forever, I rode them until the last stop before the border. There I got off and walked across some fields into France. It was a nice summer day and there wasn't a soul in sight. Other local trains and buses took me to Paris.

I was learning – how much, I was shortly to find out.

★ ★ ★

Mrs. Weissglass was at home when I rang her bell, but it was a bad time to have arrived. Although she was sobbing so hard that it was almost impossible to understand her, I eventually made out that the Germans had just arrested one of her sons on the Brussels-Paris express.

She did not know the details and it was only much later, when I met him in London, that I learned them from her other son Max, who had been on the same train. The two of them were traveling with forged Belgian ID cards like mine, and they probably would have gotten away with it had not Max's brother, when asked "*Sind Sie Jude?*" by a German officer in a routine check, lost his head and blurted out, "*Ja.*"

As incomprehensible as such a blunder seemed, I understood it. It wasn't simple to switch identities overnight. If you had been a Jew all your life and never denied it, you might easily revert to your old behavior when frightened or caught off-guard, answering such a question as automatically as if it had been put to you at a dinner party. By the time you realized your mistake a second later, it would be too late.

It was not enough to have Hendrik de Groot's papers in my pocket. I would have to be Hendrik de Groot.

Or at least to behave like him. If I walked into a café on the Champs-Elysées, for instance, I had to remind myself not to do it as Hans Kahn, who would have stepped in timidly, looked cautiously around, and chosen a corner table to wait quietly for the waiter while trying to make himself inconspicuous. The Belgian naval cadet I had become strode confidently in, chose a center table, called for the waiter in a loud voice, and sat there looking pleased with himself while ogling any pretty girls nearby.

At first it was difficult. Gradually, I learned to act the role and even to like it. It certainly made Paris more fun.

And Paris was Paris. Despite the German occupation I was enjoying my first visit there immensely, regretting only that I hadn't paid more attention to Madame Bouman-Franchimon's verbs. The atmosphere was even freer than in Antwerp. Jews walked about unhindered, there were few German uniforms in evidence, and I felt as if I were on holiday.

I walked the streets and boulevards and up and down along the Seine, taking in most of the tourist sites except for the churches. I didn't even go to Notre Dame. This wasn't a matter of piety – by now I had stopped praying and keeping the other ritual commandments, except for the prohibition on eating pork, which I still observed. But according to Jewish law a priest wasn't allowed to enter a cemetery and be defiled by contact with the dead, and since there were burial vaults in the cathedrals, I kept away from them. Whatever else, I still was Moses' nephew!

Much of my time I spent in the Jewish quarter around the rue des rosiers. It was there that I changed money when I needed to and took most of my meals, since the restaurants were kosher and didn't ask for the coupons with which the French had to buy food. And though much of what one heard there was wild rumor, one could learn a lot by culling the facts from the speculation.

One thing I found out was that, although a small strip of French coast abutting the Spanish frontier on the Atlantic was in German hands, the rest of the border all the way to the Mediterranean belonged to Vichy, the pro-Nazi French government that administered the south of France. It was from there that I would have to attempt the crossing into Spain. And since I had one last address from the Neubauers, that of friends who had fled from Paris to a small town in Vichy called Mont d'Or, I decided to make that the next station on my trek. By now I had come to realize that there was no point in thinking ahead more than one step at a time. After that, the imponderables were too great.

The restaurants along the rue des rosiers buzzed with stories about the *passeurs*, the smuggler-guides who could be hired in Paris to conduct you into Vichy. But many of these had unpleasant endings, tales of people being swindled, or betrayed and arrested, while the *passeur* disappeared with their money. Nor was this the only risk. The *ligne de démarcation* between the zones was closely patrolled by the Germans and even with an honest *passeur* you could be caught. All in all, it didn't appeal to me.

Looking at a map, I hit on an alternative.

The demarcation line, I saw, did not run evenly across France in an east-west direction as I had thought. Rather, it extended roughly from the Swiss frontier to Tours, then turned sharply south as far as the Spanish border. And since the east-west section was closer to Paris than the north-south one, it stood to reason that it was the preferred escape route. If I were a German, I would guard it more carefully.

Ergo, the place to cross was south of Tours – the further south, the better.

Studying the map further, I decided to attempt the crossing near the town of Pau, which lay just inside Vichy some one hundred miles south of Bordeaux and about half that distance from the Spanish border. The one drawback to this plan was the long train journey it entailed through German-occupied France – but precisely this would make it the less conventional escape route. "Do the unexpected" was becoming my motto.

★ ★ ★

Thus far I had avoided direct trains, but the sheer length of the journey to Bordeaux, and the need to avoid repeated transfers, made me decide to risk an express. I left Paris at midday, on a train that made one stop in Poitiers, fairly close to the *ligne de démarcation*, and then continued on a virtually parallel track to Bordeaux.

My Belgian papers were good only as far as Paris. For travel beyond that I needed a special pass – and as the train approached Poitiers and I realized that German soldiers were bound to board it for inspection, it struck me that I hadn't made a wise decision. Feeling increasingly nervous, I rose from my seat and began to pace the corridors. It wasn't just nervousness that made me do that. If I was going to have to jump off the train in a hurry, I had to discover where and how.

As I was passing through the dining car, I spotted a lone German major having a meal. My first impulse was to turn and leave. Just the way Hans Kahn would behave! Hendrik de Groot would walk casually up to the German's table and ask to join him. And somewhat to my amazement, that's exactly what I did.

I didn't quite believe I was doing it. It was as if it weren't me but someone else, someone I was watching from outside my body. I had never had such a sensation before.

"*Entschuldigen Sie, bitte,*" I began, going over to the major with a friendly smile. "I see you're having your dinner. I'm about to do the same. I thought it might be more pleasant to eat together."

"By all means, by all means," said the major. He seemed genuinely glad to have company.

I introduced myself.

"De Groot? You're Dutch."

"Belgian."

"But you speak such a good German."

"Yes. I spent my childhood years in Berlin. My father worked for a bank there. We lived on Hohenzollern Street."

"And what do you yourself do, Herr de Groot?"

"I'm a naval cadet."

"Certainly not in Bordeaux!"

"Oh, no," I smiled. "I've got a summer job there with the *Organisation Todt.*" That was the German military construction apparatus. I leaned forward confidentially. "We're building U-boat bunkers, you know."

"Really?" The major seemed interested. He was a man of about forty, blond and good-looking in an Aryan way.

"It's quite a piece of work. We're blasting them into the cliffs."

The construction of the bunkers was a piece of information I had picked up on the rue des rosiers. Fortunately, the major knew less about it than I did, since in reality the bunkers were being poured from concrete along the water line and the cliffs were entirely in my imagination.

"And how did you get to work for the *Organisation Todt?*" the major asked.

How indeed? "Excuse me while I go ahead and order before telling you about it," I said, signaling the waiter and reading the menu several times while I racked my brain. "Can I treat us to a bottle of wine, *Herr Major*? I see you're drinking *Weisswein*. Waiter, please bring us a nice Mosel." My mind suddenly shifted from my father's well-stocked wine cellar in Scheveningen to the railroad bridge near the Piet Smit shipyard that was the only crossing over the Maas connecting north and south Holland. During the German invasion Dutch marines had unsuccessfully tried blowing it up. "Ah, yes. You were asking me about the *Organisation Todt*. I was in a work brigade sent from Oostende to help repair a drawbridge in Rotterdam blown up by the Dutch resistance. They dynamited the wheelhouse. Blasted the damn place to pieces. You don't happen to have a pen on you, do you? Thanks." I took a napkin and began to draw. "Here, you see, the bridge had a pylon at either end, like this, on top of which was a huge wheel that hauled a cable attached to a railroad trestle – that's this double line over here..."

The major bent over the napkin while I felt the train reduce speed as it pulled into the station in Poitiers. Glancing up, I saw that the platform was full of *Grüne Polizei*. I went on talking as though in a trance. "The trestle slid up and down grooves in the pylon. They placed a charge here and a charge here..."

"*Ausweise, bitte.*" A German military policeman had entered the dining car and approached us.

I put my hand in my left breast pocket, looked surprised, stuck it in my right pocket, clapped it to my forehead, and said nonchalantly: "*Ach, ja*. I left my papers in my jacket. I'll go get them from my compartment."

I rose from my chair, thinking feverishly of what to do next.

The major put a restraining hand on me. "*Schon gut*," he said in an annoyed voice to the policeman, haughtily raising one eye as if scrutinizing a bothersome insect.

"*Jawohl, Herr Major!*" The policeman clicked his heels. He raised a stiff arm. "*Heil Hitler!*"

And he was gone.

Over dessert, coffee, and several brandies, our conversation continued all the way to Bordeaux. I told the major about my childhood in Berlin and he described his military career and the death of his brother on the Eastern Front.

"*Schrecklich, schrecklich*," I commiserated.

Slightly tipsy, we stepped out on the platform of the Bordeaux station. Nobody would have thought of asking for my papers in such company. "Allow me to recommend a suitable hotel not far from here," said the major, but by now enough was enough. He might decide to walk me there and order another round of drinks at the bar. Telling him that I had a French girlfriend who was dying to see me, I warmly shook his hand and wished him luck.

I checked in at a hotel that was no doubt cheaper than the one the major had in mind and made my way to the bus station in the morning. After a tedious journey involving several transfers and endless waiting for local buses that slowly wound their way through the undulating French countryside, I arrived at a village not far from Pau.

★ ★ ★

This village, whose name I no longer remember, turned out to be an agreeable little place, and I decided to spend a few days there. It had a cheap, noisy cafe that reeked of Gaulloises, the French cigarettes that smelled like fireplace smoke. Nearly all of the good-natured ruffians in the place were puffing away at these stink bombs while drinking an acidic red wine that went down less easily than the Mosel on the Paris-Bordeaux express. Most of them, I soon realized, were smugglers and black marketeers. In the German-occupied zone it was by now almost impossible to buy coffee and tobacco, items that could still be gotten in Vichy – and since supply always follows demand, numerous channels had sprung up for it to flow through. It was precisely what I was looking for.

I didn't stay long in the cafe that night. Asking the waiter what there was for supper, I was told, *"Un très bon cassoulet, monsieur."* "Fine, that's what I'll have," I said, not knowing what it was, and soon I was hungrily consuming a delicious stew of beans and an unfamiliar-tasting meat.

"C'est quoi, cette viande?" I asked the next time the waiter passed.

"Mais c'est du porc, monsieur."

I put down my spoon and sat contemplating what was in my stomach. The more I thought about it, the sicker I felt, and the sicker I felt, the more I thought about it. All at once I ran out, found a deserted spot behind the building, and threw up.

I came back the next day to find the café even more crowded. At night, it appeared, many of the customers were at work, but during the day they hung around the tables, regaling each other with their latest escapades. Listening as best I could, I gathered that most of these stories had to do with fooling the Germans while going back and forth across the border. No one asked me who I was or where I came from. Such questions would have been considered indiscreet in such a place, and besides, people on the run from the Nazis were wandering all over in those days. Everyone agreed that the Germans were bastards; there was nothing noteworthy about trying to get away from them.

While observing the clientele from a slight distance, I noticed a tall fellow in a blue beret leaning drowsily across a table by himself. Although he seemed to have just woken from an intoxicated sleep, I had a feeling that he wouldn't say no to more wine and I offered to buy him a glass. *Pourquoi pas?* He came over and sat down next to me.

His name was Pierre and he seemed more interested in chain-smoking Gauloises than in making conversation until I asked him when he planned to make his next trip across the border and whether he would mind taking me with him – for a small remuneration, of course. The mention of money perked him up considerably. It took us very little time to agree that for several thousand francs he would get me to the other side that same evening.

It proved a walkover – literally. We crossed fields and followed footpaths as far as the border, which ran parallel to a macadamized country road. There we crouched for a few minutes in a drainage ditch until a German patrol passed by. As soon as it was out of sight, we simply walked across the road in the darkness, passing the invisible demarcation line. I had never known that smuggling was so easy.

We were supposed to spend the night in a shepherd's hut, but although it was past midnight, Pierre first had some business to finish. He conducted it behind a tree, negotiating at length the purchase of a sack full of cigarette cartons. In the morning he gave me a few packs. I took them even though I didn't smoke; one never knew when they might prove useful. Not at all a bad sort!

After parting from Pierre, I walked to Pau and from there caught a train to Toulouse. Mont d'Or was in the Massif Central, the mountainous south-central part of France, and it took me several days to get there while changing trains all the time. In general, the only trunk routes ran through Paris. Connections between provincial towns were slow and tedious.

Each night I stayed in a different small town or village, sleeping in what was usually its only hotel. One night I filled the bathtub, took off my clothes, and washed them. In the morning I had to put them on dripping wet. All I had taken with me from Paris was a small handbag with my toothbrush and some shaving gear. I didn't even have a change of shirt.

The friends of the Neubauers in Mont d'Or were called the Bienstocks. They were living in an apartment in town and passing as Christians. Since they thought it would be too dangerous for me to stay with them, they put me up for a few days with a young farmer who lived with his wife and infant in a cottage that was little more than a big kitchen in which dogs, chickens, and the baby went in and out. The baby wore nothing but a smock and shat on the floor when it had to, after which its mother came, scraped the mess into a pot, threw it out, washed the pot, and used it later for cooking. There was also a barn with a few cows and a spring trickling out of the wall, whose water we drank and washed in. A ladder led up to a hayloft in which I slept.

The Bienstocks had two daughters. One, Thea, was about my age. She was lonely for company, and by now so was I, and we spent many hours together. Her older sister had a friend, a Dutch Jewish boy, for whom the Bienstocks had found a hiding place on a nearby farm. While we were walking through a field one afternoon, bending to pick the wild strawberries, Thea said to me:

"You know, Hans, we could arrange a place for you on a farm too. You wouldn't have to sleep in a hayloft. You'd be safe there."

In the green peace of that summer day, it should have been a tempting thought. But it wasn't.

"I'm not a farmer, Thea," I said. "I'm an *Engelandvaarder*."

She gave me a wistful look and let it drop.

That evening her parents suggested that I make Lyon my next stop. There was a Dutch consulate there that was said to be helping Jews to escape. One of its officials, a Jew named Sally Noach, had a reputation as a wonder worker.

I set out for Lyon the next day. It was raining when I got there and it rained throughout my stay. I had an ugly room in a small hotel with a window facing a wall, and the city struck me as gray, bleak, and depressing. On my first day there, I bought a change of clothes.

The consulate was full of Jewish refugees, all frantically trading gossip and looking for a safe haven. Sally Noach turned out to be a small, dark, energetic man with a singsong Amsterdam accent. After listening to my story, he told me that he would be glad to help me get to Switzerland. "If the Swiss don't catch you in the border zone," he explained, "they generally let you stay. And you have enough money to afford a good *passeur* who will make sure that doesn't happen. I can make the necessary contacts."

"But I don't want to go to Switzerland," I said. "I'm an *Engelandvaarder*. I want to go to Spain."

He shrugged. "I'm not a travel agent. But I have an idea. I know a wealthy Dutchman who lives outside Lyon and has connections with the French underground. I'll put you in touch with him. Maybe he can do something."

The wealthy Dutchman was gracious enough to invite me for lunch in his vineyard chateau. Better yet, he actually did run a "travel agency" offering "Spanish tours" – mostly for Dutch army officers who had fled Nazi internment camps and were trying to get to England like me.

"That's wonderful," I said. "When can I leave?"

He shook his head. "I'm sorry. I'd like to help, but I'm all booked up. Every one of our groups is full."

"But you don't understand!" I exclaimed. "I'm an *Engelandva-arder*. I'm a naval cadet who wants to fight, not just some bloody Jew running away!"

"I believe you, but I simply don't have a slot. There are more pressing cases than yours. Sorry."

Back I went to Sally Noach, who heard me out sympathetically. "There's one more possibility," he said. "Here, why don't you try this."

He wrote something on a slip of paper and handed it to me. It was the address of a Mr. van Lennep in Marseilles, plus an official title: *Haut Commissaire des refugiés Néerlandais* – High Commissioner for Dutch Refugees.

I tucked the note in my pocket and gratefully shook Sally's hand.

"By the way," he said when I was already at the door. "You didn't happen to know the Hillesums, did you?"

My heart sank. "What about them?"

"Their place in Amsterdam was raided by the Gestapo."

I was still in Lyon when I heard through the grapevine that the couple from the Rijnstraat had been arrested with their children.

I went to my hotel room and didn't come out again for two whole days. I didn't want to see anyone. Even my own company was too much for me. All I could think of was those two young parents and their lovely little boy and girl. I should never have gotten involved with them.

Chapter Five

Many years after the war, I was sitting on a terrace near the port of Marseilles, enjoying an excellent lunch with my company's French agent. It was a beautiful afternoon.

The restaurant had a fine view of the harbor. I sat sipping my coffee, debating whether to bring up memories from a past that was less pleasant than the sun-drenched day around us. After a while I said:

"You know, during the war I almost sailed from this port."

"Really?" said the agent. "As a passenger or as a seaman?"

"Neither," I said. "As a stowaway on a Swedish Red Cross ship."

The agent gave me a strange look. He opened his mouth as if to say something – and then closed it again. After a while he said:

"Tell me about it."

I told him briefly how I reached Lyon and was given the name of *Haut Commissaire des refugiés Néerlandais* van Lennep in Marseilles. High Commissioner for Pencil Pushing would have been more like it! The man was useless.

He was one of those tall, thin, aristocratic Dutchmen that I never liked, all appearance and no content. Arriving in the outer room of his office, I was told by a secretary to come back another day. Mr. van Lennep, it appeared, had important business.

"I'll wait," I said.

She shrugged.

I waited an hour, wondering what the High Commissioner and his important guest could be talking about so quietly that I never once heard their voices. Finally, he opened his door and stepped out. His office was empty. So was his mahogany desk. Perhaps he used it to keep his nail file on.

He listened to me impatiently. "I'm really quite pressured now," he said. "I suggest you come back in three months."

"Three months!" I exploded. "In three months the Germans may have won the war. I came to Marseilles because of you. I don't know a soul here, I have no food coupons, and my I.D. papers are worthless. I'm an *Engelandvaarder*. Get me there so I can fight!"

"Young man," said the *Haut Commissaire*, "I'm afraid that getting you to England isn't my problem. Mr. Noach should never have sent you here. There's really nothing I can do."

Years later I was told that Sally Noach had eventually been arrested by the Nazis, as was the wealthy Dutchman in his chateau. I never heard again of van Lennep, but I don't suppose the Germans bothered with him – unless it was to give him a citation.

I left his office boiling mad and wandered through the streets, heading instinctively for the sea. After a while I found myself on the Cannebière, the boulevard leading to the Vieux Port, the old harbor that was now a district of cafés and restaurants.

It was a hot, clear day and the girls were all in their summer dresses. The sidewalks were full of promenaders and diners eating seafood. After gray Lyon, Marseilles seemed bright and appetizing. I was in fact very hungry. Sitting down at an outdoor table of a simple fish restaurant, I ordered a bottle of wine and a bouillabaisse, a specialty of the area that I had heard about. The thick fish soup was so good that it restored my zest for life. I wasn't going to let any High Commissioner get me down. After all, here I was on the

Mediterranean – Spain was right across the water. Perhaps that was the route I should take!

While spooning down my second bowl of bouillabaisse, I noticed some small masts bobbing up and down along a quay. This gave me an idea. There was a nice sea breeze, and if I could find a boat to rent I might reconnoiter inside the new port, which was where the big ships docked. From the land side I would never be allowed to enter it, but in a boat I might slip inside.

It took some effort to convince the man renting out the sailboats that I was an experienced sailor, but a few large French banknotes eventually accomplished what my still imperfect French could not. He rigged a boat and waved jovially as I sailed off, calling after me, "Be back in two hours, don't forget!" That was more than enough for what I had in mind.

I sailed out from the old port, rounded the long breakwater, and entered the new port unhindered, continuing to tack back and forth while observing the ships loading and unloading alongside the quays. Any one of them might be my lifeline to freedom.

There were quite a few large ones, African traders to judge by their funnel markings. But Africa was not my preferred destination, and I sailed further until I reached a U-shaped basin where a number of smaller vessels were tied to the quay. One of them of them caught my attention. She was a nice-looking white freighter of some three thousand tons with the words *Croix Rouge Internationale* on her hull in large red letters beside the emblem of the International Red Cross. She was flying a Swedish flag and had on her stern the name *Emblar*, and beneath that her port of registration, Stockholm.

"The *Emblar*?" asked my French agent.

"Yes. Why?"

"Go on," he said.

Huge boxes were being hoisted from the ship's hold onto railway cars. What I wanted to know was her next port of call. Sailing past her, I tied my boat to the quay and scrambled up. Among all the sailors, stevedores, machinists, checkers, and other personnel, nobody paid me any attention. I found myself a crate and sat down to observe the goings-on from as near as possible. Not far from me sat a dockworker, a big man with a bushy mustache and the purplish nose of a heavy drinker. After a while I edged closer.

"Nice ship," I said.

He grunted what might have been agreement.

"I wonder what's in those boxes."

This time he didn't even grunt. No doubt he thought me a queer bird. He must have noticed me climb out of the sailboat and was clearly on his guard.

"Care for a smoke?" I took out a pack of my friend Pierre the smuggler's Gaulloises and offered it to him.

He took it, turned it sideways, tapped the bottom to drive out a cigarette, handed me back the pack, lit up with a match from a box in his pocket, and said by way of thanks: "Parcels for British POWs. She's back and forth with them from Lisbon all the time."

Lisbon! That suited me perfectly. I even had a sister and a stepmother there who might help me when I arrived. "When is she sailing?" I asked.

"Dunno." Although he wasn't very talkative, he didn't seem to mind my company either, since when his mates shouted that his work break was over he quietly ignored them and went on smoking. The cigarette would soon be finished, however. I had to try to continue our relationship elsewhere.

"Listen," I said, "I'm a Belgian sailor. I missed my ship when she left for Africa a couple of days ago, and I'm all alone in town.

Why don't you come after work and have a few drinks with me? My treat, of course. My name is Hendrik."

"Pierre."

Didn't the French have any other names? To my relief he accepted, and we agreed to meet that evening in the restaurant where I had had my bouillabaisse. I sailed my boat back with time to spare and went to my hotel room to wait.

Pierre II appeared as promised and even loosened up enough over several glasses of pastis to grumble about the Germans. "Those *sales boches* have screwed things up," he said. "There's not enough work in the port any more and everything costs twice as much. Pretty soon we'll be needing Red Cross packages ourselves."

I told him it was a funny coincidence about Lisbon, because that's where my mother lived. "As a matter of fact," I said, "it's the place I need to get to, because I'm low on money and she's the only person who can stake me to more. Besides, my shore pass has expired and I'll be in bad trouble if I'm picked up by the police in Marseilles. You wouldn't happen to know anyone on the *Emblar* who could help smuggle me aboard, would you? Once she's out of port it won't matter if I'm discovered, because the captain's not going to return to Marseilles because of me. He'll hand me over to the police in Portugal, and they'll release me in my mother's custody."

It wasn't bad for an improvisation, but it wasn't good enough. Pierre stared at his drink; told me that the entire port was closely supervised by the *Commission d'Armistice*, a mainly German affair run in cooperation with Italian and French police collaborating with the Nazis; murmured something about knowing no one on the *Emblar* and my perhaps finding work on another ship; and changed the subject. The time was going by. Soon we would say good night. I had to try something closer to the truth.

"Look, Pierre," I said. "I haven't leveled with you because I wasn't sure I could trust you. But I see how you feel about the Germans and I'm going to take the risk. My name is de Groot, but I'm not a Belgian sailor. I'm a Dutch naval cadet and I'm trying to get to England to join the Dutch navy. The *Emblar* is my chance. I hate the Germans so badly that I'll never forgive myself if I don't fight against them. This is your chance to fight them too."

I did trust him – but not quite enough to tell him the whole truth. I had already learned in Amsterdam that hating the Germans didn't automatically make you love the Jews.

It may have been the pastis, or perhaps he welcomed the chance to strike a vicarious blow for freedom, but when we rose to go he put his hand on my shoulder and promised to do his best. I should come back every evening to the same restaurant, he said, and when he had news he would appear.

I returned to my table in the Vieux Port two or three times, but there was no Pierre. Since my Belgian ID card was worthless, I was afraid to walk the streets during the day, especially since I wasn't sure who might have seen my sailing jaunt around the port, and so I spent the daylight hours at the cinema. I probably saw more films in that one week than in all the years that my father owned the Capitol Theater! Some of them weren't bad, and under other circumstances I might have enjoyed the suspense and the sex, but my sole thought while slouching in those dark velvet chairs underneath the dusty projector beam was to stay out of the hands of the Germans and the French police. And what I had told Pierre about money was no longer a fib. I was running up a sizable hotel bill, and if he didn't come through soon I might end up spending my last francs on a double feature.

I was despondent and almost ready to forget him when he finally turned up. He had come straight from work and was still wearing his overalls, but even through the clouds of cigarette smoke in the café I could see that his news wasn't good. None of his efforts had borne fruit. In fact, he had not been able to contact the crew of the *Emblar* at all, for they hardly came ashore and were closely watched by the Germans when they did. And that wasn't all.

"You'll have to forget about the *Emblar*, Hendrik," Pierre told me. "She's leaving for Lisbon in the morning."

Not without me, she wasn't! I had nothing to lose now. "My name isn't Hendrik," I said. "It's Hans and I'm a Jew, and if I'm caught by the police I won't just end up cooling my heels in some jail. It's a matter of life or death. You have to help."

"But what can I do, *mon ami*?"

"You can change clothes with me. Your work overalls for my civvies. It's my only hope of getting aboard that ship."

It was a long shot, and I still don't know why he agreed. It can't just have been those free drinks.

The toilet of the restaurant was quite literally a hole in the ground, and it wasn't easy to get out of my pants and keep them clean while balancing over it. Somehow I succeeded, and after prying the last of my money out of their pockets, I passed them over the partition between us and received Pierre's overalls in return. I don't know who looked funnier, me in his overalls that had room in them for two of me, or him in my pants that reached halfway around his waist, but it was no time to laugh. We exchanged a few encouraging words and went our ways.

I couldn't go back to the hotel dressed like this. So much for the new clothes I had bought in Lyon! I might as well head straight for the *Emblar*.

My plan was straightforward. I would walk right through the gate of the U-shaped basin, waving casually to the guard like a workman coming for the night shift. Such simple acts of bravado had brought me this far, and I hoped they would get me the rest of the way.

But I had miscalculated. The guard turned out to be an Italian, a real fascist bootlicker. Disregarding my wave, he stopped me and asked in broken French for my harbor pass.

"Sorry, but I left it at home," I told him. "Look, I'm already late for work, so how about just letting me in?"

He wouldn't be budged. "*Impossible*, monsieur." Either I went home to get the pass or else I waited at the gate for someone to identify me.

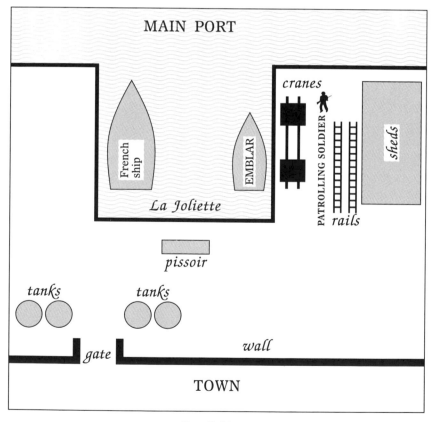

La Joliette

Neither suggestion appealed to me. "All right," I said, "I'll go look for someone myself."

I walked off until I was out of his sight and then doubled back toward the wall enclosing the basin. It wasn't all that high, and a bit further on I noticed a telephone pole within vaulting distance from the top. Climbing it easily, I soon landed on the other side of the wall. It was pitch dark there, and I had to grope my way between a number of large fuel tanks when suddenly, as if the Devil were playing games with me, I found myself facing, at a distance of twenty meters, the same Italian guard. The man stared at me as if he were seeing a ghost. I managed to keep my sang-froid and turned the nearest corner with another casual wave, after which I sprinted in the opposite direction as fast as I could, my loose overalls flapping like a sail. Close to the quayside, a providential hand had erected some malodorous public toilets. I ducked into one and waited for the coast to clear.

After a while, I looked out and surveyed the scene. The *Emblar* was moored along one of the long arms of the "U." She was lit and I could see her crew shutting the hatches and making final preparations for her departure. In the shadows across the basin from her was an old freighter that looked deserted. I walked toward it and strode unhindered on board.

It didn't take me long to discover a convenient vantage point on the starboard railing from where I could observe the *Emblar* at closer quarters. To my surprise, I was soon joined by an old Frenchman, apparently some kind of watchman. My overalls proved to be an excellent camouflage and the old geezer didn't seem to think it at all strange that some young stevedore had chosen this spot to relax. He asked no questions and even offered me a cigarette.

The *Emblar*, I now could see, was a perfectly conventional type of vessel. Midships was a deckhouse with several cabins, flanked by two gangways leading forward. At the back of the deckhouse a ladder gave access to the boat deck, on which two small lifeboats – more like dinghies – stood behind the bridge. I saw nothing else that seemed of particular interest.

Gradually, the activity aboard the ship ceased. Most of the deck lights had already been put out and the crew had no doubt gone to their bunks. If I meant to board, this was the time.

First of all, though, I had to return to the sewer-like pissoir, the only point from which I could get a safe view of the quay alongside the *Emblar*. I left the freighter, walked quickly back across the basin, and ducked once more into that dark, foul-smelling place, choking and retching while trying to keep from losing my footing and sliding into the excrement covering the floor. Peering out, I discovered that the quay was being guarded by a German soldier with a rifle, who was in the process of turning at the far end of his beat and heading back in my direction – something that had been impossible to see from my perch on the other ship.

I withdrew into the pissoir, holding my nose against the stench, and listened to the rhythm of his boots as they approached. It was absolutely regular, growing gradually louder until it came to within some twenty meters of my hiding place, then halting for a moment, and then growing fainter again. I looked out and watched the German stride down the quay until he was perhaps one hundred meters distant and then turn and start back toward me.

I let this happen a few times. His pace was so steady that you could have set your watch by it. I made a few calculations and saw that I would have to act in two stages. The first, while the soldier had his back to me, would be to make a dash for a large crane that stood opposite the *Emblar*'s stern and take cover underneath it. The second would be to wait for the German to complete another round and then clamber aboard the ship. Since the aft-deck rose only a few meters above the quayside, this didn't look too difficult.

It worked perfectly. The height from the quay to the aft-deck was even less than I had thought. I reached up, grabbed hold of the railing, and swung myself on board.

I paused to catch my breath, expecting to feel my heart pounding madly. Oddly enough, though, it had actually slowed down. It was beating as calmly as if I were in a coma, and to my astonishment, I felt more wonderfully alert than I had ever been in my life. I was totally concentrated – and so cool and collected that there wasn't the slightest twinge of fear. What was happening to me?

As in the dining car of the Paris-Bordeaux train, I seemed to be outside myself, watching some adventure film in my father's cinema in which I was playing the lead. Apart from an intense curiosity about what I would do next, the film's outcome didn't concern me. The real me, the one watching from the audience, couldn't possibly be affected by it.

I must have been literally in a trance, in a state of consciousness like a yogi's or a sleepwalker's, and the darkness on deck only heightened my sense of unreality. I have no other way of explaining the total confidence with which I proceeded to open the door of the deckhouse and enter the corridor leading to the cabins. Not until I heard loud snoring a few feet away and saw a sleeping figure through a half-open cabin door did I realize what I was doing. In another moment I would have been in the fellow's bed!

That brought me up short. I could feel my heartbeat quicken and had to tell myself to keep calm. Stealing back up to the deck, I found myself a dark, sheltered corner. From it I watched the German guard continuing on his rounds. Every now and then he let his flashlight play across the dark water and up the sides of the ship – a sharp reminder that I could not afford any more carelessness. In the shelter of the railing I crept soundlessly across the aft-deck, intending to lift a hatch and drop into a hold that had been emptied of the *Emblar*'s cargo. Damn! The hatch was closed and secured by a tarpaulin. I should have realized it would be. I pulled and pulled but it wouldn't budge. If I'd had a hammer I might have been able to knock back the wedges – and also to wake everyone aboard. I'd have to find another hiding place.

I looked about. There was only one other solution: the two lifeboats. Silently I climbed the ladder to the top of the deckhouse, untied the tarp on one of the boats, and slipped inside, making sure to return the cover to its previous position. I managed to clear some space, groped in the dark and found a flat object to use as a pillow, and stretched myself out for a few hours of much-needed sleep. My last waking thought was: I'm finally putting to sea...

★ ★ ★

I was woken by a ringing noise. For a moment, until the timbers pressing on my back made me realize where I was, I thought I was listening to the sound of an alarm clock. The ringing was the ship's telegraph, alerting the engine room to stand by for orders from the bridge. The *Emblar* was leaving – with me on it. Wasn't I a clever fellow!

Just then I heard footsteps approaching. They reached the lifeboat and halted. Someone fumbled with the tarp and four hairy hands thrust past it and began rummaging in the lifeboat. I drew my legs up to make myself as small as possible and froze. What could they be looking for?

The narrow end of a heavy crate appeared beneath the tarpaulin and I understood that they weren't looking for anything. They were simply trying to stow some extra gear. But although the crate wasn't terribly large, the lifeboat was very small, and soon the crate began pushing against me. Although I tried to make room, there was none. Why, I thought, cursing my luck, couldn't they have gone to the other lifeboat? But for that matter, why couldn't I have...

There were mutterings and muffled protests as the sailors realized that the crate was not going to fit. Then it was withdrawn and the footsteps retreated. And none too soon, for by now I was dizzy from holding my breath and sucking my ribs in as far as they would go.

I lay back with a sigh of relief.

A sadly premature one, for the footsteps soon returned. This time, to my dismay, there were more of them – it sounded as if the ship's entire crew had been summoned for some arduous task. Once again a hand appeared beneath the tarpaulin, followed by a sleeve on which were emblazoned four gold stripes. The captain's! It groped around until it seized hold of my leg, at which point an order was given, the tarpaulin was drawn back, and several strong arms hauled me out on deck.

One glance at the scornful smirk on the captain's face was enough to convince me that I wasn't a welcome guest. It did no good to beg him, in French, German, and English, to keep me on board as far as Lisbon or Gibraltar, where he could turn me over to the police. From the looks of him, he would have liked to dump me overboard tied to the crate, but this would have exceeded regulations. He barked an order and after a while the German guard appeared and I was unceremoniously marched down the gangway. Although I thought I saw a flash of pity in some of the crew's faces, he was obviously not the sort of man one argued with.

It was still very early in the morning, just getting light. The guard kept pointing his rifle at me to keep me from getting ideas but otherwise didn't know what to do with me. In the end, after asking a few questions and checking my papers, he handed me over to the French harbor police. I was, he told them, an illegal Belgian national who had tried to stow away.

Before I knew it, I was handcuffed and locked up in the harbor police station. By a nasty stroke of irony, it was located in a small tower with a balcony that offered a glorious view of the port. From it I watched the *Emblar* cast off its moorings and slowly steam away.

★　★　★

The agent threw his napkin on the table. "*Mon Dieu!*" he exclaimed.

"It had a happy ending," I assured him. "You can see that I lived to tell about it."

"Ah, yes, but *tout de même*. You see, there were three Red Cross vessels that called here regularly during the war to deliver parcels for prisoners-of-war. The *Emblar* was only one of them. I know, because I happened to be their agent."

I looked at him intently.

"What rotten luck that you picked the one of the three that had a pro-German captain. The other two were anti-Nazi. They would have taken you, *je vous assure*. Oh, I remember the bastard. Amazing that when everything else went so well, you should have ended up on the wrong ship!"

Chapter Six

It didn't look as if the French harbor police knew what to do with me either. While they were discussing my fate, the morning was getting hotter and I began to feel most uncomfortable in my baggy overalls, whose sweaty smell was becoming unbearable to me, let alone to the young French *flic* assigned to guard me. Although every now and then he brandished his revolver to warn me against making a false move, these gestures gave him such an air of insecurity that I began to contemplate the possibility of an escape.

I asked if I could go to the toilet.

"*Oui, bien sûr.*"

And my handcuffs? I couldn't very well perform my obligations with them on my hands.

This request, too, was granted and they were removed.

"Just where did you say the toilets were?" I asked.

The *flic* pointed down the stairs.

"Well, then, I'll be right back," I said.

It was no go. The *flic* came down after me with his gun and stood outside the toilet while I peed. The moment I emerged he snapped the handcuffs on again and quickly alerted a colleague to relieve him.

This proved unnecessary, however, for in the meantime the combined brains of the Marseilles police force had found a solution for me. I was bundled into a car and taken to the offices of the National Security Service, the French equivalent of the Gestapo.

The place looked more like a fortress than a police station. By now I had been around long enough to recognize the little bullies hanging around it – pitiful, toadying nonentities who could get nowhere without hitching themselves to the wagon of some greater and more power-hungry scoundrel than themselves. This was their chance to get even with life by humiliating and tormenting others. The Nazi machine was tailor-made for them.

The two French miscreants who interrogated me fit squarely into this category. As self-important as if they had caught an international master-spy, they seated themselves opposite me and went to work.

– All right. Who sent you on this mission?

– That's a good one! Who gave you the work clothes?

– Well, then, how did you know the ship was leaving?

– Suppose that's so. How did you know it was bound for Lisbon?

Their questions were so stupid that they were actually boring, and their technique for getting the answers they wanted was no less banal: a few slaps on the face and some body blows every time I disappointed them. Little by little I was pushed into a corner, where I ended up kneeling on all fours with my rear end presented to them. The only available target left, it was kicked vigorously each time I raised my head to speak.

Still fresh from my trance-state on the *Emblar*, I now discovered another mental ability – or perhaps it was a different version of the same one. The more I was hit, the less I seemed to feel it. It was as if the blows raining down were falling not on me but on somone else. I was simply there as a neutral observer.

After a while, my interrogators changed tactics. "*Eh bien,*" said one. "Why don't you get up off the floor and sit down? We don't want you to think that we have anything personal against you. It's just our job. How about a cup of coffee? Good. Now tell us what you think of France."

"I always *thought*," I said, "that France was a highly civilized country. But since meeting you two gentlemen I know better."

Madame Bouman-Franchimon would have been proud of my imperfect indicative!

I was slapped so hard that the hot coffee flew out of my hand.

After a while I began to get the hang of it. I developed a sense for when the next blow was coming and learned to ward it off by giving my interrogators worthless bits of information that made them feel they were getting something out of me. "I tell you, my name is Hendrik de Groot! I'm a Belgian naval cadet... all right, don't hit me, I'll tell you the truth. I bought the overalls from a dock worker I met on the Cannebière... He was a thin fellow, clean-shaven... No, I don't remember his name... all right, all right: it was Henri..."

That helped some, but they still refused to accept my story. What they wanted to hear was that I was a spy and that the French Resistance had planted me aboard a Red Cross ship. Just imagine the promotion they would get for unearthing something like that! The more stubbornly I maintained my innocence, the more insistent they became.

At long last, however, they seemed to get a bit weary. Besides, it was getting late and their wives were no doubt waiting at home. I was locked in a cell and left with the comforting message that in France spies were customarily shot. Yet not even this could affect my peace of mind, for at daybreak I had to be woken from a deep and restful sleep.

The interrogations and beatings continued for a few more days, but by now they hardly affected me. Each time a new face appeared, I had to tell my story all over again. I could imagine how many different reports were being written about me and how many personal descriptions were being wired to God only knew where.

The less interested my captors became in me, the more heartily they seemed to dislike me. It was as if I were to blame for not being the big catch they had hoped for. Finally, they decided to transfer me to a more plebeian prison called Le Brabant. But I only learned its name later. When I dared inquire where I was being taken as I was pushed into the van, I merely received another kick in my sore behind.

★   ★   ★

Le Brabant was a kind of halfway house, a dumping place for ordinary suspects and two-bit criminals, with appropriate accommodations. It was located in a dilapidated building in one of the poorer districts of Marseilles, apparently an old school that had been converted to a prison. The main dormitory was a large hall in which some eighty people were packed together, filling the place with the sweet-and-sour smell of sweaty socks and unwashed bodies. It was rather like being in a gymnasium without showers. Once a day we were aired in a yard separated from the outside world by a high wall topped with reels of barbed wire. It had probably once been a playground – I didn't envy the poor blighters who were pupils there.

The chief warden of the establishment was a definite nuisance. A portly Frenchman whose florid face went livid when something displeased him (which was often), making him sweat unpleasantly behind his spectacles, he also enjoyed hitting people. Every order from his superiors to interrogate one of the inmates gave him a

welcome opportunity to deal some nasty blows. Yet although I too
received my share of these, such routines no longer upset me. If
the security goons had failed to beat a confession out of me, he
certainly wouldn't either. Had I been so inclined, I could have
given him a few pointers on how to improve his tactics.

On the whole, though, we weren't badly treated. We didn't go
hungry and there were no beatings outside of interrogations. The
worst part of it was the lice, cockroaches, and bedbugs, the likes of
which I had never seen in my life. The mattresses were crawling
with vermin, and the prisoners spent long hours trying to smoke
them out by burning strips of paper or anything else inflammable.
To my intense relief, I soon saw that the little buggers didn't like
the taste of Jewish blood and left me alone.

Except for a few real criminals who formed a social élite – the
"heavies," as they were called – most of my fellow inmates were
small-time: black marketeers, pickpockets, pimps, and smugglers.
The "heavies" were clearly well provided for. Some had their own
private rooms with radios and gramophones, and were actually
"sirred" by the guards. They were even, from time to time, allowed
to relieve their itchiness by going to a brothel or visiting a girlfriend. It was, from the chief warden down, quite a freewheeling
place.

With such company to choose from, I kept largely to myself. I
particularly tried to avoid a short, dark, stocky Turk who fell in love
with me and tried seducing me with chocolates. He followed me
around everywhere and called me "Mademoiselle Hendrika," and
it wasn't easy to get rid of him.

The one friend I made in the place was also a homosexual –
perhaps my slim build made me attractive to such types – but of a
very different nature. He was an Austrian named Franz, a blond
and charming young man with genteel airs. A good storyteller, he
entertained me for hours with supposed escapades from his past

that were all contradictory. One day he was the son of a Polish count and a Viennese courtesan who ran away with an Armenian opera singer; the next day his father was a German beer manufacturer from Prague. He had been arrested for dealing in contraband while living in Antibes with an exiled Russian cousin of the Romanoffs; he had been apprehended for writing anti-Nazi slogans on a wall while touring the Basque country with a ballet dancer from Chicago. None of it added up or made sense.

Franz was very elegantly dressed and had a private room like the "heavies" in which he kept a large wardrobe, from which he sold me a silk shirt and a pair of black-and-white checked pants with which to replace my stevedore's overalls. He often took his meals in this room too; they were brought in from restaurants, complete with wine and real china. Sometimes he asked me to join him. Occasionally he made little advances by trying to hold my hand or stroke me, but he was discreet and desisted when asked.

With such a murky past, I never understood where he obtained his money from. One day, however, I awoke in the morning to find that the last of my cash was gone; it had been cleaned out of my pockets while I slept. Since Franz was the only person who knew of its existence, I naturally suspected him, but there was no point in making accusations.

Although being penniless made my prospects for survival in the outside world far less cheery, it was clearly time to depart my life of idleness in this corrupt sanitarium, whose daily routines were interrupted only by the solicitations of the obscene Turk and an occasional audition with the florid Frenchman. I had used my days to case the joint, and my conclusion was that the best escape route was a tree with a few sturdy branches that was growing near the wall of the courtyard in which we had our daily airing. The scenario was clear: a brief sprint, a leap onto the closest branch, a scramble up to the higher ones, and a jump down on the other side.

Once I succeeded in breaking out, I was unlikely to be missed for quite some time, since the prisoners in Le Brabant were never counted – not only out of sheer laziness, but because this would have exposed the aptly named system of "French leave" that was so profitable for the warders. The problem was to get over the wall unnoticed. The odds seemed against me, and though I cast longing glances at my tree, each time I promenaded in the courtyard, whose every blade of grass I knew by now, I did not feel ready to risk it.

And then some workers began digging a hole near the tree. It might have been for a sewer line or whatever – I couldn't have cared less. What interested me was the building materials they had brought and the small truck they had parked near the wall, which created one or two temporary hiding places alongside it.

I waited for the whistle that summoned us inside and then slipped behind the truck while the prisoners trooped back into the building. As soon as the last of them had disappeared, I dashed to the tree, swung myself onto the first branch, clambered up until I reached the wall, and vaulted over it... almost straight into the arms of a policeman who had been posted below for precisely such an eventuality. They weren't as dumb as I had thought! Worse yet, I had twisted my ankle as I landed and couldn't do more than hobble.

Although he was every bit as astounded as I was, the *flic* kept his presence of mind. Taking a firm hold of me, he pushed me to the office of the chief warden. I was back in prison as quickly as I had gotten out.

The warden's face turned its usual livid color. His eyes narrowed to slits. *"Alors, petit crétin, ça te plait pas chez nous?"* he hissed at me. "Let's see whether we can make you a bit more comfortable so that you'll like it better." He snapped out a command, and I was locked up in a dingy cupboard that was too narrow to lie down in and too low to stand up in. All I could do was squat or sit with my knees pulled up to my body. When the door was opened twenty-four hours later and I was released from my cage, I had to agree with *monsieur le directeur* that my lice-infested mattress was not so disagreeable after all.

Soon afterwards I was transferred. It may have been because of my failed jailbreak, but I suspected it had more to do with the Germans. By now the Nazis had, to all intents and purposes, taken over the administration of Vichy, and very likely they had concluded that I did not fit the category of inmates housed in Le Brabant.

I was summoned to see the warden. Although at first I thought that it was simply to receive another dressing down, I realized better the moment I saw a uniformed gendarme in the room. The warden gestured in his direction as if to formally introduce us and announced with evident satisfaction:

"Well, now. The two of you are going on a little picnic together."

Before I could ask where, I was handcuffed and marched out to an unknown destination.

A few minutes later I was walking down a street in Marseilles, mingling with the pedestrians – and manacled to a policeman. It was a gorgeous day. Although I had lost all track of time, it must have been autumn by now, because the leaves on the trees were yellow. That must also have been the designers' choice that year, because the girls were all wearing it too. They looked awfully pretty in their print dresses, and I couldn't help noticing how they glanced away as I approached, as one does with a beggar or an invalid. It was as though if they did it fast enough, I didn't really exist.

Those few minutes of walking to the train station were worse than all the days in Le Brabant. As a prisoner among prisoners, it now struck me, one's situation was not yet totally intolerable. Deprived of all contact with the outside world, there was a kind of comforting normalcy about it, as if such were merely the human condition and one was sharing it with all other men. But to be dragged like a leper through the sunny streets of a city, surrounded by ordinary people going about their ordinary lives – ordinary people who were disgusted by the sight of you – this was the ultimate humiliation. Suddenly I understood that a radical gap had opened between me and the world. I had become a non-person.

And the girls in yellow just made it worse. In prison I hadn't had a sexual thought. Nothing could have been further from my mind. Now, looking at these creatures who were like some species of once dear flower that I hadn't seen for a long time, my sexual feelings reawakened... into a sense of total impotence. There was not only no question of approaching them physically, there was no question of even approaching them mentally, because I was now a resident of another universe. A white-hot anger shot through me.

It was going to be a long journey. This was all the policeman was prepared to tell me when we reached the railway station. As he had obviously received strict instructions not to unlock the handcuffs on the train, we remained chained together like Siamese twins. At least now, though, I was not such a marked man, because he sat by the window with me next to him and the manacles hidden between us where the other passengers couldn't see them. It was a long trip and people kept getting on and off. One of them, a farmer's fat wife, sat squeezed against me for a long while.

The policeman was a dull fellow and hardly spoke a word to me, although perhaps he was just acting under orders. But dutifully keeping the warden's promise of a picnic, he shared his lunch with me, passing me from time to time a chunk of bread with thick slices of greasy garlic sausage to be washed down with a swig of wine. By the time we reached our destination, a small, run-down station seemingly in the middle of nowhere, we both reeked.

It was getting dark. We were the only passengers to descend from the train, which had probably stopped only for us. Although I had no idea where we were, our arrival was clearly expected, for transportation had been provided in the form of a wooden cart with two horses. Still cuffed together, we climbed aboard and drove off.

It was a slow ride along deserted country roads, and I was grateful for being spared the humiliating glances to which I had been subjected all day. The nature around us, with its good smell of fields and woods, offered a measure of consolation too... until some distance ahead, the beam of a searchlight raked the treetops. A few minutes later I saw that it was mounted on a watchtower.

The wooded terrain turned into a bare, sandy plain, in the middle of which stood some barracks surrounded by barbed-wire enclosures.

My most elemental nightmare, the dream that had ever haunted my sleep, was about to become a reality. I was entering a concentration camp.

The driver cracked his whip above the sweaty backs of his horses, urging them to a final effort as if impatient to enter a haunted castle whose terrifying apparitions could not bear the light of day.

The effect on the policeman was altogether different. His dour face actually creased into something like a smile, and he even hummed some tune under his breath. With the camp gates in sight, his mission was completed. I heard the rattling of a chain as the gate swung open.

I felt weak and dizzy. Slowly, my mind began to clear and I mumbled something that no one could have understood. It wasn't a prayer – I had given up that nonsense long ago. It was simply a few words of encouragement to myself. I was going to get out of this place alive.

Chapter Seven

The gate shut behind me. *"Wieder so ein Jude?"* asked a bored voice.

Yes, another Jew. And my life depended on no one knowing it.

That same evening I found out that I was in a place called *Camp disciplinaire Vernet d'Ariège*. The name meant nothing to me. It was like a blind spot on the map of France. But the next morning, when a bright sun rose in the sky, I made out the white peaks of the Pyrenees on the horizon to the south. We weren't far from the Spanish border. My morale rose considerably.

I was taken to a room in some kind of administration building, where a fat German with close-set eyes was sitting behind a desk. He addressed me in German. By now I was becoming quite expert at being grilled by sadistic nobodies. *"Pardon,"* I answered. "I don't speak German. Here are my papers. As you can see, I am Hendrik de Groot from Belgium."

This forced him to resort to a French sentence he knew well. *"Vous êtes juif?"*

Although I did my best to stare as though he had suggested something indecent, my thoughts were racing ahead. What would I do if I were asked to drop my trousers?

I wasn't. Looking at my papers, the German simply growled, "Hendrik de Groot. *Cadet officier de marine.* Caught stowing away on a ship en route to Lisbon." He shook his head, mystified why anyone would want to flee the new order bestowed by the Master Race on its lucky neighbors, and ordered me sent to the political prisoners' wing. While I would have preferred an immediate parole, this was infinitely preferable to the Jewish barracks that had recently been added to the Vernet camp. From there I would have been put on a train to unknown destinations, never to return.

Vernet, I soon learned, was divided into what were called *quartiers*, compounds of ten barracks that were separated from each other by barbed wire. Each barrack had three tiers of "beds," broad wooden platforms on which 20 to 30 men slept. By comparison, an ordinary prison cell was an island of privacy.

The camp's original inhabitants were Spanish refugees, men who had fought in the Republican army and escaped across the border after its defeat. Equally loath to hand them over to Franco's police and to grant them the freedom of France, the democratic French government had restricted them to makeshift housing under the rubric of *"residence forcée."* There they had squatted, accommodating themselves to their refugee quarters and feeling almost at home in them – until one day, France having fallen to the Germans and Vichy, they found themselves in a full-fledged concentration camp. Their new rulers, pleased to be in possession of such useful property, had decided to upgrade it, complete with transit facilities for Jews.

Already in jail in Marseilles I had learned that, no less than civilian society, prisons have a rigorous hierarchy. But there were two crucial differences between Vernet and Le Brabant. The first was that status and rank were a matter of life and death here. The second was that, whereas in Le Brabant the élite had been formed by the criminal "heavies," in Vernet it was composed of the Spaniards. Most were socialists, communists, and anarchists who had fought the good fight but had long ago abandoned whatever ideals they had had in the jungle of camp life. It was them you had to befriend if you wanted to eat or simply to avoid constant harassment. They had mastered every trick in the book. Or, as they liked to say, "*Il y a des combines*" – you had to know the angles.

The first of these was finding yourself a Spaniard.

While I was looking for one I observed that food, roll-calls, and defecation were the three main themes of camp life. And while the former was scarce, the latter two were in abundant supply.

We shat into metal barrels placed beneath a wooden platform with holes in it. You simply squatted above a hole and let go. Given the food and the condition of our bowels, it was not surprising that the barrels filled up fast. And most of the inmates not only had chronic diarrhea from the diet, which consisted mainly of beets, cabbage, and turnip soup, but were also chronically hungry. Although physical torture was not practiced in Vernet, starving its population to death was considered quite legitimate.

Even worse than helping to fill the barrels was the task of emptying them. The two men assigned to this chore were each given a long pole. After wedging themselves beneath the platform in a dark underworld of awful stench, they stuck their poles through the barrel's two handles and carried it to a nearby ravine. The guards stood watching from a safe distance, laughing heartily whenever a jerky movement caused the stinking mess to slop over the rim and befoul the prisoners' rags.

Not having many volunteers, the latrine detail was generally assigned to inmates guilty of some infraction. Yet when I heard that the ravine into which the barrels were emptied was situated outside the camp perimeter, the loathsome procedure started to look attractive. On one of my first mornings in the camp, I decided to be late for roll-call.

My punishment was indeed prompt, but so was my letdown. As soon as our French guards opened the gate to the ravine, they were replaced by a platoon of heavily armed SS soldiers. The latrine detail held no prospects whatsoever. Unless I intended to do it by suicide, I would have to escape the camp in some other way.

The morning roll-call or *appel* took place in front of the barracks at six o'clock. Or rather, it was supposed to take place then, but in fact we were often left standing outside for hours. As a rule of thumb, the colder it was, the longer we were made to wait.

After the *appel* came breakfast. This consisted of a chunk of gray, moist bread about as big as the back of your hand, and something black and hot that went by the name of "coffee" and was ladled out by our barracks head, a Spaniard named José, into the tin mug that was each prisoner's all-purpose utensil. The bread was the only allotment of solid food until the next morning. You had to choose between swallowing it immediately, which meant filling your stomach and having nothing left for later, or trying to make it last.

Since I liked the idea of at least simulating regular mealtimes, I chose the latter course on my first morning, priding myself on my self-discipline as the men around me wolfed their entire ration. Dividing my bread into a few portions, I stuck them underneath my straw mattress. But when my rumbling stomach urged me to retrieve the last of my ration that night, it was gone. It wasn't weakness of will, it dawned on me, that had made the others eat their bread at once, but simple experience. The next morning I gulped mine down too.

Lunch was *la soupe*, ladled into the same tin mug by a prisoner while José looked on to make sure that no one snuck back into line a second time. He also picked the ladler, a job coveted by all, since it allowed one to barter for favors by scooping portions from the bottom of the *marmite*, the big vat, where bits of potato, cabbage, and beet root – a vegetable generally fed in France only to pigs – were to be found.

As for supper, there was none. Nor was the rare potato or bit of fatty sausage that we sometimes got for "Sunday dinner" enough to make a difference. You couldn't survive without a *combine*.

After a while I developed a defense against hunger. It consisted of perfecting the technique I had developed under interrogation in Marseilles. When my hunger pangs grew too bad, I withdrew into myself, letting myself drop into a voluntary stupor. Besides making them more manageable, this rendered me impervious to my miserable existence in general. I simply closed my eyes and stopped seeing and hearing what was around me; it was like putting a filter in my brain so that nothing came through from the outside world. "Enough for today," I would say and go off into a kind of meditation. It was a useful skill, but it couldn't change the fact that if I didn't find a way of getting food, I would sooner or later die of starvation.

Men died all the time. Sometimes they dropped to the ground during roll-call and were dragged away by the French gendarmes. Sometimes they were too weak to get up from their mattresses and were taken directly from there. There was one fellow who literally smoked himself to death in a matter of weeks. A tobacco addict who claimed to be a Polish diplomat, he traded all his food for cigarettes and was soon a corpse.

You could see doom in such people at a glance. I tried to keep away from them. There was a barber in our *quartier*, a man who had gotten hold of a pair of scissors and cut hair for money or barter. One day I went to him for a haircut, took one look at him, and walked away. I feared being contaminated – not by the dysentery he had come down with, but by Death itself.

There were various ways of scrounging for extra food. One was hunting the emaciated specimens of cats that occasionally wandered over the camp grounds. A "syndicate" would be formed for this purpose, lengthy negotiations being held to determine who would put up a piece of sausage for bait in return for an extra share of the profits. The arguments over this could be fierce enough to make men stop talking to each other.

Once the sausage was secured, it was laid in a corner. Then we waited for the cat. If it approached, we pounced on it and killed it in any way we could. Each of us was given a piece of raw meat to cook in his mug, the sausage owner getting a double portion. A shared soup was made from the head and tail.

Sometimes the cat got away, leaving bruised heads that had collided. When it was caught it was delicious, a cross between chicken and rabbit. It amused me to think that I, who not long ago had been made ill by a bit of pork, now ate with relish the flesh of cats.

It was November 1942. Although the battle of Stalingrad was raging and the British had turned back the Germans at El Alamein, almost nothing was known in the camp about the progress of the war. Occasionally someone swiped or obtained a French newspaper, but these were so heavily censored as to be worthless. Perhaps this was why José, eager to hear about the outside world from which I had recently arrived, began taking an interest in me. I had been hanging around him for several days, disappointed by my lack of success in gaining his attention, when, as he was eating his polenta one day, he almost imperceptibly crooked a finger as if inviting me to join him.

José's polenta was a sign of his high station, no ordinary prisoner being able to obtain the corn meal for this pudding that was the specialty of the Spaniards in the camp. More than once I had enviously watched him prepare it in his "apartment," the little cubicle by the entrance to the barracks that was his unchallenged domain. Fitting a smaller metal can into a larger one, the bottom of which was kept hot with pieces of burning charcoal, straw, paper, or anything else that caught fire, he patiently stirred the meal and water in circles with his single arm until it became a thick mush whose steamy smell drove me mad.

This "apartment" was also José's store, in which he sold and bartered pencils, stationery made from heavy gray paper, and cigarettes. You could buy a whole cigarette, a half of one, a third, or a stub or *mégot*. José also manufactured *espadrillas*, the Spanish sandals that he wove from bits of rope and string while sitting in front of the barracks in good weather.

He was a strong, muscular man with a broad, friendly face who had lost an arm while fighting with the Anarchists. As kapos went, he was a good one. Although he caught hell from the guards if he didn't turn us all out for the *appel*, his strongest measure to get us up in the morning was shouting "Let's go, Let's go" as he rapped on the bottom tier of the bunks. And while he never tried to be a leader or to intervene in barracks quarrels, it being strictly your own lookout if someone stole from you or abused you, he was fair in distributing such chores and privileges as carrying the *marmite* or performing KP duty – another sought – after task that enabled one to steal potato peels, bits of cabbage, and other things.

Over that first polenta he asked me all kinds of questions: where I came from, why I had been sent to Vernet, what I had seen "abroad," and in particular, whether "that lousy war is getting anywhere" and which side was winning it. He was hungry not for food, of which he had plenty, but for news and stories that would help break the monotony of his existence.

I told him not only all I knew of what was happening in the world, but everything that had happened to me since the day I left Amsterdam. It was the first time I had bothered to take stock of my adventures and I quite enjoyed the opportunity to relate them. The next day I was invited for more polenta.

It took a while to penetrate José's crusty exterior, but eventually a degree of friendship and even affection developed between us.

"Muy bien, come, poquito," he would say, placing a plateful of hot pudding in front of me. It was a mystery to me where he obtained the small bags of finely ground corn from, but I knew it would be indiscreet to ask. From time to time he even managed to add a few slices of sausage. He was a regular magician!

Since I no longer needed the watery camp soup, I began to pass it on to the fellow in the bunk beneath me, a slightly-built youth named Marcel. He was not much older than I and had dark, soulful eyes that seemed familiar. I must have guessed right away why that was. His real name was Maximilian and he was a Jew from Budapest who had been caught without his papers during a raid in Aix-les-Bains, where his family was staying.

On hindsight the lack of papers was Max's salvation, since it enabled him to spin a story about his Hungarian Gentile origins that landed him in Vernet rather than on a train to Poland. Every Jew who lived through those years had experiences like that – you never knew when seeming bad luck would turn out to be its opposite and vice versa. Nor could you know what the French police, who were less efficient and determined than the Germans, would think or do when they arrested you. Although they had been crazy enough in Marseilles to believe I was an Allied spy, it had never occurred to them that I was Jewish.

Max and I had much in common. Not only were we Jews, we both came from Orthodox families and were Zionists. Yet though I had long ago gotten over any qualms I might have had about denying my origins, this continued to be a moral dilemma for Max. He was, unlike me, still religious. Three times a day he turned to the East to say his prayers. He did it so unobtrusively, moving only his lips, that only I could have noticed, but somehow it irritated me.

I had become a different person. The months spent eluding the Germans had left me no time to think about such things, but now that I was immobilized in Vernet, with nothing to do but sit, shit, and play coma, my mind reverted to the philosophical questions that had always occupied it. And when it did, the boy who had been genuinely convinced of his special relationship with the Creator and had never doubted His covenant with the Jewish People, discovered that his beliefs were empty. The God with whom I had communicated daily in my prayers as if He were on the other side of a telephone line had turned out to be a fake: if He was not a criminal, He was impotent. Everything I had ever held to be true had vanished like a fata morgana.

The less credence I put in all that, the more all kinds of things weighed on Max's conscience. The wet dreams he had, for instance, which made him feel sinful but which he loved to tell me about, describing the women in them in great detail. Or the food packages that he received from his parents, which were opulently packed with goodies. Informed by José that one of these was waiting for him in the *quartier*'s office, he would retrieve it, swallow as much of its contents as he could, hide the rest, and return to tell his barracks mates that he had been sent only a few dry cakes. Yet afterwards he felt guilty for not sharing it and poured out his remorse in my presence.

I had, it so happened, gotten such a package myself – from Thea Bienstock, to whom I had written, on José's stationery, one of the two letters I was allowed to send from the camp. (The other was a complaint to the French police, which was of course never answered.) And I had with a clean conscience gobbled it all down right away, cutting its hunk of Mont D'Or cheese so greedily that I stabbed my thigh and was left with a scar that I still have.

"Max," I said, "you're completely nuts. There's no such thing as morality in our situation. And I don't want to hear about your women and your dreams. I want to get out of here."

So did he, but he thought he could do it by praying.

Still, we spent a lot of time together. It was comforting having a fellow Jew around. Until one morning when we witnessed, through the coils of the barbed wire, the first deportation from the *quartier juif*. A train arrived, the wagons were shunted alongside the platform, the doors were opened, and people were bundled inside. The entire process took several hours. I had no illusions about where they were going. It was a macabre spectacle.

My whole being revolted. Where was the God of Max – the Almighty God of Israel? If He could allow this, I no longer wanted to have anything to do with Him.

I was also filled with revulsion for the French, who were always talking about *honneur* and *la gloire de la Patrie*. So this was their idea of *gloire*... disposing of human beings as if they were so much garbage. Just sweep them all inside the wagons, *alors*, and off to the dump with them!

It was quiet in our barrack that evening. The grim scenes of the morning had affected the other men too, although along with the pity there was a sense of relief. It was others who had been taken away; fate had struck down strangers, not oneself. I felt the same way, and at the same time I felt despicable for feeling it. I tried pulling myself together. "Stop hating yourself," I thought. "Your only duty is to live."

Just then Max entered the barracks and began mouthing his evening prayers. That was already too much for me. I jumped down from my bunk and hissed:

"Whom do you think you're talking to? Whom are you praising and thanking – that all-knowing God of ours who didn't see fit to lift a finger while they were loading Jewish children into those freight cars?"

My voice was choked with emotion.

Max didn't answer at once. First he quietly finished his prayers. Then he said:

"No, you shouldn't see it like that. Why don't you think of all the good things that you owe Him?"

"Well," I snarled, "if there is indeed a God the way you imagine Him, and you think we owe Him for the good things He has done, you should also hold Him responsible for all the suffering in the world, including the misery we're in up to our necks! As far as I'm concerned, thanking Him is pure blasphemy. It means that every last drop of human unhappiness is because of Him too."

Too upset to continue the argument, I went outside to cool off.

"Yes, I'm finished with all this nonsense," I told myself. "And even if an omnipotent God should exist, it's pure megalomania to suppose that He would be in the least bit interested in such pathetic little bugs as us."

I sat brooding under a sky studded with bright stars. And suddenly, looking up at them, I had a vision. I had shrunk. I actually saw myself sitting on an electron, like the one in Niels Bohr's atomic model, which was revolving around its nucleus just like the earth that I lived on supposedly revolved around the sun. And looking up into molecular space, electron-borne Hans saw millions and millions of shiny dots all around. Each was an atom, in which spun more electrons, on each of which sat millions and billions of tiny Hanses! And perhaps at this very moment some of those Hanses were staring into space, convinced that they were seeing millions of suns with planets revolving around them. And perhaps, too, all the electrons on which those tiny Hanses sat formed a little object in some universe – a soup ladle, for example. Yes, perhaps a Very Big Hans was standing somewhere right now and ladling cabbage soup from a *marmite* while holding trillions of tiny Hanses in his hand.

I burst out laughing – and with that laughter came the realization that I was now, for the first time in my life, a free man: free of illusions, free of wishful thinking, and free of all the granny tales invented by men to create a God in their image to serve their needs and desires.

I realized something else at that moment, too, which had never crossed my mind before: that if push came to shove, I could not only punch, but kill. I would kill whoever stood in my way. From now on, I would make my own moral laws.

★ ★ ★

I had never in my life touched a pistol or a rifle, but I was determined to learn to use one. And I had already decided on my teacher: he would be none other than our *Commandant de quartier*.

This was a self-important and rather preposterous sergeant of the French gendarmerie, who clearly regarded his present position as the peak of his career. Among the prisoners he was known as *petit Napoléon* because of the grandiose postures he struck as he paraded up and down the camp. And for good measure, he sported a small, tightly clipped mustache that would have done Hitler proud.

The first step was to be introduced to this character, who was vain, greedy, and corrupt. Knowing that some of the prisoners had hidden valuables, he had opened a trading post and let it be known through the Spaniards that watches, gold rings, and other objects could always be exchanged for bread, a handful of corn, or even some sausage. It was, one had to admit, a nice little business, with no overhead to speak of. And when it was slow, a slight reduction in our rations soon boosted the turnover!

The Spaniards played a key role in these transactions, both as intermediaries and as advisors. No one held it against them if some of the profit stuck to their fingers, for the camp's barter economy played an important role in keeping us alive. Yet at the same time, there was a certain distrust of the Spanish camp élite in general, as a result of which not everyone was prepared to disclose his possessions to them – especially since many of the prisoners, particularly the newcomers, had no clear idea of how the system worked.

This gave me an idea. Over polenta one day I said to José:

"Did you notice that new shipment of Poles or Czechs, or whatever they are, that came this morning? They don't know any Spanish or French, but they probably speak a bit of German. Why don't I try to make contact with them? They're sure to have something to trade."

"Hmmmm," said José. "Could be. But what makes you think they'll tell you what they have?"

"First of all, my being a newcomer myself. And secondly, the fact that thanks to you, I'm not going hungry. What better proof that you can be trusted?"

José said he needed time to think about it.

A few days later he brought up the subject. "*Muy bien, amigo.* But how do I know that you'll bring everything to me and won't cut me out by starting your own *combine* with *petit Napoléon?*"

I gave him an injured look. "How could I do such a thing? I would never go to Napoleon without you. I'll tell you what. Why don't you take me with you the next time you go see him, so that he'll know we're in this together?"

It was not a very logical argument, but José was a decent type and the thought that some prisoners didn't trust him injured his pride. Besides, what did he stand to lose? "All right," he answered grudgingly, "we'll see how it works. You can tell them they'll get an honest deal from me."

My plan worked in more ways than one. By acting as José's agent, I was helping him, myself, and others, but even more to the point, I was getting a chance to suck up to *Monsieur le commandant.*

I succeeded beyond my wildest hopes. Besides being greedy and vain, *petit Napoléon* was intensely lazy, and I immediately took advantage of this by little gestures like placing a chair underneath his behind when he sat down. He was also extremely untidy, and his room was littered with empty cups and dirty plates. This gave me an opportunity to offer to do some dishwashing while proposing that, as long as I was at it, I might as well sweep and mop the floor as well. *Petit Napoléon* was only too happy to agree. There was nothing like a lickspittle to keep his ego inflated.

Before long, I was more or less acting as his valet–cum–personal secretary. I filled out endless lists and forms that he was too indolent to attend to himself and even polished his boots as soon as they showed the slightest stain from his expeditions in the camp – all with praiseworthy zeal and servility. And without the slightest sense of shame.

Even more than in his shiny black boots, *Monsieur le commandant* took great pride in his new German Mauser pistol. He spent hours disassembling it, cleaning and oiling the parts, and putting them back together. I had never seen a gun up close, and I was fascinated by the sight of it and the accompanying clicks of its shiny mechanism. I carefully followed every movement out of the corner of my eye, hoping the knowledge might stand me in good stead.

Meanwhile, a new plan was hatching in my head. By now I knew from José that the source of his polenta was a farm several kilometers away at which the Germans responsible for securing the camp were lodged. And at the *commandant*'s office I had learned that considerable amounts of vegetables, fruit, potatoes, eggs, butter, and cheese were produced there. While most of this went to feed the Germans, there was a surplus that was bartered inside the camp.

From my point of view, the most important thing was that this operation was run with forced labor recruited from the inmates of the camp. Despite my feelings about farming, this was no time to stand on principle. Located well beyond the last barbed-wire fence, the farm was definitely the place for me. The only problem was that work there was reserved for the most privileged prisoners, and that despite having wormed my way into the *commandant de quartier*'s good graces, there were others with far more seniority. Without the help of the Spaniards, there was no hope of getting to the front of the line.

Once again, fortune smiled on me. A few days later a rumor reached our barrack that there were several openings at the farm. I had seen and heard enough at Vernet not to get excited by every bit of hearsay, but when I saw José in serious conversation with his fellow Spaniards the next day, I was sure something was up. And indeed, he soon confirmed the rumor and said that, since the camp management owed him a favor, he was allowed to choose one or two of the lucky candidates.

This was my chance. I begged to be one of them.

"Oh, no, *poquito*," said José. "I'll miss your nice stories and business skills too much."

Thank heavens he was joking, although I would like to think he meant the part about missing me. He knew what I was planning to do without having to be told. Apart from Max he was the only person in Vernet to whom I had confided that I was Jewish, and he knew perfectly well that the longer I remained, the greater the chance of being found out.

The next day I was called to the camp commandant, whom I hadn't seen since my first day in Vernet.

"Well, de Groot," he said. "We're considering transferring you to the farm."

Appearing too eager was the only thing that could spoil it now.

"*Monsieur le commandant*," I protested, "I'm a naval cadet, not a farmer. All that hard work and long hours aren't for me. Besides, I suffer from hay fever."

That did it. "Don't argue," said the German. "You'll go to the farm."

Sadists are so predictable!

★ ★ ★

A few days later I left the camp on the same cart that had brought me there. Although I had decided not to look back at a place I intended never to see again, once outside the gate I couldn't resist a last glance. One thing was clear: I would risk my life before letting myself be returned there.

The first days at the farm I had to pinch myself to make sure I wasn't dreaming. The conditions were paradise compared to those I had left behind. Of course, we were under constant guard, but we had a lot more freedom of movement, and there was none of the discipline and humiliation to which I had been subjected during the past few months. And while the food wasn't plentiful, it was sufficient. After all, it was we who produced it.

We were roused early each morning from our straw mattresses, and after a reasonable breakfast we took our pickaxes and hoes and departed whistling for the fields. (I don't remember whether we were ordered to whistle, or whether it was simply suggested that it might be appropriate, but yes, whistle we did!) Not that the work was a lark. It was hard and lasted all day, and you couldn't be choosy about doing it. The slightest sign of idleness, let alone insubordination, meant an immediate return to barbed wire. Still there was no reason to complain. Sooner or later my moment would come.

The nights were the worst part. After supper we were herded into a barn that served as our living quarters, and the windows and doors were securely bolted. There was nothing to do but shut your eyes and go to sleep. Still, I told myself, it was a lot better than a cattle wagon!

In the morning we were released like a herd of sheep, and after breakfast we returned to the fields to go on hacking, hoeing, weeding, ploughing, or whatever. Much of the time, I think, we were working with potatoes, although to tell the truth, any vegetable having green leaves seemed like a potato to me. To keep my mind from going numb, I invented various imaginary devices to reduce the effort expended. But not even the most brilliant invention would have interested our masters. Not when they had us.

For a while I was put in charge of the rabbit hutches. This was definitely an improvement, since I was no longer under continual supervision. Nor was there much to do. I put green stuff into the rabbits' cages and cleaned brown stuff out of them. For that you had to remove the rabbits first, which was done by grabbing them by the ears. Although they didn't bite, they could give you a good scratching, pawing frantically with their claws, if you weren't careful.

One day one of my fellow workers came to me with a long steel pin that looked like a very thin knitting needle. God knew where he had gotten it from. "You take care of the rabbits, don't you?" he said with a broad wink. "Here, maybe you can take care of one with this." By way of demonstration he put one end of the needle to his ear and mimed ramming it into his head.

As soon as I was sure that nobody was looking, I hauled one of the largest and fattest rabbits out of its hutch, put the steel pin in its ear, and banged it right through its brain. The animal didn't even bleed, though it did manage to have a last shit. Making a virtue of necessity, I ran toward the nearest German guard, holding the rabbit and its soiled tail at arm's length while shouting in my most melodramatic voice: "*Kaninchen krank, kaput, krepiert!*"

The man was not about to make an issue of it. All he needed was to be accused of negligence by his bosses! "Well, bury the damn thing," he said, waving vaguely in the direction of our barn. As soon as he was looking the other way, I strolled toward our sleeping quarters and threw the rabbit into a dark corner. That night we ate a fine stew, prepared on a little stove by the fellow who gave me the needle.

But the rabbit interlude was of short duration and soon I was back in the fields again, scratching away at them until dusk. It would have been terribly boring had I not spent much of the time studying the layout of the farm in the hope of finding an escape route. Finally, I saw a way.

A considerable distance from the vegetables was a large, rectangular field that was used for growing field crops and tilled with a horse and plow. Better yet, it was bordered on three sides by dense woods. If I could somehow manage to get in among those trees, I would be invisible. Even if the Germans shot at me, their chances of hitting me would be nil.

Luck was with me this time too, for soon after this discovery I was assigned to the plowing detail. There were two of us: one man guided the horse while the other steered the plow in a straight line. Following us was an SS soldier with a carbine slung across his shoulder and a heavy pistol in his holster. Whenever we arrived at one end of the field, the horse and plow were turned around and back we went in the other direction. It was up and down like that all day, every run finishing close to the edge of that dark woods.

Each time we turned, I kept my eyes on our guard. It was my only chance to observe him, because now, instead of walking behind us, he stood still while we pivoted around him. And while the horse made a wide turn away from him, the back of the plow, which was the fulcrum of the pivot, came quite close to him as it swung round.

I noticed two things. One was that the German sometimes took advantage of these turns to light a cigarette – an activity that, if only for a few seconds, engaged his two hands as well as his eyes. The other was that his holster flap was unbuttoned.

As I had been given the job of leading the horse, my first objective was to switch jobs. Since like all Germans, I assumed, this one too must love neatness and order, the best way to accomplish this was to make a mess of the job I was engaged in.

Suddenly, I could no longer walk a straight line. The furrow began to run a little this way, and then a little that way; in fact, it looked like a boiled stick of spaghetti. And swearing at me, I made the guard realize, didn't help. Somehow, I just couldn't control the horse. We were too far from the rest of the farm to send for a replacement. There was nothing for it but to order my mate to take the reins and give me the plow.

It wasn't as easy as I thought. As long as I had led the horse, the plow had seemed simply to follow it; only now did I perceive that steering it was the more difficult of the two tasks. Every clump and uneven patch of earth made it swerve, and I needed all my strength to keep the blade down and guide it straight. And this time there was no nonsense: my incompetence had already lost me any chance of another day on the plowing detail, and if the guard retired me now all was lost. Before long, my body was a bundle of raw nerves. I always knew I wasn't meant to be a farmer! The tension grew unbearable. The nearby edge of the woods that was supposed to be my safe haven became a dark and menacing blotch that frightened rather than encouraged me.

"Do it now, Hans!" I urged myself each time we approached the edge of the woods. But I couldn't get myself to act. For a while, too, the German had lit no cigarette, and his hands remained free as I pivoted close to the gun sticking out of his holster an arm's length away. It was the same type of Mauser that belonged to the *Commandant de quartier*.

We crossed the field again while I fought to keep the plow in line until we reached the furrow's end near the woods. With the guard at my back, I pressed down on the plow's rear and let its front swing around behind the horse. At the end of the turn I was facing the German. He was lighting a cigarette, one hand holding a match and the other cupped against the breeze. Fleetingly I glimpsed his face. It belonged to a man no longer young, too old to be at the front.

"Yes, NOW! Do it, NOW!" My head pounded with the rhythm of my steps. "NOW! NOW!" I knew that if I waited any longer my fear would get the better of me and the opportunity would slip away for good.

And then it happened again. I suddenly went into slow motion. Everything was reduced to a crawl, my heartbeat too. All fear was gone. I was as though standing outside myself, watching from a vantage point in space, my only emotion a feeling of suspense. "Now I've got you, you dirty bastard!" I heard myself say, although in fact I must only have thought it. The gun was already out of the holster and in my hand. For a second I shut my eyes, as if loath to see the consequences of what I knew was about to happen. Then I opened them again while my finger found the trigger and my thumb released the safety catch, as I had watched *petit Napoléon* do many times.

The German had dropped the match and was staring with stupefaction at the pistol pointed at him. He slid his hand to his holster, failing to grasp that the Mauser was no longer there. Then he moved toward me as if to grab it.

I fired. I saw the panic in his eyes as the bullet found its mark. Although the impact threw him backwards, he tried coming at me again. I kept firing until the Mauser was empty. A feeling of exultation washed over me, such as I had never known in my life.

The gun felt red-hot. As soon as the last echo faded, I threw it away. The horse had bolted, the plow skidding crazily in its wake like a fish floundering on dry land. My dumbstruck partner set out behind it, leaving the German outstretched on the ground. And then suddenly the prostrate body twitched. As if flung by an electric shock, I turned and started running, jumping across a ditch and into the protection of the dense and gloomy forest.

I ran faster and faster, picking up speed. And yet I felt as if I were standing still and the trees were racing past me. I could hear them whistling in my ears. I plunged deeper into the forest, hardly knowing where I was going. Branches scraped my face and once or twice I ran into a tree. Brought up short, I took a few seconds to clear my head and pushed on, scaling fallen branches and undergrowth, deeper and deeper into what began to seem like an endless tunnel. As in a feverish dream, I no longer walked but was suspended, floating from tree to tree. My chest felt filled with a hot, searing gas. I imagined dogs and SS soldiers, even tanks and airplanes, on my heels. I was no longer running but stumbling. In the end, I found myself creeping on all fours like a crippled animal.

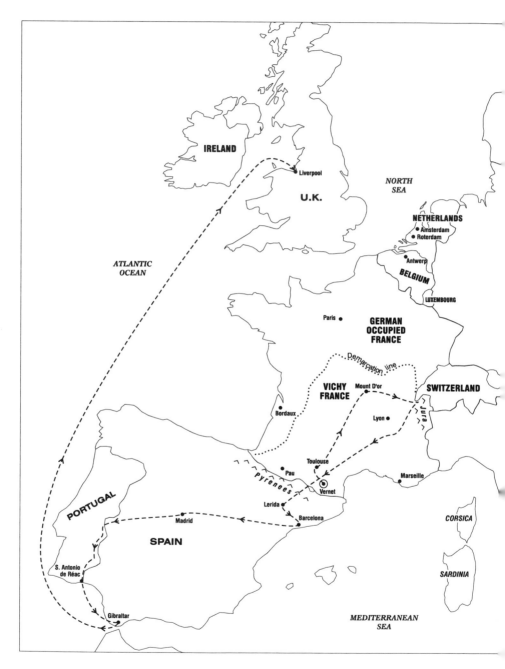

The Escape

Chapter Eight

I must have passed out from exhaustion. When I awoke, dawn was breaking. I had slept for the better part of a day and had no idea where I was.

I looked about. High above me was a power line dipping above the trees, and a little further on, a pylon. I decided to follow them. Electricity meant people, and people meant possible help. I couldn't stay in the woods forever and I now had a price on my head. The next time I fell into the hands of the police I would face a firing squad.

I dug a hole, took my Belgian papers from my pocket, and covered them with earth. *Tot ziens*, Hendrik de Groot! He had been a faithful friend, but it was time to bury him.

The power line led me to a narrow country road. I crouched in the bushes alongside it, not knowing what to do next. After a while, I heard slowly approaching wheels.

It was a horse-drawn cart driven by a farmer with a large load balanced on the back of it. He looked friendly enough and something told me to take a chance. I must have looked quite a sight, jumping out of the bushes to flag him down in Franz's checked pants and silk shirt, both torn and smeared with dirt, and José's *espadrillas* on my feet.

He stopped his horse and waited.

"Where to?" I called.

"Toulouse."

"Can you give me a ride?"

He scrutinized me for a moment, nodded wordlessly for me to climb aboard, and clucked his horse back into motion.

Not a word passed between us. That was just as well, because I was in no mood to talk. I had just killed a man and it wasn't anything I felt proud of.

Not that I felt sorry for the bastard. He shouldn't have had that lousy job. But I would rather have killed a German in combat.

We entered a village and the cart halted in front of a church. Still without a word, the farmer pointed with his thumb, first at the ground, as a sign for me to climb down, and then toward the church. With a crack of his whip he moved on, leaving me in the street.

He must have known I wasn't legitimate. Perhaps he even realized that I had fled Vernet. But had he brought me to safety or had he simply dumped me in the first place he could?

And yet if he had only wanted to get rid of me, why would he have given me a ride?

It was the first church I had ever been in. I felt a shock walking into it, as if crossing a physical field of force. It was cool and very dark inside, and there was a strange smell, musty and sweet. After a while my eyes got used to the darkness and I made out a crucified Christ on the wall and a statue of the Madonna and child in front of the altar. The whole thing was unreal. I, a Jew accused by those who would send me to my death of having killed that man on the wall, was seeking refuge from them in his sanctuary!

A priest was rearranging a rather sad-looking bunch of flowers in front of the statue of the Virgin. Although he must have seen me come in without crossing myself, he didn't show the slightest sign of acknowledgment. Only when I began walking toward the altar did he glance directly at me with a quiet smile that was both questioning and kind. He was younger than his severe black habit suggested, with finely carved, dark features. After a few seconds of facing each other, he took my arm and guided me to the sacristy. I followed, unsure but unresisting.

The walls of the sacristy were lined with high cupboards whose open doors revealed clerical vestments. The same sickly-sweet odor of incense assailed me here too, accompanied by a smell of mothballs. The effect on my empty stomach was such that I collapsed into the nearest chair. Apparently, I couldn't have expressed myself better, for the priest disappeared and returned a minute later with some bread and sausage and a bottle of wine. It took me no time to wolf the food down under his approving gaze.

I felt a great peace. Like the farmer, he hadn't asked me a single question. To be simply accepted like that, as a fellow human being, after so many weeks of humiliation... it filled me with gratitude.

At last a question came:

"What are you planning to do next, my son?"

I didn't know what to say. For the first time since leaving Amsterdam, I had absolutely no plans. All I knew was that I was at the end of my strength. Swallowing the lump in my throat that suddenly threatened to choke me, I answered:

"I'm very, very tired. I've been through a lot. What I would most like is a place to rest for a few days."

"Just stay here," the priest said. "I'll see what I can do for you."

He turned and left the sacristy, turning the key from the outside. For a moment, I felt panic. I had better get out before it was too late and the man returned with the police or a German soldier! Looking around for a means of escape, I noticed that the window had been left open. This calmed me, for there were no bars and it was a cinch to climb down on the other side.

Relax, I told myself. Of course he had to lock the door. How else could he make sure that someone else didn't walk in on me?

I shut my eyes and fell asleep.

After what may have been minutes or hours, I awoke with a start: they had come to get me! Jumping blindly off my chair, I almost knocked over the kindly curate. With his quiet, understanding smile, he surveyed me and said:

"Come, we'll find something that fits you."

From one of the cupboards he took a cassock that was more or less my size. "Here, put this on," he instructed me.

Dutifully, I obeyed. In a few seconds I was dressed as a priest. Had any Jew ever risen so quickly in Christianity's ranks?

"And now this," said the curate, hanging a silver crucifix around my neck.

At that I almost rebelled. I had to give myself a good mental kick to keep from tearing it off. Hans, I told myself, it's just a costume – pretend you're in a school play.

"And this." I was handed a little black book.

"Hold it with both hands and walk behind me. Do whatever I do. You'll be all right."

It took us almost an hour to reach the center of Toulouse.

The priest walked slowly ahead of me, the skirts of his cassock swishing around him, while I shuffled a few paces behind with my hands clasping the book and my eyes demurely on the ground. Now and then the priest nodded in response to the respectful greeting of some passer-by. After a while, I began to nod gravely myself.

We finally arrived at a quiet square, where my guide halted before an imposing mansion. He rang a bell and the door was opened by a servant girl who led us into a large, high-ceilinged parlor furnished with a number of richly plush-upholstered sofas. A heavily made-up and rather blowzy-looking lady stepped forward to greet us. She kissed the prelate's hand respectfully and acknowledged my presence with an amused smile.

I had to pinch myself. From my first church to my first brothel, all in one morning!

I was told to wait on a sofa while the madame and the priest went off to another room to discuss my case. I was beginning to feel rather like a boy whose father had brought him for his sexual initiation and then gone off to negotiate the price. And my discomfort only grew as the doors of the adjacent rooms opened and their occupants, in various states of semi-nudity, peeked out at my black dress and withdrew with an audible giggle. Better to have been in my underpants like them than in such a ridiculous outfit!

My embarrassment didn't last long, because I was soon whisked upstairs, past a second and third story, and ushered through a trapdoor into a stuffy attic room in which I was at last permitted to disrobe.

This room was to prove my entire world for the next several days. In it was a bed with brass-knobbed posts and a small table beneath a skylight. The trapdoor had two rails on its upper side, to which was fastened a ladder that slid to the floor below when the door dropped down. Since it was latched and unlatched from below, I was again a prisoner, but for once in my life I didn't mind. I was too exhausted to do much but sleep and would have hardly wanted to explore the premises anyway, since they belonged to – as the priest informed me before taking his leave – the most luxurious bordello in the whole of Toulouse, one reserved exclusively for German officers.

I nearly climbed right back into my cassock. "A house full of German officers is the last place I should be," I protested.

"On the contrary, my son," smiled the priest. "It's the last place where anyone will look for you. I'll be back in a day or two. I hope you get a good rest."

I did indeed – until later that evening, when I was woken by bumping and banging from the floor below, accompanied by grunts and muffled cries. It went on until the wee hours of the morning and started again the next day at the same time. The whorehouse was a gold mine. The entire German officer corps of Toulouse, so it seemed, had nightly orders to report to it for duty.

In the off-hours, I sometimes had visits from the girls below. Curious about their mysterious guest, they would "drop up" to say hello, looking as unkempt in their morning frocks as any housewife who has just seen her husband off to work. The quaint sight of a man who thought beds were for sleeping in seemed to appeal to them. Sometimes they brought me a newspaper. As dull as these censored French rags were, I welcomed them as my only reading matter. Without them there was nothing to do when alone but lie in bed daydreaming or sit at the table staring through the skylight.

My food was sometimes brought by the serving girl, an ugly thing in a gray smock, and sometimes by Madame herself. It wasn't haute cuisine, but I was so hungry after the months in Vernet that I would have eaten horseshit with sugar. The serving girl also came each day to empty my chamberpot and bring me a pitcher of cold water and an earthenware basin to wash with.

One of the girls brought me chocolates, too. She must have gotten them from the German officers. Her name was Yvette, and unlike the others, who just peeked in on me and left, she liked to sit on my bed and talk. Perhaps she was more curious than they were, and perhaps she felt a connection with me. We were the two youngest inhabitants of the brothel, and at seventeen or eighteen she was even younger than I was, a pretty country girl with peach-colored skin and a very nice, plumpish figure.

She had beautiful little breasts, which were clearly visible through the transparent blouses that she wore. She could not have been in the establishment for very long and was as rosy and innocent as a young bride on her honeymoon. Her work didn't depress her at all; in fact, she seemed to like it. So might the others have felt too if they were, like her, in such demand that they could pick and choose their customers.

Our conversations didn't go very deep. We were both tactful or bashful enough not to ask about each other's past. I told her that I had escaped from Vernet but not that I had killed a guard, while all I knew about her was that she was a farmer's daughter. I didn't feel she would enjoy being questioned about whatever sordid episode had brought her to this place, which she evidently regarded as a step up in life.

She didn't behave like a whore. She had nice, soothing fingers, and sometimes she ran them over my thigh as she sat on my bed, and we necked and petted like high school sweethearts. It was all gratis of course, and she clearly was ready for more, but to my great chagrin, I wasn't. I just couldn't get my bloody prick to stand! Yvette was very nice about it. "Don't worry," she said. "It's probably just something they put in your food at Vernet."

I didn't want to tell her that it was more likely the thought of her being fucked by all those Germans.

I don't know what made me feel more awkward – my incapacity at such moments, or my chamberpot full of a day's deposits on the mornings when Yvette came to visit me before the serving girl had emptied it. I would quickly shove it under my bed when I saw her head of blond hair coming up the ladder.

After a few days of such loving ministrations, I was rested and ready to move on. True to his word, the priest came to see me. By now I trusted him totally and assumed he had connections, possibly via some Catholic network, with the Maquis. "Could you put me in touch with them?" I asked. "They're the only ones who can get me across the Spanish border. If you need a reference, I know a Dutchman working with them near Lyon who can vouch for me."

I gave him the name of the chateau owner who had refused me a ticket to Spain. Perhaps if he received an SOS from Toulouse, he would take me more seriously.

I never found out whether he was contacted, but when the priest came a second time he had news for me: a place had been found for me in the Jura Mountains and I was to depart for there immediately.

"The Jura?" I wasn't sure I had heard right. "But that's near the French Alps, next to the Swiss border! It's in the wrong direction."

The priest gave me his first and last disapproving look. "My son," he said, "there are times when one doesn't argue where a helping hand is coming from. And Toulouse is not the safest area for you to stay in while waiting to get to Spain."

He handed me some money for the trip and I slipped back into my cassock and went downstairs, leaving my room for the first time since arriving. All the girls were waiting in the parlor to say goodbye. They plied me with small presents and delicacies for the road, and I suddenly realized that I would miss them.

The last to kiss me goodbye was Yvette. She pressed a sturdy pocket knife into my hand. "*Tiens, on ne sait jamais,*" she said. "You never know."

She gave me a strange look. Although I couldn't be sure, it seemed to me that I wasn't the only one with tears in my eyes.

★ ★ ★

There was no problem in getting me safely to the station, out of my cassock, and onto the train, but without papers I now was like a fly on a kitchen table, expecting the swatter to descend at any moment.

And in fact, somewhere between Toulouse and Clermont-Ferrand, a German patrol boarded the train. I managed to duck into an unoccupied toilet, but once inside it I realized that I was trapped. Even the most stupid ticket inspector always checked the toilets, and the soldiers were sure to do no less.

I had to think fast. My only chance was to make it seem that the toilet was out of order and that the door had been locked from the outside to prevent it from being used.

Normally, the toilet door locked from the inside by means of a copper hammer that dropped into a slot in the door jamb. Taking a hurried look at the outside mechanism, I saw that it consisted of a revolving disk, half of which was hidden behind a metal plate when the other half was showing. One of these halves was green and said *Libre*, while the other was red and said *Occupé*. When the hammer dropped, the disk turned in a semi-circle, exposing the red half and concealing the green one.

I took out the knife Yvette gave me, opened it, and jammed the blade into the slot while wedging the handle tightly against the hammer. It worked perfectly. While the door was now locked, the *Libre* sign remained showing.

I sat down and waited. A regular passenger who needed the toilet would give the handle a few tries and give up, but I was about to be faced with German thoroughness. Footsteps sounded in the corridor. Then someone rattled the door. I held my breath and heard a voice say in German, *"Französische Wirtschaft,"* "What a French mess!" There were a few more rattles and the footsteps receded.

"Thank God," I almost whispered, fighting back the words just in time. Whoever He was, I'd be damned if I'd give Him the credit.

★　★　★

It was a bitterly cold night when I arrived by local train at the mountain village of Jeurre. The directions given me by the priest were to leave the railroad station and follow the only road into the woods, "up and up and up and up" until I came to a crossing. The right-hand side of this junction branched off to the village. The left-hand side led through thick forest to the farm of yet another French-domiciled Dutchman, Jaap van der Post, who would be expecting me.

These days Jaap's farm is easily accessible by car. Except for the final few miles, all the steep and winding mountain roads have been paved. Even so, I almost lost my way when, on my way to Geneva a few years ago, I decided to pay a surprise visit.

Jaap recognized me immediately. He was much older and smaller than I remembered, but as soon as he placed both hands on my shoulders, the long years that had passed seemed to vanish. It was the same gesture with which he had wished me Godspeed when I set out for Spain. Never a man of many words, he remained true to style now too. "Hello, Hans. So you finally came to have another look? Yes, we're still here. Good to see you."

Later, over a bottle of nice wine, we reminisced. "I remember exactly how you turned up here," he said. "It was the end of 1942. It was pitch-dark outside and we saw your shadow through the windows, walking around the house two or three times. What a queer character you seemed! I guessed that you were too scared to knock, so in the end I went out and brought you in. We were expecting you and we had just sat down to supper, so of course we invited you to join us. Your first response was: 'Well, I have no food coupons, and actually I'm not very hungry.' Only it was quite obvious to us that you hadn't eaten for days – you looked thin as a rail. It wasn't until I explained that we didn't need coupons and that everything on the table came from our own farm that you started to smile. The quantities of food that you managed to stash away after that were quite amazing!"

Jaap's farm was indeed self-sustaining. It had about twenty cows and some horses and pigs, and even produced its own sausages and firewood. The main building, a two-story house, stood at the back of a big farmyard that was flanked by long rows of sheds.

To the rear of this house, toward the woods, was a converted stable, in which I shared a loft with several fugitives like myself. One was a big, fat fellow called Billy, who had been in the Dutch resistance until his group was betrayed. Another, tall and slim, was a young Frenchman named René. He too had been in a rolled-up resistance group and owned a Beretta pistol, which seemed a very useful thing to have; I had often regretted throwing away the Mauser with which I shot the guard in Vernet. Both of them were awaiting transport to England like me.

Although we had good relations, we didn't become friends. Despite all we had in common, we never talked about ourselves. Experience had taught us the value of silence. It was as dangerous for you to know too much about others as for others to know about you.

There was another Jew beside me on Jaap's farm, a young blond woman who lived in the main house and did the cooking and brought it to us. She and her husband had attempted to escape to Switzerland and were already across the border when they were picked up by the Swiss police and returned to France. Shortly afterwards her husband was caught by the Germans. She was very quiet and I often saw her cry. She clearly had reached the end of her rope and had no strength left to flee again, not even if the Germans were to raid the place – an eventuality for which, further back in the woods from the stable, stood a well-camouflaged hut half sunk into the ground.

We all had our chores. Mine was feeding the animals, helping split the logs that Jaap felled in the woods and brought to the farmyard with a horse and wagon, and cleaning out the barn – a job that I liked even less than tidying the rabbit hutches in Vernet. Because it was winter and the cows stayed indoors, I had to hoe the shit out from between each animal's legs, which kept shifting as if to mock me, and then flush the stall out with a hose. I disliked the stupid beasts as much as they disliked me. There was a young bull that I particularly loathed. Once, when he kicked me, I broke the wooden handle of the hoe over his back.

When it was too cold or snowy for us to be outside, Jaap had special work for us. In one of the sheds lay a huge pile of wooden toys that he had bought for such occasions, and handing out brushes and paint, he would tell us to spend the day coloring little dolls, pushcarts, and what not. We called it "Jaap's kindergarten." From time to time he would take these gewgaws down to Jeurre to sell and come back with cigarettes, flour, newspapers, and other supplies.

Once in a while a German patrol would climb the mountain on growling motorcycles. We could hear it coming and observe it through binoculars almost half-an-hour beforehand, laboring up the slow and only ascent, which gave us plenty of time to hide in the hut. Sometimes the soldiers dismounted from their cycles and came into the big house for a friendly chat. If he had extra food, Jaap sold it to them.

Although the farm was an ideal hiding place, the nearest neighbors being several kilometers away through thick, virgin forest, he was running an enormous risk. He would have been shot had the Germans found out about us. And yet so successfully did he stay on good terms with them that after the war the same neighbors accused him of being a Nazi collaborator! Later, when the truth came out, he was awarded the French Croix de Guerre.

Jaap had a wife and two small children, and though I couldn't make out the exact words of the quarrels that I sometimes heard between them, it was obvious that she wasn't happy with his hiding us. She never talked to us, and everything about her bespoke a silent protest at our presence. I couldn't blame her. Still, it made the atmosphere less comfortable than it might otherwise have been.

Even this, though, couldn't spoil our Sunday night dinners, the one time of the week when we all ate together around the large kitchen table in the main house. When we had put away all the food that we could, we sang songs: Dutch songs, the French ballads that were a specialty of René's, and even a few Hebrew songs from Palestine that I had learned in Zichron Ya'akov. I can still sing one of them to this day. It had a melody more like a march than the lullaby of the waves, but its words went:

> *For distant lands the ships now leave the shore,*
> *Thousands of arms load their cargoes aboard;*
> *We are the sailors and the stevedores,*
> *We are the men who are building a port.*

I even remember the second stanza:

> *The derricks are raised and the concrete is poured,*
> *The lighters arrived with their loads to the shore:*
> *The sky is bright blue and the sea even more –*
> *This is the way we are building a port.*

Corny? Perhaps. But if you think of it sung on a winter night in the Jura by a Jewish sailor from Amsterdam who had never been to sea, the flickering light from the fireplace throwing shadows across his face and the faces of those humming with him... No, it didn't seem corny at all.

★ ★ ★

A few months after my arrival at the farm, when I was chafing at the bit to move on and feeling increasingly frustrated by my dependence on unknown others who did not seem to share my sense of urgency, I returned from cutting wood in the forest to find Jaap drinking wine with two strangers. Even René, who habitually kept an eye on the mountain path for any sign of danger, had been surprised to see them suddenly appear behind the house. With their berets and sturdy walking sticks, they looked like ordinary French farmers, but since none of the locals ever visited us, they had to be something else.

As simple and innocent as they appeared, the instructions they proceeded to give Billy, René, and myself were of a military precision. We were to get ready to set out at once and were to do everything we were told – *et puis, c'est tout*. Baggage? Out of the question: nothing! René even had to surrender his Baretta. To my surprise, he didn't protest.

We were given mountain boots for crossing the Pyrenees – unfortunately, there were none my size, and I had to settle for a pair that was too small – and a few brief minutes in which to say goodbye to Jaap and his family. Our two Résistance guides were real disciplinarians. But the entire expedition, we soon realized, had been meticulously planned and from now on every minute counted.

For some reason, I remember less of our trip to the Pyrenees than of any other episode from this period. Perhaps this is because others were in charge and I could let my mind relax without paying attention to the details. All I recall is a series of local trains and ramshackle buses, some running on gas produced by large charcoal-burning contraptions mounted on their backs, interspersed with long marches on foot. We spent the nights with farmers who showed no surprise at our arrival and asked no questions. In this way we traveled from village to village with no idea of where we were or were heading. At no time did we pass anything that remotely resembled a city or town. I enjoyed immensely not having to think or make decisions.

★ ★ ★

It was nearly midnight when the five of us alighted at a small railroad station close to the *zone interdite,* the 30-kilometer-wide strip along the Pyrenees from the Atlantic to the Mediterranean that the Germans had declared off-limits to non-residents. To my astonishment, at least a dozen other men, types looking very much like us, got off the train too and walked with us to the exit. The two helmeted German soldiers at the gate, bayonets on their rifles, didn't even blink as we passed.

We turned to the right outside the station and walked for about a kilometer until we came to a bridge and took cover underneath it. Little groups speaking Dutch, Polish, French, and English began to form. While stamping my feet to keep my toes from freezing, I made the acquaintance of some of my new companions: a short, middle-aged French Jew; two American airmen, a navigator and a half-Indian tail gunner, whose Flying Fortress had been shot down over northern France; a Polish soldier who had escaped from a prisoner-of-war camp; and a tall, powerfully built, good-natured Canadian wing commander from the RAF. Off to one side stood a group of young Frenchmen.

I liked the looks of the Canadian. He struck me as the kind of person who would definitely survive a mid-winter trek at high altitude, and I decided to stick close to him.

A car came to a halt on the bridge above us. Although we were expecting to be met, we all tensed. There was always the possibility of betrayal, in which case we might be confronted by a squad of Germans or French Vichy police.

But the party that approached us in the dark was cordially welcomed by our French guides and the newcomers immediately began to divide us into groups of five. I made sure to be in the same group as the Canadian.

"*Allez-y, et bonne chance!*"

Our guides from the Jura took their leave and were swallowed up at once in the dark.

Our little group was the first to be sent on its way. The five of us were crammed into a black Citroën with front-wheel drive and the car took off at once without lights, turning off the road into a narrow country lane. What followed was the bumpiest and scariest ride I have ever taken. Our driver simply floored the accelerator and gunned the souped-up-sounding engine at full speed, disregarding potholes, sharp descents, and curves in the road – or sometimes, all three together. The speedometer never dropped beneath 120, and here and there, while racing through some dark village whose houses flashed dementedly by, it touched 150. Crouched in the rear seat with the sweat pouring down my back, I felt like a pair of dice being rattled in a cup.

Suddenly the car shrieked to a halt and we were told to get out. Our feet had barely touched ground before the Citroën spun around and raced back for its next load of passengers.

From here on we had to walk. Following a mountain trail that was barely visible in the dark, we were brought to a cabin and handed over to the *passeurs* whose job it was to lead us across the

Pyrenees into Spain. Although we were allowed a few hours sleep, the cold and our nerves – particularly the latter – kept us from getting a real rest.

Months later, when I was already in England, I heard that the driver of the Citroën and the rest of his underground unit had been caught in a subsequent sortie by the Germans and shot by a firing squad.

★ ★ ★

We were a motley band that set out on the final trek across the mountains. There were about fifteen of us, a large enough number to guarantee that there would be at least one problem case. This turned out to be the middle-aged French Jew, who, despite countless warnings that he would require every ounce of energy, had insisted on lugging along two suitcases of what were presumably his last worldly possessions. Worse yet, he suffered from asthma, and from the beginning he had difficulty keeping up with the *passeurs* as we started up the first and lowest of the three mountain chains that we had to cross. As luck would have it, these ran in an east-west direction, perpendicular to our north-south route, so that we had to ascend and descend each one of them in turn instead of following a single ridge.

Before long we were climbing through loose snow, which gradually became deeper. The French Jew started falling further behind, and several times I had to turn around and retrace my steps to prod him along. He was slowing us down and making me angry... and I became even angrier when it occurred to me that I was the only one bothering to go back for the idiot. Of course! It was because he was a Jew. He was endangering us all with his stubbornness – and most of all me, because of the stupid bond that I felt for him! I could have strangled him with my own two hands.

"Stop carrying those goddam suitcases," I snapped the next time I turned back for him along a narrow path flanked on either side by steep ravines.

He just clutched the suitcases more tightly and plodded on.

I seized one of them, tore it from his hands, and flung it into a ravine. Then I lunged for the other.

"No!" he shrieked. "Let go of it! It's none of your business!"

I wrestled it from his grasp and heaved it after the first.

He let out a moan and seemed about to throw himself after the suitcases. I grabbed him and pushed him ahead of me until they were out of sight.

Even without his luggage, he was unable to keep up. Our next stop was a log cabin in which we were again allowed a few hours' rest. Here two Spaniards relieved our French escorts, hard-as-nails professional smugglers who would be taking us up to a height of 3,000 meters. The snow, they said, was very bad there. They took one look at the French Jew and shook their heads.

"Next time you'll be luckier," I tried consoling him as he started down with the French guides on his return trip.

He gave me a hateful glance. Although only he knew what was in those suitcases, back in France and without them he could only be worse off than before.

★   ★   ★

That night we descended the first ridge. At the foot of it lay an open meadow cut by a stream. There was a ford there where the Germans sometimes lay in ambush, and we waited until we were all gathered at the meadow's edge and ran across it and through the ice-cold water like little rats, scuttling up the other side.

The nights were moonless. We took advantage of them to move on, sleeping during the days within the protective walls of shepherds' cabins. Despite the hard floors covered with only a thin layer of straw, we were utterly thankful for a few hours' shelter from the biting cold wind outside. But the winter days were short, and all too soon we had to stretch our chilled arms and legs and head out.

The third and last night seemed the longest. Well above the tree line, with nothing to serve any more as a windbreak or support, we slogged up the highest ridge in snow nearly up to our waists. How heavy can my legs get, I wondered, zigzagging exhaustedly behind our guides, before I reach the point where I can no longer lift them? My muscles had cramped up and each step was agony, especially since my boots rubbed fiercely against the blisters that had formed. The pain was excruciating. How much longer could I keep it up?

My strength was giving out. I needed to rest. Right here, on this snug blanket of snow... there, that was better... I would shut my eyes just for a minute...

Something cracked me hard across the cheek.

"Come on, little Dutchie." It was the Canadian wing commander, pulling me out of the snow. "You don't want to quit now. If you do, they'll have to chip you out of the ice like a mummy."

I rose and staggered on like an automaton, almost unconscious from the cold, in the lee of his giant frame that seemed unaffected by the elements. From time to time he turned around to lay an encouraging hand on my shoulder and say: "Hang on, lad. We're almost there."

Once he joked:

"If you'd grown up with some mountains instead of all those dikes and polders, you'd be better at this."

Then we were no longer climbing but following a knifeback that ran in a westerly direction. The snow was hard under our feet. Our little group had disintegrated; there were only the two of us, alone in a world resplendent with snow and ice. We had reached the very top of the mountains. In the starlight, they fell away beneath us. The sky was a deep, dark blue that sparkled with diamonds of all sizes, and below us was the faint reflection of a glacier. Far away were the lights of towns. It was unbelievably beautiful. Suddenly I felt totally elated. I was outside myself, up among the stars. Whoever it was who had walked this far was somebody else, not me. *I* was the deep, deep blue of ice and sky.

Intellectually, I knew, it made no sense. But there was nothing intellectual about it. It was a purely physical experience.

"Let's go, little Dutchie!"

We had no sense of being lost. The steep ravines on either side kept us to the ridge with the Pole Star on our right. Some time during the night we came to a southward-running spur that descended gently to a valley. This was the way that led to the Spanish towns below. Fortunately, it was easy to spot by the snow churned up by passing feet, because missing it would have meant walking on until we dropped.

As we started down the slope, we almost collided with a large outcrop of rock. Behind it, where he had sought protection from the wind, was slumped the body of René. I didn't need to be told what had happened.

He was still breathing, very slowly. We did all we could to revive him, slapping and shaking him and rubbing his frozen nose and ears with snow. When he failed to come to, the amazing Canadian picked him up, slung him over a shoulder, and marched on.

After a while, though, when the downhill path began to slope more steeply and we entered another deep snow drift, the burden proved too much even for the wing commander. Nor, hardly able to walk myself, was I of any help. It wasn't easy, but there was only one thing to do. We propped René against some snow in a sitting position and pushed on in the hope of finding help.

We hadn't gone far before we discovered footprints in the snow, pointing downhill. We pressed on as fast as we could, but even then it took several hours before we finally caught up with the *passeurs*, who showed us the way to a large farmhouse standing in a clearing between tall trees.

"We made it, Dutchie," I heard my wing commander say, giving me a smart slap on the back. "Rather close shave for you, but here we are. And now they will get it, the bloody, fucking bastards!"

The *passeurs* headed back to get René and I staggered into a warm kitchen with a roaring fire and plenty of food and wine.

The next thing I remember was waking up in a huge bed, lying between two strange men. Every bone and muscle ached.

René was lucky, too. In Lerida they only had to amputate one leg.

Chapter Nine

I had made it. The Third Reich lay behind me. The next time I saw its representatives, I hoped it would be through the sights of a Dutch naval gun.

Despite our warm reception on the Spanish side of the border, there were still Franco's fascist authorities to deal with. True, the regime was not anti-Semitiç – having expelled them all in 1492, the Spaniards had no Jews left to hate – and was said to accept Jewish refugees; but nobody in the farmhouse seemed able to tell us what would happen next. All questions were answered with an uncomprehending smile and an invitation to enjoy some more delicious food and excellent Spanish wine.

At long last the authorities appeared in the form of a company of the Guardia Civil. With their black patent leather hats perched at a funny angle on their heads, they looked like soldiers from an operetta. Without removing the rifles slung on their backs they marched us to the nearest road, where a bus was waiting to drive us to Lerida, a provincial town at the foot of the Pyrenees.

In Lerida we were put in the local jail, four of us to a cell. The iron doors swung shut behind us and we were left to ourselves. It was a discouraging beginning.

For a few minutes, we sat glumly on the beds. Then one of us shook the iron cell door angrily.

It opened.

So, almost simultaneously, did the other doors in the cell block and out walked our contingent of border crossers.

The building was deserted. Before leaving it, our jailers had made sure all the cell doors were unlocked. They had done their job and taken us into custody. Who could blame them if, despite their best efforts, we managed to escape?

We were still standing there, trying to decide our next move, when a man appeared out of the shadows, wordlessly handed us tickets to the train for Barcelona, and pointed in the direction of the station.

We trooped up the street to it. Who would have thought the Spanish were so efficient?

★ ★ ★

Once in Barcelona, it didn't take long to recover my verve. Not until I was given a brand new passport from the local Dutch consul with the name "Hans Kahn" on it, however, did I feel that the process was complete. After all the months of wandering, deprivation, want, and imprisonment, I was officially my old self again.

Billy, myself, and the other *Engelandvaarders* in our group were told to report to the Dutch embassy in Madrid, where we were given ample pocket money to exist on. We were a mixed lot – students, escaped officers, and a few lower-class types from Rotterdam whom we called "the Stickyfingers" because of their habit of walking off with whatever wasn't nailed down.

While we were waiting to move on we did a lot of promenading and bar-hopping. To help pass the time, I took lessons at a local fencing club. My partner was named Carlos; after lessons he often invited me to the dives where he and his friends hung out. There, in a place near the Opera House, I met Isabel.

She was sitting by herself at a small table, her dark green eyes and shoulder-length mane of chestnut hair making her seem like a jaguar among alley cats. I couldn't take my eyes off her.

After a while she returned my stare with an amused smile, which I took as an invitation to introduce myself in French. She spoke it perfectly, and being told her name I declared that she was so beautiful that I would turn it backwards and call her Bellisima. Much too soon she said that she had to go home, but we arranged to meet the next evening by the performers' entrance of the Opera, where she was rehearsing with a ballet troupe.

I was there an hour early, pacing the back alley in a fine drizzle that gradually soaked me through and through. When she finally appeared, she smiled, took my hand, and said as if scolding a school child:

"Silly boy! No umbrella, no coat! Come quick, before you catch cold."

I let her pull me along. Hand in hand we ran along a maze of narrow streets until we reached a courtyard where she started to climb a wooden staircase. Higher and higher we went, until we reached a top-floor room. She closed the door behind us and turned the key. Then we were in each other's arms. I started to tremble like a tree in a high wind.

A violent thunderstorm released in a few moments all the hunger, longing, shame and fury of many months. It might have scared anyone but a jungle cat. Isabel's warm body understood all. And afterwards we floated in a sea of infinite tranquillity.

Our romance lasted two or three weeks, for as long as I remained in Madrid. I waited for Isabel every day after rehearsals and even went to one. There was a lot of tutu-ing around that didn't impress me very much, and I was impatient for it to end. When it did we ran back to her room.

When I think of her today, she seems a dreamlike figure. Perhaps that's because I knew so little about her. Even now that there was no need to live in fear, we hardly talked about our pasts. And despite the intensity of our feelings, we knew they had no future. That was the way it was during the war years. Everything took place in the present tense. You never knew where you would be in another month or year, or if you would be at all, and you protected yourself and others by staying on the surface of things. You didn't ask questions and you didn't expect to be asked any. In an odd way, it was like continuing to live underground.

Isabel did tell me that she was a refugee too, the daughter of a Hungarian father and a French mother. Perhaps they were communists. She herself, once she trusted me enough to express them, had strongly anti-Franco views. One night, without telling me where we were going, she took me on a bus to a dreary high-rise project on the outskirts of town. We walked down a dark, narrow street until we came to the wall of a prison, and there she stopped and began to sing in a strong, loud voice.

I stared at her. It was unworldly.

"For a friend," was all she said when she had finished.

Then we rode the bus back into town.

★ ★ ★

We never even said goodbye, because at four o'clock the next morning our group was awoken and told to pack and head for the railway station. Once more I found myself on a train, this time with padlocked doors. We were obviously a secret cargo.

After a few hours we came to a halt and our car was uncoupled and shunted onto a siding. It took several more hours before we were hitched to another train that took us on the next lap of our journey. The next day we were uncoupled again and left standing at a small rural station. By now there were murmurs of protest in the group, but I knew that everything was all right. I had smelled the sea.

It wasn't my imagination. When at last the doors were slid open, we were in San Antonio de Real, a small Portuguese port just across the Spanish frontier. The afternoon sun was still shining, the population was friendly, and the wine in the tavern by the quay was truly good – but before I could start to relax a British destroyer came steaming into port at high speed. Within fifteen minutes we were aboard.

Portugal being a neutral country, the ship flew not the white ensign of the British Royal Navy but "the Red Duster," as the flag of the British merchant marine was called. Its cannon were covered with tarpaulins and the sailors on deck were even dressed in civilian clothes. But as soon as we were outside territorial waters, the charade came to an end: the white ensign was hoisted, the cannon were uncovered, and the Oerlikon guns were manned and elevated in readiness for an air attack.

These guns were to accompany me for the rest of the war – and beyond. They were heavy, Swiss-made machine guns with round magazines that emptied in eight seconds, a very fast rate of fire for those days, and though they could hit only low-flying planes, they were fired anyway to keep the pilot up high, where he had less chance of hitting you. Noticing my interest as I watched him heft a metal canister with 20-mm. shells to load the gun, a bearded seaman invited me onto the gun platform.

"Just press your shoulders against these stirrups," he instructed me. "Now pull that little black handle toward the right."

With an ear-splitting roar, the Oerlikon started pumping bullets into the sky while kicking me in the shoulder like one of Jaap van der Post's bulls. The bearded Englishman almost choked with laughter at my reaction, which must have seemed even funnier when I tried picking up one of the shell cartridges that had scattered on the deck. It burned my fingers so badly that they blistered, but the entire experience left me with a powerful sensation.

The voyage was a short one, for we disembarked in Gibraltar to await the arrival of a convoy on its way to Liverpool. Grilled there by British intelligence, I decided to bluff a bit about my "naval education" – the name I gave to the few months I had spent at the Rotterdam Nautical College. Turning these into a few years, I told my interrogators that I would have been an officer by now if I hadn't been forced to break off my studies. It must have sounded convincing, since from then on I was treated as an officer with all due privileges.

★ ★ ★

The convoy, when assembled, was a huge armada of over one hundred ships, from giant tankers and passenger liners turned into troop transports to brand-new mass-produced Liberty ships and dilapidated freighters, with every kind and size of vessel in between.

It looked like an impossible task to line up this floating chaos into columns. Slender destroyers flitted back and forth, issuing instructions through their bullhorns like sheepdogs corraling a flock. The better part of a day went by until the signal flags were raised on the Commodore's vessel, a large troopship that steamed at the head of the central column. The signal was repeated by the other ships, and as soon as the Commodore's flags were lowered the vast fleet set sail. Large Sunderland amphibious planes droned back and forth above it, their job to spot surface and underwater assailants and keep them at a safe distance.

It was an awesome spectacle. Our ship was steaming near the center of the convoy, and in every direction, as far as the eye could see, loomed other hulls. Far ahead on the horizon I could barely make out the low-slung profile of the largest destroyer, carrying the Senior Officer of the Escort. Other destroyers and frigates were strung out in a protective screen around us.

Sticking up in the middle distance behind our ship was a row of gigantic cannon barrels. Even a greenhorn like me understood that battleships didn't normally sail in the middle of merchant convoys. A young British naval officer was leaning over a railing near me, and I asked him about it.

"Oh, that's the old *Warspite*," he answered.

The *Warspite*, he explained, was a legendary ship from World War I that had been de-mothballed and sent to the Mediterranean to help defend the beleaguered island of Malta against General Rommel's invasion plans. During an Axis air attack she had received a direct hit and a bomb had gone off in one of her boiler rooms. "That would have sunk anything else afloat," the young officer proudly told me. But the *Warspite* had managed to steam back to Gibraltar and was now on her way to England for repairs.

Since the Spanish border town of Algeciras, across the bay from Gibraltar, was swarming with spies who would report our departure at once, we headed straight into the Atlantic to put as much distance as possible between ourselves and the coast. Unfortunately, it wasn't enough.

Having been for an hour a Catholic priest myself, I was in the middle of a theological argument with the two Catholic chaplains who shared my cabin when several squadrons of heavy Heinkel bombers swooped down on our convoy. They seemed particularly interested in the *Warspite*, toward which they peeled off one by one from their attack formations.

All hell broke loose. Every ship began to fire all its guns at once, and the old *Warspite*, fighting once more for her life, let loose a spectacular barrage. The boom of the cannon and the clattering of countless machine guns totally numbed my senses. Soon there was so much smoke that I couldn't even see the German planes. It was total bedlam. I stood in the midst of it transfixed.

So this was war! I was finally in it, if only, alas, as an observer.

I was itching to get my hands on one of those guns myself. But my time had not yet come.

★ ★ ★

It didn't seem in any hurry to. As soon as we set foot on British soil we were put on yet another train to London and secluded on the grounds of an old private school, a cluster of low buildings situated in a park and separated from the outside world by a high wall.

We were in quarantine. The rule in Britain was that all escapees from Europe had to be carefully screened, and we *Engelandvaarders* were being held until a British intelligence officer could be found who spoke enough Dutch to interrogate us.

After six weeks of waiting for one to turn up, I had had it. I had managed more difficult escapes in my life, and one evening I waited for it to grow dark, found a sturdy creeper that reached to the top of the wall, and was over it in a few seconds.

There followed a pleasant evening in an English pub, after which I could have found another creeper to climb back on. But being full of beans and beer by now, I decided to take the path of most resistance. Walking straight to the gate, I politely asked the guard to let me in. Although this was beyond his mandate, he was a decent enough bloke to allow me to telephone the base commander.

The fellow almost burst a blood vessel and ordered me marched into his presence – which was exactly what I wanted. Before he could get a word in, I exploded:

"Look here! I didn't risk my life crossing half of Europe to spend the rest of the war in a school grounds! Who ever heard of anything so ridiculous as making us wait for an Englishman who speaks Dutch? Don't you realize that nearly every one of us speaks English? What bloody language do you think I'm talking to you now!"

The base commander flushed with anger. Then the corners of his mouth relaxed. Then they started to twitch with laughter.

"You have a point there, old chap," he admitted. "I'll see what I can do."

Whatever he did, we were soon being questioned by British intelligence – in English. Compared to the third degree I was now given, my interview in Gibraltar had been a lark. I practically had to give a day-by-day description of my life from birth – and when my insatiable interrogators were at last satisfied, I was turned over to the Dutch intelligence service in London and the whole rigamarole began again.

Finally, I was taken to an army barracks, where during the next few days the rest of our Dutch group came trickling in, and told that I had been inducted into the Princess Irene Brigade... as an infantry soldier. It was a cruel blow, made worse by our new drill sergeant, who put us through our paces while bawling:

"Down! Get down! Who the bloody hell do you think you are anyway? Wanted to come to England to play soldiers, did you? Righto, mates, I'll show you what that means. Down, dammit, on your bellies – now forward, keep down, never mind the mud – go on, underneath that barbed wire – lower, dammit, rifles ahead and behinds down – touch that wire and I'll blast your bloody arses off!"

He appeared to mean it, too, for several times he fired off a volley. No doubt he was shooting blanks, but none of us was inclined to call his bluff.

Drills aside, we weren't badly off. After hours we made frequent sorties into town, where life – despite, or perhaps because of, the war – resembled a gigantic party. London was a city of females: the postmen were women, the policemen were women, and women deftly steered the heavy double-decker buses through the streets as if wheeling baby prams. Everywhere you were surrounded by a flutter of skirts – and although many of their wearers were probably carrying passionate letters in their handbags from husbands or boyfriends at the front, they had clearly not taken vows of chastity. For many of the younger girls the war was an opportunity to escape their bourgeois homes by throwing caution – and frequently, virginity – to the winds. You couldn't walk through Hyde Park at night without stumbling over dozens of couples locked in a close embrace.

Our interest was particularly directed at girls in uniform. We had opportunities galore for meeting them in the Service clubs, where ATS girls in khaki gear, WAAFs in light blue air force uniforms, and Wrens in dark blue naval uniforms and little white hats were much in evidence. The pert little Wrens were the most sought-after but also the least approachable, and after several failed attempts at trapping one I decided to cut my losses and befriend an ATS girl who worked in a hospital. We must have made love in every bed in the place. When none was available, we used the operating tables.

We *Engelandvaarders* also had our own club, located in a posh mansion near Hyde Park Corner, where we read, played chess, and drank tea. One day we were visited there by Queen Wilhelmina's son-in-law, Prince Bernhard, and his aide-de-camp. While the prince was busy conversing, I approached the aide and told him that my talents were going to waste. "I'm a sailor," I said, "not an earthworm. I wasn't made to crawl around in the mud."

At once he reached for a pad and asked for my name and serial number, calming my fears that I was about to be court-martialled for insubordination by telling me that as a naval man himself he thoroughly sympathized with me. He had a friend, a rear-admiral, whom he would talk to.

It worked, and early in the spring of 1943 I joined the Dutch navy and was sent to sea.

★　★　★

Although the United States had entered the war in December 1941, German U-boats continued to roam the Atlantic, turning it into a vast graveyard for the Allied shipping that was enabling the British to hold out. Only the fastest and most modern ships could risk sailing alone. The others had to seek the safety of convoys, guarded by escort vessels.

The Dutch navy played only a minor role in all this, since most of its fleet had been lost in the Java Sea in a heroic but fruitless attempt to halt the Japanese invasion of the Dutch East Indies. There were, however, a few Dutch support ships available, one of which was the *Ondina* – a justly famed vessel to which I was now assigned. Originally an oil tanker that had been fitted with cannon and anti-aircraft guns at the outset of the war, she had been attacked in the Indian Ocean by two Japanese cruisers and a squadron of Zeros. Although one of the cruisers was hit and forced to withdraw by her guns, the second damaged her so badly that she caught fire and – after a final pummeling by the Zeros – was left by the Japanese to sink. The saga of how her surviving crew members put out the flames and brought her safely to an Australian port had made her a floating legend.

The minute I reported to her in Liverpool and saw her moored in her wartime camouflage colors, I fell in love with her. Staring awestruck at the heavy cannon on the rear deck and the clusters of machine-gun barrels pointing skywards like warning fingers, I felt immensely proud to be her junior officer. Not even having to share a cabin with "Sparks," the Australian Third Radio Officer – I was apparently too lowly to rate quarters of my own – could dampen my enthusiasm, especially when the cabin turned out to have a private toilet and a shower.

My problem was to keep from giving myself away, for I had done some pretty outrageous fibbing to get where I was. Ironically, although I had given up being Hendrik de Groot many months ago, here I was once more under a false identity! And, as I soon saw, it wouldn't be easy to play this part well either.

The very first time I entered the officers' mess I must have been late, because all the officers were already seated. Looking for an inconspicuous place, I spotted an empty chair at the end of a long table in the back and sat down in it. Nobody said a word or even looked my way until a huge fellow with half-a-ton of gold bars on his shoulders entered the mess and headed straight for me. It was the captain – who in a booming voice demanded to know what I was doing in his place. Only then did the poker faces around me break into broad grins.

And so, told shortly after this to report to the captain, I feared the worst. What comeuppance was I in for? Hastily brushing my uniform and straightening my cap, I headed worriedly for the upper deck.

My suspense continued even after entering the captain's cabin, for I couldn't tell if my reception was encouragingly friendly or ominously taciturn. The captain offered me a seat and sat regarding me in a profound silence that I did not dare violate. Could he be contemplating the rare spectacle of a seagoing Jew, of which I might well be his first? After an unconscionably long time he nodded and declared, as if summing up a lengthy conversation:

"Well, yes. Your duties. Oh, I take it you'll be all right."

He rose, took two large glasses and a bottle from a cupboard, filled both with an amber liquid, handed me one, and said:

"Welcome aboard, young man. Cheers!"

Not wanting to be outdone as he poured the contents down his gullet, I swallowed mine in one gulp and felt as if someone had stuck a red-hot poker down my throat. I was nearly twenty-one years old and had never tasted whisky before! The next day I awoke with a hangover, but I felt that I had come through with flying colors when told that the captain was heard remarking:

"That Kahn may be a Jew, but he can drink with the best of them!"

Further trials were in store for me. As the *Ondina* was waiting for a U.S.-bound convoy, our First Officer decided to prepare a new deviation table – two columns of numbers indicating the compass error at different headings of the ship, caused by her own magnetic field. And what better person to prepare it than the new junior officer?

Starting to sweat, I went off to the platform where the large standard compass stood. *Compass error? Deviation table?* I desperately thought back to my few months of nautical college, ready to jump into the water and disappear... when miraculously, entire pages from one of my textbooks suddenly leaped into my mind. With a bit of help from the First Officer, who proved not at all a bad fellow and took the ship around in a full circle several times while I checked the deviation at different headings, I passed this test too.

My first real job once we set sail was as a standby on the First Officer's watch, ceaselessly scanning the horizon twice a day on the eight-to-twelve watch. This meant looking in particular for the tiny black dots in the sky that could within seconds become large and vicious bombers, and for the slender metal rods between the waves that betrayed the periscope of a lurking submarine.

Rather than take the shortest route to New York, we steamed along the coast of Scotland to stay within range of the British Coastal Command for as long as possible, and then proceeded northwest toward Greenland. By the time we reached the Atlantic it was getting pretty nippy, and I had frequent recourse to my balaclava, a long woolen cap with a narrow slit that left only the eyes exposed. It had been especially knitted for us sailors by the Dutch ladies of Curaçao, and it certainly came in handy, even though the cold wet air soon froze it stiff. When you were finally able to peel it off your face in the comfort of your warm cabin, it remained upright for a while before collapsing slowly like a sagging erection.

Sometimes I had just managed to thaw my freezing bones when the "Action Stations" alarm shrieked through the ship. Pulling the soggy balaclava back over my head and donning a steel helmet over it, I would run on the double to my post on the compass platform, from which I had an unobstructed view of the ship. From this spot I was supposed to help coordinate the firing of the Oerlikons, although the veteran machine-gun crews hardly needed my assistance.

Often the weather made open-air watches impossible. Ferocious gales roared out of the polar ice at us, threatening to blow overboard anyone venturing on deck. Fortunately, lookouts were now hardly necessary, since the more furiously the storm raged, the less likely we were to be attacked by enemy submarines. In such tempests they simply bottomed, as blind and helpless as newborn kittens.

To my great surprise, I never suffered from seasickness like many other members of the crew, no matter how badly the *Ondina* was rolling. From behind the protection of the bridge windows I gazed in fascination at the endless dark green mountains of waves that came sweeping in from the horizon towards the ship. It was a mighty spectacle, and every time a wave met our bow, the ship vibrated along her entire length before disappearing, groaning and bucking, under the foaming cauldron. A few seconds later she would rise at such a speed that your knees buckled under you, only to slide giddily into the next trough, making you almost weightless. And before you had a chance to catch your breath, another wave was already curling above the bow. Once again the deck vanished, followed by the rest of the ship.

It went on and on in the same thunderous cadence. I loved it. It was awe-inspiring. There you were, alone on a small, tossing island, surrounded by elemental fury. Nothing on land could compare to it.

At such times the rest of the convoy was spread out over the horizon except for one corvette behind us whose bow was thrown so high into the air that you could sometimes even see her keel. Corvettes were the smallest type of escorts and had to be refueled along the way. As soon as the weather calmed, they steamed close behind the *Ondina* and refilled their tanks through a fuel hose like calves sucking from a mother cow.

By now I had proved myself, and when we entered a zone of heavy fog near Newfoundland, a precarious situation in which the slightest deviation in direction or speed by any ship could produce a nasty collision, I was sometimes left in charge on the bridge. Slowing down or accelerating the *Ondina* by a few revs was enough to maintain a proper distance from the next vessel, but after a few hours of staring into the woolly gray blanket ahead of me, I felt as if my eyes were popping out of my head.

And just to keep me from getting too cocky, there were reminders that I wasn't out of danger yet. For example, our ship pulled something behind it called a "Walker patent log," a cigar-shaped contraption with wings that trailed at the end of a long, plaited rope. Spinning in the water like a propellor, it torqued the rope and turned a clock on the aft taffrail that gave us our distance traveled through the water, and by calculation, our speed. As we were about to enter New York, the chief officer said to me:

"Go with the bos'n and take in the log."

The two of us went to the taffrail. The rope was attached to the clock by means of a hook, but having no clear idea what to do with it, I waited for the bos'n to take the next step. When he failed to, I ordered:

"All right, take it in."

He looked at me and made no move.

"Well, come on," I repeated sharply. "Take it in!"

He shrugged and began to haul the rope in, and pretty soon all 200 meters of it had become one hopelessly snarled mess. Only later did I learn that, as he hauled in the line with the log attached to it, he should have let out the free part to enable the line to untwist. But without an explicit order from me, he was not about to do anything of the sort.

We managed to unsnarl the rope, and since crew members didn't talk to officers about anything they weren't asked about, none of my superiors heard of my gaffe. The bos'n must have had a fine time, though, entertaining his mates with his story of the junior officer who didn't even know how to take in a Walker patent log.

★ ★ ★

Almost a hundred miles out from New York, we could already see the faint reflection of the city's lights in the clouds above the horizon. Next emerged its distant silhouette followed by the contours of its brightly lit towers that resembled a collection of asymmetrically arranged building blocks. The sight came to me as a physical shock. I couldn't help comparing the war-torn, blacked-out Europe I had left behind with the splendor and affluence of this city. Even from afar America looked like a land of exuberance and plenty.

Once we entered the port, the same picture recurred in close-up. Manhattan was pulsating and swinging with night life. The entire city seemed to be on the move, with the red and yellow lights of endless files of cars weaving luminescent chains through its avenues.

The convoy was disbanded and our ship dropped anchor in the Hudson River. I was already standing on deck, freshly scrubbed and decked out in my fancy togs, ready to jump ashore and join the happy turmoil. And I had another reason for being eager to visit New York, too, which was that I had learned while in London, via an old friend of my father's, that my sister Ellen was now married and living there, having reached America by a long, roundabout route.

We were assigned a berth alongside a depot of oil tanks, and when the mooring cables were made fast a company of armed American sailors swarmed aboard to secure the ship. Then, without further delay, the *Ondina* started pumping. It seemed that we had been ordered to begin the return journey within twenty-four hours, loaded with fourteen million liters of high-octane aviation fuel – enough to keep hundreds of bombers in the air for months.

Before I could brood about it, I was told to change from my dress uniform into overalls and supervise the filling of the *Ondina*'s tanks. While the deckhands opened and closed valves, it was my job to watch the gauges and make sure that the volume did not rise above a red line. The tanks filled at an astounding rate, and a single mistake on my part could have made them overflow and risk blowing the *Ondina* sky-high. We worked non-stop, and in seemingly no time the "Ready to depart" order was given and I found myself at the telegraph, ready to pass on instructions to the engine room below. A sense of bitter disappointment overcame me. After all these years here I was, a few minutes' ride from my sister, and I wasn't even going to get to say hello!

I shifted the telegraph to "Slow ahead" and an answering ring sounded from the engine room. And yet though the engines should have started pounding, nothing happened. Had I made some mistake? I repeated the order: "Slow ahead..." After a while the engines came to life, coughing and spluttering unhealthily.

"Half ahead," I signaled. The clamor became louder and the steel deck started to vibrate under my feet. Something had to be wrong. A few seconds later the engine room reported serious trouble. There was nothing to be done but shut down the engines and vacate the berth by towing the *Ondina* into midriver, where she dropped anchor.

The damage turned out to be serious. Repairs would take at least a week. There were smiles in the mess room, for I wasn't the only one who had craved some rest and relaxation.

"Well, Kahn," said the First Officer, "you can see your sister now. I don't know how you fixed it, but my compliments."

To show that he bore me no grudges, he gave me a 72-hour pass.

An hour later I stood on a quay near Battery Park, dressed again in my good uniform and white cap. I hailed the first taxicab I saw, and seconds later I was floating on the cushiony springs of an American limousine through the fume-saturated streets of Manhattan.

The cab driver, a large, jovial black man, leaned back in his seat comfortably, guiding his vehicle with gentle pressure from his thumb while plying me with questions: Where did I come from? How long had I been in the States? How did I like New York? I was flattered by his interest. What a friendly people! No taxi driver in Europe would have dreamed of such behavior.

Ellen and her husband Lou were having a late Sunday morning breakfast in their apartment in uptown Manhattan when I arrived without warning. We had last seen each other in the autumn of 1939; it was now the summer of 1943.

She opened the door and burst out crying.

I couldn't think of the right words. Perhaps there weren't any. I let her cry and then listened to her story.

The first part of it I already knew in a general way. She had been in Monte Carlo with Bichen and Bichen's mother when the Nazis invaded Holland, and the three had then moved to Lisbon. What I didn't know – although it hardly surprised me – was how Ellen had been humiliated there. While the two women took up residence in a luxury hotel, she was tucked away in a seedy boarding house and given so little money that she practically went hungry. And when they all received visas to the United States, Bichen and her mother booked first-class cabins and made Ellen travel steerage in the bowels of the ship, a dilapidated Spanish steamer.

In New York it was just as bad. Bichen soon found a comfortable apartment with a room in it for Ellen – for which my sister was required to pay fifteen of the twenty-five dollars that she earned each month by looking after the children of a Jewish family. It was her luck that she eventually landed better work as a dental assistant, through which she met her husband Lou and was at last rescued from Bichen's clutches.

"Have you heard anything about father?" I asked.

Ellen shivered and started to cry again. "He was arrested in The Hague," she almost whispered. "That's all I know. Nothing has been heard of him since."

So much for the lunatic asylum!

"What else do you know?" I demanded.

Perhaps it was the harshness of my voice that made her cry harder.

"What about Uncle Georg and Aunt Rosa? What about Uncle Bernard?"

Sobbing, Ellen left the room.

"You mustn't mind her, Hans," said Lou. "She can't sleep nights thinking of these things. We've tried everything we can to find out more, but basically we know very little. Georg and Rosa were last seen in Westerbork. Bernard made it to France and was caught and deported from a place called Gurs. That's all we can tell you." He went to console Ellen, leaving me in their little living room. A wave of grief swept over me; then, helpless rage. How I wanted to go out and destroy the criminals who had done this, one by one!

After a while Ellen and Lou returned. Now it was my turn to tell about myself. I tried to do it in order: Amsterdam, Antwerp, Paris, Mont d'Or, Lyon, Marseilles, Vernet...

"Hans! I sent you parcels there via the Red Cross. Did you get them?"

Word of my being in Vernet, but not of my alias, had apparently reached her indirectly from the Bienstocks. Her packages mailed to "Hans Kahn" must have ended up in some German stomach.

"And the visa to Cuba! You didn't get that either?"

She had actually saved up months of hard-earned wages to buy a piece of paper with a Cuban stamp that she thought could save me from the gas chambers!

"It wasn't just my money. I had a little help. You must know we have cousins in New York. You probably remember Alfred; he's a big shot on Wall Street, so I went to see him in his fancy office. He didn't even want to talk to me. Then I tried Walter, who also earns a lot, and he wouldn't chip in either. Only Arno was decent. He didn't believe it would do any good, but he did give me something."

Poor Ellen! I didn't have the heart to tell her that it was just as well her efforts had come to naught. If the Germans had discovered my real identity, I would have ended up not in Cuba but in a cattle car to Poland.

We sat up talking past midnight. Then, saturated with emotion, I went to bed to get some needed sleep.

★ ★ ★

The following morning Ellen took the day off to show me some of the sights of New York. We went to Rockefeller Center, and even to Coney Island, but I couldn't get excited over any of it. The towering buildings first bored and then depressed me; after a while I felt as if I were surrounded by the walls of enormous prisons. Even the American friendliness began to pale after I met a few of Ellen and Lou's friends. It didn't take long for me to realize that all the pretended interest was an empty ritual of politeness. If you actually tried telling anyone where you came from, you saw at once that they weren't listening.

What did I have in common with these people? What did we have to talk about? They had never been under bombardment and they had as much to eat as they wanted. An ocean of water – of experience – separated them from the world of death and destruction I had left behind. And still they dared complain about the minor sacrifices required to keep their war industry turning at full capacity! It was sickening to hear them go on about the difficulties of buying new tires for the gas-guzzling monsters they called cars, or about the minor restrictions imposed on the sale of sugar. I understood better now the American sailors I had met in England who threatened to go on strike because there were only two flavors of ice cream served aboard their ship. There was not the slightest grasp of, or empathy with, the oppression, misery, and hunger in Nazi-occupied Europe – or for that matter, of the true heroism and sacrifices of the British civilian population.

We were living on different planets. I could have slugged the man on the subway who, noticing the patch saying "The Netherlands" on the sleeve of my uniform, came up to me and said with the very best of intentions:

"Don't you worry, pal. We'll win the war for you."

Maybe it wasn't being very nice to Ellen, who was trying so hard to give me a good time, but I could hardly hide my happiness when my three days of leave were over and it was time to rejoin the *Ondina*. She had been moved to the Brooklyn Naval Yard to complete the repairs on her engine, and I was quite satisfied to stand watch on board while the other officers went into town to look for fun and sex. I wasn't in the mood for it.

Not that there was much to stand watch over – but still, here I was in the port of New York, a Jew thrown out of nautical college by the Nazis, guarding a ship vital to winning the war effort. Just seeing our flag race up the mast every morning with the flags of the other ships nearby gave me a profound sense of satisfaction.

Chapter Ten

The return convoy to England carried mostly U.S. Army tanks and fuel needed to keep the RAF flying. In it were quite a few of the spanking new Liberty ships that were now rolling, as though on conveyor belts, out of U.S. dockyards faster than the German U-boats could destroy them.

We were taking a more dangerous route this time, "going round the south" to England by the coast of Ireland, where there was less wind and fog but more chance of U-boats. Judging by the large number of American destroyers and frigates that supplemented our British admiralty escort, we were considered very important.

Since she had been assigned the role of a rescue ship that would pick up survivors of torpedo attacks while the rest of the convoy steamed on and left her behind, the *Ondina* sailed at the convoy's rear. Apparently we were chosen for the task because, with 14,000 tons of high-octane fuel beneath our feet, if a torpedo hit *us* there would be no survivors to pick up.

The mental techniques I had mastered in Vernet came in handy now, for I learned to repress all morbid imaginings by simply drawing a mental line around them. And as an extra safeguard, I surrounded this line with a second barrier composed of anything I could concentrate on: erotic fantasies of my ATS nurse or – what was even more effective – mathematical problems like proving Pythagoras' theorem or constructing a spherical triangle using the elements needed for calculating your position at sea according to the method of Marc-St. Hilaire. Whenever a depth charge made the *Ondina*'s steel plating tremble as if pounded with giant sledgehammers, I could stop my thoughts from running amok with such themes – unless I happened to be doing duty on the bridge, in which case the Commodore kept me hopping with his constant flag-signals, sending messages like: "Ship Number 18, Stop Making So Much Smoke," or "Emergency Turn, 30 Degrees Starboard."

The most dangerous vessels during these maneuvers were the Liberty ships. Because of inexperience or whatever, they invariably kept moving straight ahead, threatening to ram every vessel near them. And to add insult to injury, they would then signal "dot-dot-dash" – international Morse Code for "You are steering a dangerous course"! It didn't surprise me to hear that their deck officers were allowed to keep watches after a mere six-week crash course.

We arrived in Liverpool safely, except for the second engineer, who had to be carried off the ship in a blue funk. In the middle of the Irish Sea he had suddenly abandoned the engine room and appeared on the bridge, shaking with fear and ranting:

"I just heard a freaking torpedo pass underneath the ship. I'm not going back down there again!"

Given the noise in the engine room he could not have heard a school of whales, but the poor fellow's mental defenses, which had held since the war started while he crossed the Atlantic countless times, had simply collapsed all at once.

★ ★ ★

After discharging part of our cargo at Liverpool, we continued up the Mersey and into the Manchester Ship Canal. Halfway along it we moored near a railway bridge at Runcorn, from where we were to continue the next morning. There was to be a party in a local hall that night organized by the United Services Club with lights, bunting, paper chains, barrels of beer, and large numbers of females from all over the district. The spiffing up on the *Ondina* was great.

I danced most of the evening with a willowy divorced blonde named Gladys. We didn't talk much, but she clung to me langorously, and as I walked her home I was already counting on a night in bed with her.

We entered a working-class neighborhood and soon Gladys halted in front of some dreary row houses. What a dismal place to spend your life in! You could feel the soot settling on your shoulders. Even worse, by the time we reached Gladys' front door dozens of curious eyes were peering out the neighboring windows. Disconcerted by so much attention, I let her give me a prim kiss before she vanished inside.

Several days later, on our way back to Liverpool, we moored at Runcorn again. The moment I was free, I set out for Gladys' house. Before she could express surprise at my appearance, I was through the door. She apologized for not having let me in the last time and began to explain that, living alone, she had to watch her reputation... but there was really no need for apologies. Prim Gladys was the most passionate of women. She had that cool English demeanor that can be so deceptive, and although she didn't look it, she was quite a lot older than me – and more experienced. From then on we saw a lot of each other between one Atlantic crossing and the next. I remained faithful to her until my final journey on the *Ondina*.

★ ★ ★

By the spring of 1944 I had completed several such crossings and the trip was almost routine. I had also gotten used to the real officer's stripe that I now sported in place of a cadet's. Even the steamy nights with Gladys were losing their excitement. All we had between us was sex – a lot of it while it lasted. But there had to be more to life than dodging U-boats on the Atlantic and coming home to a squalid working-class house and a woman as familiar as a wife.

I felt that the war was passing me by. Though I knew our convoys were important, they weren't what I had been an *Englendsvaarder* for. Waiting to be hit by a torpedo was too much like waiting for a Nazi knock on the door or a German patrol to board your train. Someone like myself, who still had recurrent nightmares in which I felt the breath of my would-be killers on my neck, had an almost violent need to fight back. Hence my mood improved as rumors increased of an impending invasion of Europe in which the *Ondina* would take part.

Not that we needed rumors to be aware of it. Great Britain had become one huge parking lot filled with tens of thousands of vehicles – jeeps, personnel carriers, armored cars, and rows and rows of tanks, tanks as far as the eye could see, many of them carried by our convoys. It was a thrilling sight.

London was now swarming with Yanks in uniform. They had completely taken over the town. No, they could not win the war for us – by then Germany, its armies retreating in Russia and its air force defeated by Britain, had already lost the war – but they could certainly shorten it.

The big moment was almost at hand. The *Ondina* was ordered to steam to Loch Ewe, a large naval base in the north of Scotland.

It was beautiful spring weather when we entered a scenic fjord and dropped anchor amid several hundred vessels of the most varied kinds: Liberty ships crammed to the gunwales with tanks and cannons, landing crafts of all sizes, ancient cruisers and shiny new frigates and destroyers – all part of the biggest invasion fleet the world had ever known.

Several weeks later, on June 6th, D-day arrived. By now we were at a fever pitch – but there were still no orders to sail. Nor, as the days went by and the Allied beachhead at Normandy was expanded, did we get any. It soon grew clear that part of the fleet, including the *Ondina*, was being held in reserve. Although this showed the enormousness of the Allied forces, our morale plummeted. How many dice or card games could we go on playing while listening to radio reports of the fighting along the French coast?

Our boredom and frustration grew by the day, and the captain, aware of the time bomb ticking among his crew, must have spoken to the First Officer, whose plan to release our pent-up tensions by organizing a party aboard ship was greeted with wild enthusiasm. Finding the women for it was no problem, since the signal station at the entrance to our fjord was exclusively "manned" by a large contingent of Wrens, who like us had been confined to their quarters since D-day and were getting just as itchy.

Unfortunately, although the mother Wrens were agreeable to our invitation, they insisted that their little birds be back in their nests by 10 p.m. How could a party end by such an hour? The answer was simple: start it at four.

By five the *Ondina* was a madhouse. There were lots of pretty faces among our guests, but we didn't have the patience to be choosy. From the word go, it was catch-as-catch-can. Every corner of the ship, not to mention the cabins and the life boats, was occupied by entwined couples and swamped by puddles of whisky and beer. The *Ondina* had become one vast mattress. Surely it wasn't just our imaginations that made us feel her heaving and rolling in the quiet fjord.

The next day we were out for the count. We wouldn't have felt it if they had wiped the decks with us.

The real hangover, however, came several days later, when we learned that we had definitely been excluded from the invasion. In fact, we were to steam to Glasgow and return to convoy duty.

I decided to ask for a transfer.

★   ★   ★

Specifically, I asked to be assigned to one of the squadrons of motor torpedo boats, operating out of Dover, that attacked German naval movements in the English Channel and along the North Sea Coast.

For a while it looked as if I would get my wish, since after yet another round trip between England and the United States I was told to report to a naval base near Falmouth for a gunnery course.

Although I was quite familiar with the Oerlikon guns, I was now also introduced to the new two-inch Beauforts, popularly known as "Pom-Poms" because of their double barrel, one side of which fired while the other recoiled. Even more novel was the "Stalin Organ," a Russian invention that unleashed a battery of rockets at low-flying planes. There were ten of these to a box, each in its own compartment as in a wine carton, and you had to fire them all together – after which, if you missed your target, you were out of luck, since it took half-an-hour to reload. Definitely low-technology, but highly effective against Stukas... once, that is, they were on top of you.

The Stuka was the most hated and feared of German airplanes. Small but powerful, it came tearing straight down from a great altitude, dropping its bombs at what almost seemed mast level. The closer you let it get, the better your chances of hitting it – but of course, of being hit too. To teach you to wait until the last moment, Falmouth had something called a "simulator."

This instrument consisted of a large dome like a planetarium's on whose interior was projected a film of a group of attacking planes. Standing at your rocket launcher inside it, you waited for one of these planes to peel off and dive at you. It was all terribly realistic, including the rapidly increasing dimensions of the plane on the screen, the ear-splitting roar of its engine, and the flaming red points of its machine guns. However, the most sadistic little touch, aimed at paralyzing the victim, was the Stuka's siren. Activated by the pilot halfway down his descent, its piercing wail increased in frequency until you felt your brains were about to burst. The only defense was to shut your ears and concentrate on keeping the approaching plane centered in your visor while your finger rested on the trigger. No... not yet... not yet... *now!*

Bull's-eye!

At which point, your tattered nerves were frayed even more by hearing the laconic voice of your instructor say:

"Four hundred yards... not bad, but it should have been three hundred. Let's do it again."

To my great disappointment, I didn't make the torpedo boats. The Dutch navy, it appeared, had more seamen than ships. Instead, I was mustered as a junior deck officer, with special responsibility for anti-aircraft defenses, on the S.S. *Nijkerk*, an ancient Dutch merchantman that had been placed at the disposal of the British admiralty. The ship had been armed and was now being used to transport ammunition to the Mediterranean – and not just your common, garden variety of explosives, but sticks of gelignite. The *Nijkerk*, in short, was one enormous floating bomb: a single direct hit and the entire crew would be singing madrigals with the angels.

★ ★ ★

Just before we set out to sea I had a visit from a social worker attached to Netherlands House in London, the seat of the Dutch government-in-exile. He brought me news of my father, who by some miracle was still alive. Following his arrest he had been sent to Bergen-Belsen, but he was now in Biberach, a camp in a small German town not far from the Swiss border that was under the supervision of the Red Cross. Although there were no further details, it seemed that he was not in danger and would be kept safe until the end of the war. (Much later I learned that he had managed to use his semi-diplomatic status to save him from certain death in an extermination camp.)

I was also handed a letter from my mother, whom I had not seen since she left us for another man when I was a small boy. It was posted from Italy, where she had been hidden in a monastery with her second husband, a man oddly named Kahn too, who died before the Allied liberation. I was almost beginning to feel sorry for her when she dropped her bombshell: following her husband's death, the nuns had been so wonderfully caring that she decided to become a Roman Catholic.

It was unbelievable. She even asked me what I thought about the fact that she was already baptized.

I told her what I thought. I wrote back that besides being shocked by her stupidity in converting to such a faith, I was ashamed to have as my mother a person who had betrayed her people in its darkest hour.

I received no answer to that.

★ ★ ★

The *Nijkerk* turned out to be the commodore ship of the convoy. It was a truly impressive sight when we left for Gibraltar at the head of the central column, with some 150 ships in tow. The sea was smooth, with a bright blue sky overhead and the ship's ancient steam engines pounding their reassuring beat beneath our feet. Given the difference between the Mediterranean and the Atlantic, and the changed fortunes of the war, the journey promised to be far more peaceful than my crossings on the *Ondina*.

After a few days, during my afternoon watch, the gigantic rock of Gibraltar loomed on the horizon, rising straight out of the sea. Nothing disturbed the perfect calm but the drone of some Sunderland flying boats skimming the water.

At four o'clock I was relieved from my watch as usual. "Not a cloud in the sky," I said to my replacement. "Gibraltar's dead ahead. Have a nice time."

The words were scarcely out of my mouth when, turning to go down the stairs to my cabin, I was picked up, as if propelled by a giant hand, and slammed against the deckhouse. For a moment, everything went black around me. Then I opened my eyes to see my relief standing motionless, staring horror-stricken toward starboard with his mouth hanging open. How he had managed to stay on his feet was beyond me. I crawled toward him and picked myself up. Following his stare, I understood what had happened. Where a few seconds ago a fair-sized ship had plowed the water, only a seething maelstrom was visible. The torpedoed vessel had carried a full load of gelignite like ourselves.

It was sheer pandemonium and there was no time to think. We were the commodore ship and had to take charge. Already an order arrived from the Commodore: "Emergency zigzag code 3." This called for opening the code book, preparing and running up the signal flags, checking the time, making sure that every ship repeated the signal, reporting back, and checking the time once again. There followed the order "Execute," which meant that our signal flags had to come smartly down while we began the maneuver and hoped that the entire convoy fell in line.

There was no time to worry about the unlikely prospect of survivors. The convoy started to zigzag toward the safety of Gibraltar while its destroyer escorts coursed through it like crazed terriers, dropping their depth charges left and right. This didn't do much good, for within a short time the U-boat lurking beneath us succeeded in hitting two tankers. They were left behind wreathed in smoke while we steamed on.

Only after we had anchored in Gibraltar and I was able to go to my cabin did I feel something sticky in my pants. I had shat in them like a little boy! And yet not only hadn't I noticed it at the time, I hadn't felt a moment's fear. My body had. But I wasn't my body. *I* was something else, just like on that night in the Pyrenees.

★　★　★

Gibraltar's main street was a rather savage place in those days, frequented by thousands of British and American seamen whose sole purpose was to drink themselves senseless. As usual under such circumstances, the evenings began amicably enough, with much toasting and fraternization, and ended in violent brawls. I don't imagine many pub interiors in Gibraltar survived the war.

Even after the pubs had closed, the streets were far from safe. Drunken Limeys, Yanks and Aussies roamed about in them, brandishing guns and threatening to settle unfinished scores. Even more dangerous were those still sober enough to aim and shoot at each other. There were times when it seemed to me that a new front had broken out.

On the voyage across the Mediterranean to Egypt, I made a point of not thinking about the torpedoed gelignite ship. One afternoon, standing watch over a smooth blue sea, I suddenly noticed a large number of half-submerged spherical objects ahead of us. Floating mines! Without hesitation, I hit the red alarm button. Alarm sirens wailed up and down the ship and the entire crew ran to its action stations.

In no time the captain was on the bridge to see what the emergency was about. I pointed agitatedly to the menacing globes. Barely bothering to glance at them, he quietly pressed the "stand-down" button to cancel the alarm.

I couldn't understand what he was doing.

"Sorry, Kahn," he said, putting an arm on me with a friendly smile. "I should have warned you about the sea turtles in these parts."

★ ★ ★

Entering the port of Alexandria, I spied a small, ancient-looking vessel bearing the name *Amal* in Hebrew letters and flying a blue flag with a white circle that had a capital "P" in it. There could be no mistake. It was a Jewish ship and the "P" stood for Palestine! I felt tremendously excited.

As soon as we had docked, I went off to meet its crew. The first of them I encountered was a young man with a single stripe on the epaulet of his white tropical shirt who went by the biblical-sounding name of Malachi Efrati. I thought it so beautiful that I couldn't stop rolling it around my tongue. He told me that the *Amal* was one of three ships belonging to the Atid Navigation Company in Haifa, which was controlled by the Borchards, a family of German Jews who had been the only Jewish shipowners in Europe. They had gotten the ships to Palestine before the war, and these had subsequently been requisitioned by the British admiralty and were now being used for the dumping of old land mines and other obsolete ammunition out at sea.

It wasn't an impressive job and the *Amal* wasn't an impressive vessel, but that wasn't the point. Not only was I no longer the world's only Jewish sailor – here, before my eyes, was a Jewish ship, owned by Jews, manned by Jews, and carrying a Hebrew name! I had always believed that we could learn to be a seafaring nation. Now I had seen proof.

My excitement mounted when we left Alexandria for Haifa, our next port of call. It wasn't even deflated by an unpleasant incident aboard ship of the sort I sometimes had to cope with.

I was having some canned fruit for dessert in the officers' mess when – perhaps remembering my Uncle Nehemia and the Jaffa oranges – I remarked:

"You know, citrus is a big crop in Palestine and it keeps for a long time. We should put in a big supply of it in Haifa."

"I'll bet," said one of the senior officers. "And be cheated blind. They'll sell us rotten fruit at double the price with their *joden streken*."

Jodenstreek was a Dutch slang-word meaning "Jew trick." It wasn't the first time I had heard it aboard ship.

If we hadn't been in uniform, it wouldn't have ended peacefully. As it was, I rose and walked away from the table. I went to the First Officer and told him that I wasn't eating in the officers' mess any more and wanted to be served in my cabin from now on. This led to my being summoned to the captain.

"What's this about wanting your meals in bed, Kahn?" he asked.

"I'll eat them sitting up, sir," I answered. "But I will not share a table with a contemptible bigot." And although he had undoubtedly heard what had happened, I told him the story again.

"Oh, come," he said, not unsympathetically. "You mustn't take such things personally. You know that remark wasn't intended for you. You're not that kind of Jew at all."

This only made me angrier, but how could I explain that to him?

"In any case, Kahn," he concluded, "we're not a hotel with room service. You'll continue eating in the mess."

Quite a few sailors on the *Nijkerk* were anti-Semites. For the average Dutch seaman, Jews were clever traders, shrewd lawyers, and unscrupulous financiers. And yet not even the worst of these characters was at all virulent about it. They were after all Dutch. While they may not have thought Jews were to be trusted, they would never have dreamed of denying a Jew his rights.

I returned seething to the officers' mess, but as the *Nijkerk* was slowly being towed into port my feelings turned into something close to ecstasy. There in front of me, along a gently curving bay, lay the city of Haifa, its houses ascending to the top of Mount Carmel like a shimmering white staircase. I remembered my sister Ellen shouting "My windmill! My windmill!" long ago in the back of my father's car. If I had dared shout now on the deck of the *Nijkerk*, it would have been: "My country! My country!"

We hadn't been docked for long when someone came aboard to look for me. It was a local tugboat captain named Hans Windmuller, a short, heavyset Jew from Amsterdam who had immigrated to Palestine before the war. Hearing of a Jewish officer on a Dutch naval ship, he had decided to investigate.

During the next few days, while the *Nijkerk* was unloading some of its gelignite, I spent a lot of time with him. He showed me about the city and we spent hours chatting on his tug, which to my disappointment had an Arab crew. He was very fond of Arab sweets like *halva* and *baklawa* and sometimes sent his crew members to the Arab souk to fetch them for us. Together we dreamed of a Jewish merchant marine and even of founding a Jewish seaman's cooperative, a kind of seaborne kibbutz.

On one of our walks through the downtown port area, he pointed out some Jewish whores to me.

"So you have them here too," I said, not knowing whether to feel pleased or disturbed by this sign of the Jew's normality in his – that is, her – own land.

"Yes," Hans said. "But not enough of them. For the time being, they have to be imported from Tel Aviv."

There were plenty of Arab whores too. Frankly, I couldn't imagine going to either type.

While sitting on the tug, I told Hans about the incident of the oranges.

"I have an idea," he said. "I have friends in a kibbutz near here that grows citrus. Let's go get a truckload for the *Nijkerk*."

I put the proposition to the captain. No doubt trying to make up for my hurt feelings, he gave me not only permission but a wad of British pound notes for the purchase.

Hans Windmuller got hold of a truck and we drove it to the kibbutz and filled it with ripe, juicy fruit. When I mentioned the *Joden streek* remark to the kibbutzniks, they refused to accept money from me.

"Take it," I protested, waving the captain's pound notes. "Why lose income because of some Jew-hater?"

They wouldn't budge and we drove back to the *Nijkerk* with the oranges, which were served for dessert that night in large, colorful baskets. I waited for my fellow officers to begin greedily attacking them and then pulled the pound notes from my pocket and handed them to the captain in front of everyone.

"Your change, sir," I said.

My triumph was complete. I had never seen so much fruit eaten so quietly.

★ ★ ★

Our next port of call was Aden. We still had a sizeable quantity of gelignite on board, and I had no idea when and where we would dispose of it.

First we had to pass through the Suez Canal. In Port Said the *Nijkerk* joined a line-up of ships, enabling most of the crew to enjoy a few hours of shore leave.

My brief excursion was a shock to me. The beggarly throngs crowding the streets defied description. They clung to us like flies, hawking every imaginable kind of merchandise, and the only way to get rid of them was to swat them off. Like flies they kept coming back, though, and for every one you chased away there were ten others with fake gold jewelry, cigarettes made of straw, shoes manufactured from cardboard, dirty pictures. I had been among rich Jews and poor Jews, and I had never doubted that there were rich Arabs and poor Arabs; but thinking about it afterwards in the officers' club on De Lesseps Quay, under fans operated by pitch-black Sudanese boys who pulled their heavy strings in an automatic cadence while leaning seemingly fast asleep against the walls, I no longer understood how Jews and Arabs could live together.

And though it was fascinating to see the long column of ships shepherded through the sixty-mile-long water trough of the Canal like a floating camel caravan, the Gulf of Suez was a hellhole when we reached it. There wasn't a breath of wind and the sun stoked the air to over 45°C degrees. Nor were the nights much better, for besides being very humid, they brought out legions of flies.

These disappeared upon our entering the Red Sea – only to be replaced by armies of locusts. The creatures formed a dense black cloud as far as the eye could see, whirring like squadrons of monoplanes. They blacked out the sun, turning day into dusk. The scrubbed teak decks of the ship were covered with layers of them, so that every step was accompanied by a loud crunch.

Halfway between Suez and Aden we made fast to a rickety quay and watched part of our remaining explosives carried ashore by swarms of black porters. What they could have been used for along that desolate coast was unimaginable, but the more of the nasty stuff disappeared over the side, the better we all felt.

In Aden we moored next to an immense mountain of coal, for the *Nijkerk* was an old-fashioned vessel with coal-fired boilers and Aden was the bunkering port for Asia-bound vessels. Across narrow gangplanks, endless rows of emaciated little men scurried back and forth like ants, carrying baskets of coal on their heads. After shuffling on board, they emptied the baskets into chutes that fed from the deck into coal bunkers. One of these was situated behind my cabin, and the noise of the heavy lumps clattering down it day and night was indescribable. After spending hours on my bunk to escape the black clouds outside, I could no longer stand it and escaped on deck. The entire ship was covered with soot. I stood there breathing coal dust and air in equal quantities, but at least the noise was now bearable.

By now it was the beginning of May, 1945, and our humdrum existence was punctured one day by a radio bulletin announcing that the war in Europe had ended. The Germans had surrendered and the Nazi monster had been beaten!

I tried to picture what was going on in Europe: the cheering crowds, the dancing in the streets, the dazed souls emerging from their hiding places. I wondered who was still alive and who was not. Yet while all I wanted was to get back to Holland to find out, we soon learned that the war was not yet over for us. The Japanese had decided to fight on. We received orders to proceed with the remainder of our cargo to Bombay.

★ ★ ★

We had, we discovered as we prepared to set out again, become a passenger ship. First to board was a group of Sikhs, quiet and impressive fellows with neatly trimmed beards, white uniforms and turbans, who spent most of the day sitting meditatively on the deck with their legs folded beneath them. Of greater interest was a party of British officers, including several Wrens. One in particular took my fancy, a young Third Officer with long legs and dark blond curls. She had an attractive, open face with a pair of shining eyes that peered candidly at the world. I fell in love with her at once.

She might easily have escaped me, for there were quite a lot of competitors for her favors, including the First Officer – who, fortunately, was twice my age. In the end, it was the seating arrangement in the mess that did it. Since she was closest to me in rank we were placed near each other, and in no time we were the best of friends.

Her name was Evelyn, and this was her first trip so far away from home. Together we experienced for the first time the magic of tropical nights, through which the ship drew its luminous trail across placid waves. Soon we exchanged tentative kisses in the shadow of one of the lifeboats. Realizing almost immediately that she had never been to bed with a man, I was for a while satisfied with our innocent caresses, but nature quickly took its bolder course. As junior officer, I had the middle watch from noon till four p.m. and the midnight watch till four in the morning. When I entered my cabin at the end of it, Evelyn would be there waiting for me.

She left the ship in Bombay. Our goodbyes were short and to the point. We promised to write each other regularly, but neither of us had any illusions. No one did in those years. There were no guilty consciences. You took what life gave you, never knowing when it would be the taker.

As if to remind me of that, a few days before reaching Bombay we held a firing drill with our four-inch guns. One of them jammed, and as its crew opened the gun breech to extract the unfired shell and throw it overboard, the ship rolled on a wave and the shell fell to the deck and began careening around. Since it had already been primed for explosion on contact, it could have gone off at any second. Everyone stared at it mesmerized.

Without knowing it was going to happen, I suddenly went into my "slow motion" reaction. As unhurriedly as if I were a vehicle in reverse, I walked across the deck, picked the shell up perfectly calmly, and flipped it over the side. It took only a few seconds, but for me time had stopped entirely. Or else, the space between one moment and the next had become so great that I could take as long as I wanted while remaining safely inside it.

★   ★   ★

Bombay was another rude shock. The poverty and misery were worse than in Port Said. At first I was hurt and outraged; then I realized that it was my duty to ignore the putrid mass of humanity, the begging children and misshapen creatures, filling every corner and alleyway. If you were not to go crazy with frustration, you had to shut it all out and accept the enormous differences between human beings. It was a matter of self-preservation.

During the next few weeks the *Nijkerk* meandered southward along the Indian Coast. We had long ago unloaded our last crate of gelignite, and I had no idea what we were doing; neither did anyone else. Madras was no better than Bombay. The same skeletal hands were outstretched toward me everywhere, as if I alone had the power to ward off hunger, sickness, sores. All I could do was withdraw into myself.

Studying a map of the town of Cochin, however, our next stop along the coast, my eye was caught by the words "Jewish Quarter." I had never heard about Jews living in India and thought at first that it might be a reference to some old, abandoned ghetto. Nevertheless, I decided to look into it.

To my surprise, I entered a district of quiet streets lined with neat little houses. Silence reigned. There were none of the usual milling crowds and not a single beggar to be seen. Small oil lamps were burning in niches beside each front door.

It suddenly struck me that it was Friday night and that these must be Sabbath candles. Like a long-lost son, I felt they had been lit just for me. The feeling grew stronger when a few minutes later, entering a tiny synagogue, my first since my religious days in Amsterdam, I felt that I had come home. There, against the wall where it had always stood, was the Holy Ark with its Torah scrolls. The only difference was the *bima*, the cantor's podium, which was placed in the synagogue's center, with the congregation seated around it on colorful cushions.

Questioning looks were sent my way as I came in. It clearly wasn't often that a European visitor arrived here, let alone one dressed in a white naval uniform. But as soon as I uttered the traditional *"Shabbat shalom,"* several of the men moved smilingly aside and invited me to join them. At the conclusion of the service I introduced myself to the *Chacham*, as the rabbi was called, a venerable figure with a long white beard. I was even able to talk some Hebrew to him, since, contrary to the prevailing Ashkenazi custom in Holland, the Palestinian pronunciation we had learned in Zichron Ya'akov was of the same Sephardi type used by the Cochinese.

Perhaps he saw how happy and excited I was, or perhaps it was his custom to collect stray souls for his Sabbath dinner as I had done for Mrs. Neubauer on the Nieuwe Kerkstraat. In any case, he invited me home with him and even gave me the seat of honor beside him at the beautifully laid table. Not that it was easy to sit, since every nook and cranny of the room was filled with relatives and friends. After a while indeed – whether from the heat, the overcrowding, the busy gesturing, or the incessant talking – my head began to reel and I had to leave. They were lovely people – they were *my* people – but after years at sea, with only distant horizons and no Jews around me, I appeared to be suffering an acute attack of claustrophobia.

Yet the next day I returned to the synagogue and had the honor of being called up to the Torah. After the service I was again invited by the *chacham* to his Sabbath meal. This time his home was less crowded and we had the opportunity to converse. Told by him that Jews had lived in Cochin for thousands of years in isolation from other Jewish communities, and that their relations with the surrounding Indian population had always been excellent, I asked:

"Do you mean to tell me that you have never been humiliated, persecuted or harmed?"

"On the contrary," said the *chacham*. "The Indians respect us for wanting to remain ourselves, and we are on the best of terms with them."

The sense of Western superiority that I had been feeling since Suez was deflated all at once. To think that a Europe that had spawned an Adolf Hitler should have the conceit to think itself better than these people!

★   ★   ★

Eventually, we received instructions to sail to the British naval base of Trincomalee in Ceylon – a stroke of good luck for me, since Evelyn had been posted there. We dropped anchor inside an enormous bay and waited for what would happen next.

Although we were doing nothing, we were doing it in excellent company. Our neighbors riding at anchor included the enormous British battleship the *Duke of York* and the Free French flagship *Richelieu*, as well as a super-modern Italian cruiser whose crew had hastily changed sides after the fall of Mussolini and – much to our contempt – hung its laundry out to dry on its cannon barrels. A launch from the naval base shuttled all day between these ships, picking up and returning crews from shore leave.

My own first leave was devoted to trying to find Evelyn. After losing my way along the beach and being pelted with coconuts by monkeys, I managed to find out that she was stationed in an office in charge of Allied merchant vessels in the Indian Ocean.

I hesitated before entering it. How did I know that she hadn't meanwhile found herself another naval man? There were, after all, some 20,000 troops on Ceylon and only a handful of Wrens.

It turned out that I had no reason to worry. In fact, Evelyn already knew that the *Nijkerk* was in port and had devised a scheme to keep me close to her. Her boss, it seemed, was continually complaining about being short-staffed, for not only had there been a considerably increased workload with so many ships being routed from Europe to the Pacific Theater, many of these were foreign vessels manned by Dutch and French crews. And the Frenchies in particular had the beastly habit of sending all their paperwork in French, a language that no self-respecting Englishman could read! In short, since I knew French – and, needless to say, Dutch – and had also taken a gunnery course at Falmouth...

A little shyly, Evelyn told me that she had gone out several times with the base personnel officer, quickly reassuring me when I made a doubtful face:

"It's nothing serious, you silly boy. He's simply damned useful around here. I'm sure he'll fix things up for us."

The captain of the *Nijkerk* saw no reason to refuse the base personnel officer's request to borrow me for some urgently needed shore work. Before I could say "Jack Robinson," I had changed my cabin on board for a room in bachelor quarters on land.

It turned out to be a cushy job, shuffling papers and paying an occasional visit to some of the ships out in the bay. And to top it all off, Evelyn had the use of a jeep, in which we made excursions to Colombo and around the island. We also regularly visited the Allied Officers' Club, situated in a luxurious hotel with palm-fringed terraces descending to a clean white beach. Not a day passed without some party or other event that lasted till late in the night. The atmosphere was hot and sultry. One night, as Evelyn and I drew up at the Club in our jeep, we nearly ran into a stark naked couple at the entrance, jumping up and down and shouting: "Taxi! Taxi!"

★ ★ ★

Immediately following the bombing of Hiroshima and Nagasaki, World War II came to an end. I thought of my old physics teacher Pukki chalking $E=mc^2$ on the blackboard. He had imagined every use for atomic energy except the first to which it was put.

The next morning I was told to report to the *Nijkerk* for our return voyage to Europe. On our way, we were to steam to Tamatave in Madagascar to pick up part of a Free French battalion. There was even less time to say goodbye to Evelyn than in Bombay.

Tamatave was a sleepy town, hot and humid. I was just about to abandon hope of anything interesting happening there when the Free French began to board. Every one of them was a woman!

I am certain that the crew of the *Nijkerk* will never forget that last journey. Ahead of us loomed a new and peaceful world full of hope, but also of new responsibilities before whose onset we had one last pleasure cruise. Our young passengers felt pretty much the same way. For them, too, this was a last chance to enjoy the tropics and their soft nights before their return to the humdrum realities of Civvy Street. The *Nijkerk* became a floating sex club.

But all good things come to an end. As soon as we entered the Mediterranean, carnal activity ground to a halt. It was as if we all had the same thought at once. "Well, there's home just ahead. The rules are different there, and we had better start getting used to them!"

Chapter Eleven

Our first sighting of liberated European soil was a grim one. Steaming up the Garonne in the direction of Bordeaux, we gazed awestruck at the devastation. Both river banks were lined with burned-out and collapsed ruins of factories and warehouses. The river itself was littered with sunken ships, and on several occasions we had to maneuver carefully between wrecks. Once we even steamed right through the two halves of a ship. Only by pulling them apart had the French been able to create a temporary channel in the river.

The quay at which we moored was a scrapheap of twisted and scorched metal, remnants of which had once been warehouses and cranes. The concrete paving had enormous craters where it had been hit by bombs. One huge hole, flanked by several overturned railway cars, hid an entire locomotive that had been unable to keep from plunging into it.

But the strangest sight among all this havoc was the local brass band ranged along the quay, tootling an off-key welcome to *les demoiselles de* Tamatave. The musicians had obviously not had enough rehearsal time under the German occupation.

It was quite amazing to see the same young ladies who had spent much of the voyage in Dutch arms jump to rigid attention upon hearing the first strains of the Marseillaise. Here and there, while marching down the gangway, a few of them threw us a wink, but then it was back to the kitchen stove and a pair of nagging parents, or a dull husband and some screaming brats.

Dommage!

★ ★ ★

As soon as I was able to go ashore, I went to the nearest post office. The only people whose whereabouts I had any idea of were the Bienstocks in Mont d'Or. After an hour on the telephone, I found some local clerk who was able to tell me that they had moved to Paris. He even knew their address, although not their telephone number.

I immediately requested forty-eight hours leave and was soon on a train to Paris. Less than a day after the *Nijkerk*'s arrival in Bordeaux, I rang the bell of an expensive-looking apartment near the Boulevard Haussmann. Papa Bienstock had always been what we Jews called a *macher*, someone with a gift for pulling strings. Quite obviously he had pulled them again, and more power to him! It was the only way to survive in this world.

Mama Bienstock opened the door. For a few seconds she simply stared at me. Then she pulled me to her bosom and burst into tears. It was as if only by holding me tight could she convince herself that I wasn't a ghost. While I stood there, clasped in her embrace, Thea entered and started dancing around the room.

I hadn't come empty-handed. In Madagascar I had laid in a stock of good coffee, which now proved a most welcome present. Preparing it delayed by a few minutes what I most wanted and feared: to hear what the Bienstocks knew.

Very soon they began to tell me – slowly and with difficulty at first, then more freely until the words came tumbling out.

It was easier to start with the good news. My father had returned safely to The Hague. Others had survived too. Miriam Neubauer and her mother had been rescued from Bergen-Belsen by the Americans at the last possible moment, while Hannah had gone underground and worked for the Dutch resistance, forging documents. After the liberation, she had joined her older brother and sisters in Palestine.

Then came the bad news.

Dr. Neubauer had died in Bergen-Belsen of starvation.

"And Yehoshua?"

"Yehoshua too."

The Neubauers were rounded up in the last *razzia* and detained in the Joodse Schouwburg, the building of Amsterdam's main theater. Hannah and Yehoshua decided to try to escape, but were persuaded there was no chance. At the last minute, as they were being marched away, Hannah pretended to have forgotten her bag, slipped back into the theater, and hid. Yehoshua failed to go with her.

I stood up and said that I would like to be alone for a few minutes. Thea took me to her room, and I lay down on her bed and wept as I had not done since I was a child.

Plucky Yehoshua, who had been like a little brother to me!

At least he had not died in the gas chambers. He would not have gone willingly, I was sure of that. Others might have, but not Yehoshua. He would have fought to the end.

And Dr. Neubauer, that wise and wonderful man! Even after my "vision" in Vernet, I had continued to believe he would survive. Someone that good and that pure *had* to. His whole life had radiated a profound faith in man and God.

Here was his reward.

And to what did I owe *my* survival? For a moment I hated myself. I had thought only of my own life. While doing everything to preserve it, I had let my friends go to their doom.

Yet what, besides saving myself, could I have done? And what better example could I have given others? Had others acted as I had, might not they be alive too? Had not doing everything in one's power to save one's own neck been the best – the only reasonable – strategy for everyone?

★ ★ ★

Papa Bienstock had the address of Miriam and her mother in Amsterdam, and the next day he got hold of my father's address in The Hague. It was time to return to my ship. I said my goodbyes, promising Thea to visit her again soon in Paris.

The next day I was back at sea, steaming in the direction of Southampton under a storm-laden sky.

The quay at Southampton was crowded with the women our Dutch crew members had found themselves during their years of being based in England. Gladys wasn't among them. But there was no time to think about her, because almost immediately I was busy supervising the transfer of our remaining ammunition to the Royal Navy.

I must have been one of the few people aboard ship who were not in the mood for celebrating during those early post-war days. I wasn't the only one, though. Our First Officer broke down in front of the whole crew as we *Engelandvaarders* left England for the last time. The poor fellow stood with tears streaming down his face, having just said a final farewell to his British war wife.

★ ★ ★

On a drizzling November morning in 1945 the lock-gates of IJmuiden closed behind us and the *Nijkerk* was towed into the North Sea Canal. Low, wet clouds and water-logged polders were our only greeting.

I was back in Holland.

Several hours later we made fast along an empty quay in Amsterdam harbor. We were too late for the flags and brass bands. There were only half a dozen stevedores in oilskins, casting accusing glances at us for having forced them to go out in such weather. By now it was some six months since VE-Day and our *Nijkerk* must have been a curious sight with her camouflage paint, armor-plated bridge, four-inch cannon, and ack-ack guns.

The crew was unusually silent. What could they have said, these men, many of whom had been at sea for five whole years, exposing themselves to a host of dangers in order to make this moment possible? Never had they imagined a return to such gray and barren unconcern, such eerie indifference.

Even after our arrival in Amsterdam, it took twenty-four more hours before we left the ship with our discharges in our pockets. After collecting my back wages, which made me suddenly rich compared to a Dutch population living in post-war poverty, I hitched a ride on a Royal Dutch Navy personnel carrier to The Hague.

I was dropped off in a quiet street of terraced, middle-class houses. For a while I stood there, a sick feeling in the pit of my stomach. I didn't have the courage to ring the bell.

But I couldn't just go on standing there. Here and there lace curtains were being pushed aside and unseen eyes were scrutinizing me. I walked up to the door and rang.

It was opened by a woman. She asked me to follow her. The moment I entered the shabbily furnished living room, I realized that my fears had been justified. In a large armchair in a corner sat a shriveled bundle of clothes. I went over to it.

"Hello, Papa," I said. "I've come back."

The head slowly turned its half-closed eyes in my direction. "Hans?"

I bent over the chair and let a pair of thin, dry hands explore my face. I kissed the tautly-drawn skin of the forehead and pulled up a chair.

I had so much to say to him. And perhaps there was much he had to say to me. But the words did not come.

We talked in silence, through our thoughts.

★ ★ ★

On my twenty-third birthday, a cold, wet winter day, I went for a walk through the old Jodenbuurt of Amsterdam. It was gone. Not just its Jews, nearly all of whom were dead, but even its houses, cannibalized during the hungry winter of 1944 when Amsterdamers had died of cold and malnutrition in the streets. Desperate for anything to heat their homes with, they had ripped out window frames, doors, ceilings, entire floors of the empty Jewish quarter. Nothing but skeletons were left. The few returning survivors were living elsewhere.

I had found Mrs. Neubauer and Miriam in a dingy, one-room apartment. All their possessions were gone. In a dejected and bitter tone unlike that of the woman I remembered, Razi Neubauer told me that she had lost all faith in Europe and that she meant to start a new life with her children in Palestine. I could not bring myself to ask about her husband and Yehoshua.

I had also gone to look for my old classmate Joop Chazan. He had disappeared without a trace. A Christian family had moved into his old home. *Chazan?* No, they had no idea.

And what was *I* going to do? There was no one left to ask for advice. To sail and own Jewish ships, of course. But how to accomplish that?

I hadn't noticed that my feet had led me to the old harbor, where stood the Amsterdam Nautical College whose cadets I had enviously regarded as a teenager after my strolls down the Jodenbreestraat following Sabbath services. Hardly stopping to think, I walked in and asked to see the headmaster. Perhaps it helped that I was still wearing my blue navy uniform, both out of habit and because it looked smart and because it was almost impossible to buy decent clothes in Holland. Following a brief review of my wartime experience, I managed to get accepted to a six months' course for the state examination for the certificate of Ocean-going Second Mate. "I'm bending the rules for you," said the headmaster, "but I want to give you a chance."

I quickly settled into my new routine. My father was now living in Bussum, where he had found a caring home with a Jewish family of survivors, a grandmother, daughter, and granddaughter who occupied a small private house with an attic room into which I moved. Every morning I took the train to Amsterdam, and in the evenings I did my homework in the living room, where I sometimes stole a glance at the pretty granddaughter. Her name was Mary. Thinking that inappropriate for a Jewish girl, I promptly began calling her Miriam.

After a while I began to get bored. The lessons at the College proceeded at a snail's pace, and the daily train journeys were tiresome in the extreme, especially as there were frequent delays due to the Germans having stolen most of the rolling stock before their hasty retreat. I started to cut classes and to do my studying at home, subjecting myself to a rigorous nine-to-six schedule. The next state examinations were scheduled for February – which meant that if I wanted to save time and pass them, I had to cram six months' study into six weeks.

Still, my evenings were free. Miriam and I began to go out together, often riding our bicycles to Hilversum to go dancing in the fashionable Hotel Gooiland, recently converted into the "Allied Forces Officers' Club." American swing was then the height of fashion, and the orchestra's massed trumpets were audible from afar. Canadian forces were still stationed in Holland, and at the entrance to the hotel was a continuous picket of Dutch girls hoping to catch the eye of some Canadian officer who would invite them inside. Dressed in my uniform, I had no problem getting in with Miriam's arm clasped in mine.

She had spent the war in hiding. Suffering the fears and longing of puberty and budding womanhood in isolation, she had a craving for company and physical contact, which resulted in our often ending up in bed after our return from the Gooiland. But the atmosphere of the war days was over; I felt uneasy at the thought that she might be taking the relationship more seriously than I was and worried what would happen if her mother and grandmother found out. Yet although it was almost impossible for them not to have an inkling of the traffic between our two adjoining rooms, they never let on, not even when our sleepy faces the next morning should have given us away. Perhaps they simply didn't mind.

Not that our companionship was purely physical. We had long and serious discussions about the future. Miriam too wanted to leave Holland and explore the world, but her sights were set on the United States, not on Palestine. I often lectured her about this. "Don't you have any pride?" I would ask. "Haven't you learned anything from what happened?" If we Jews didn't work to establish our own country, it could happen to us again.

Perhaps I convinced her, and perhaps she had fallen in love with me. One night during dinner she announced that she had changed her mind and was planning to go to Palestine. I watched her mother's face drop and said nothing. I didn't want them to think that I was behind it, or – worse still – to encourage Miriam to hitch her fate to mine. Although I truly liked her, the idea of living with her as man and wife in Palestine was the furthest thing from my mind.

One wintry morning in February I reported to a government building in The Hague for my state examinations. The written part of the exam was a cinch, but an oral interview on the subject of marine engineering threatened to be my undoing, since my examiner, a long-retired Naval Chief Engineer, insisted on a detailed explanation of the workings of the condenser of a steam engine – a subject I knew absolutely nothing about. For goodness sake, who still cared about steam engines?

"Well," I stammered, racking my mind for something to say about condensers, "the point is, uh, that a steamship doesn't have unlimited quantities of sweet water to keep the boilers humming, so a way has to be found to recirculate the available water..."

Suddenly I had a bright idea. "Of course, that's only a very general outline," I added, facing my grizzled questioner. "I daresay that there are only a few specialists who know everything about these things, and I wouldn't be surprised if you were one of them."

He fell for my flattery totally and spent the next half-hour explaining his favorite subject while I sat there, carefully nodding at appropriate moments to keep him going and prevent myself from falling asleep. The result was a juicy 8 out of 10 for marine engineering.

Several weeks later I received a beautifully hand-written document in the name of Her Majesty the Queen stating that Hans Kahn had earned the Certificate of Competency as second mate on ocean-going merchant vessels.

★   ★   ★

Following a lengthy depression, my father had rebounded. He had already left Bussum and installed himself in the prestigious Hotel Wittebrug in The Hague as soon as General Eisenhower and the Allied Forces' temporary headquarters moved out of it – a useful address if one needed to impress people. He had also taken steps to recover his property, and first and foremost, the old Capitol Theater. He had even had time, unknown to me, to devote some attention to my affairs, for one day when I was invited for dinner at the Wittebrug he introduced me to the Director-General of the Dutch Ministry of Transport and Shipping.

With growing astonishment and not a little consternation, I listened over several courses as my father – Dr. Isidor Kahn, as he billed himself, the former Portuguese Consul in Berlin and a man with considerable international standing in diplomatic and financial circles – expounded a wholly imaginary scheme to his guest. With the help of his far-flung connections, he explained, he wished to help restore the war-crippled Dutch shipping industry to its old eminence and put The Netherlands back on the international map... and speaking of shipping, had the Director-General ever thought of doing business with Palestine? Of course, this might not be the moment to go into details... but nevertheless... yes, there were some very interesting possibilities...

"Please do go on, Dr. Kahn," said the Director-General, snapping up my father's bait. "What sort of possibilities?"

"Well," replied my father importantly, dabbing his lips with his napkin, "I should think that, given the current depression in world trade that is the result of a worldwide shortage of finance capital, the Dutch government would be giving serious consideration to the encouragement of barter transactions. The potential is enormous." Naturally, he couldn't go over his whole list of contemplated projects right now... If Mijnheer would care to visit

him in his office... Would Mijnheer care for a brandy by the way?...
But perhaps one example...

"Yes, of course," urged the Director-General.

"Well," lectured my father, taking a sip of his brandy, "we Dutch
have the shipyards and would like to build ships. And we also badly
need fruit and vitamins. Are you aware, Mijnheer, that in Palestine
the vitamins are falling off the trees right at this very moment? Yes,
yes, I mean that quite literally. Tens of thousands of tons of the
highest quality citrus fruit rotting on the ground for lack of
shipping to get it to European markets! Now suppose that our
Dutch yards were to build fruit carriers for Palestinian growers in
return for large shipments of oranges and grapefruits to Holland...
My son Hans, it just so happens..."

Incredibly enough, I was soon after invited by Her Majesty's
government to prepare a report on such a possible barter
agreement. There was no remuneration involved, but besides
opening doors in Palestinian economic and shipping circles, my
letter of recommendation from the Dutch ministry of transport
would get me a British visa – a commodity in such scarce supply
that hundreds of thousands of European Jewish refugees were
making desperate attempts to enter Palestine without one.

I set out on my way within a few days.

Chapter Twelve

Since there was no direct flight to Tel Aviv, I traveled via Cairo. It took several days of waiting there before I managed to book a seat on a small, single-engine Misr Airlines plane that flew across the Sinai desert.

This was my second time in Palestine. Once again, I felt immediately at home. The energy, sense of purpose, and warm, blunt camaraderie contrasted strongly with the cold formality of Europe.

Harebrained though my father's scheme might be, I had come to try and implement it. The first step, I decided, was to contact Ernst Birnbaum, a nephew of my father's who had immigrated to Palestine in the early 1930s and now bore the name of Moshe Bar-Ilan. He was a big shot in the Haganah, the semi-clandestine Jewish army, and knew everyone.

Cousin Moshe received me warmly and immediately made me feel one of the family. Such hospitality, I was to learn, was common in Palestine, and one received it not only from relatives and their friends, but even from chance acquaintances. People never refused you a bed, even if it meant opening the sofa in the living room, and everyone had some practical advice for you.

Moshe Bar-Ilan introduced me to Bar-Kochba Meirovitz, the man responsible for maritime affairs, fishery, and ports in the Jewish Agency, the governing body of the country's Jewish community. A prototype of the Zionist *apparatchik*, Meirovitz knew next to nothing about the things he was in charge of. Still, Dutch ships for Jewish oranges sounded like a fine idea and he scribbled a letter of introduction for me to Dr. Naphtali Wydra, the director of a new shipping company called Zim that was partly owned by the Histadrut, the Palestinian labor federation.

Dr. Wydra was the same story. An amiable fellow, his sole expertise in water transport came from having once owned a soda water factory in Germany. "Why don't you try the Citrus Marketing Board?" he suggested.

I did – and soon realized that it too was unable to help me. Indeed, the circular nature of the problem was beginning to emerge. If the citrus growers were paid in Dutch ships, they would have to sell these ships to someone else; the only prospective buyer for them was Zim; Zim was Dr. Wydra; and Dr. Wydra had already referred me to the Citrus Marketing Board.

I dispatched an extensive report to Holland in which I explained that the times were not yet propitious for my father's visionary plan, and I proceeded to forget about the entire project.

★ ★ ★

Since I couldn't go on sponging off friends and relatives forever, I had to find a profitable occupation. In search of one I took to hanging around the Seamen's Club in Haifa, where I could meet people who were actually working on ships, as opposed to writing memos about them in an office.

One of them was my friend Hans Windmuller, the tugboat captain, and together we revived our old idea for a sailors' collective based on equality and social justice. To tell the truth, I had never had the slightest belief in either of those things since my teenage debates with Betty Kanner, but if joining a maritime kibbutz would make me even a partial Jewish ship owner, I was willing to give it a try. Hans and I promptly founded the Israel Seafarers' Union and issued ourselves membership cards Nos. 1 and 2. I don't recall if there was a third.

There seemed no choice but to put off owning ships for a while and go back to sailing on them, and so I put on my best officers' whites and went to the Haifa offices of the Atid Navigation Company, whose ship the *Amal* I had visited in Alexandria. Suitably impressed by my credentials, they said they would put me at the top of their waiting list.

I was down to my last pennies and reluctantly thinking of stowing away on a freighter back to Holland when Hans Windmuller came to the rescue. Through his port connections he had heard that a small British tanker, which transported oil from Libya to the Haifa refineries, was looking to replace a second mate who had gone ashore and disappeared. Taking my brand-new Dutch merchant marine diploma, I went at once to see its captain. He was lying in his cabin in what seemed a state of light but ongoing intoxication, which may have explained his respectful examination of my document. Turning it over and over without rising from his bed, he kept repeating its first words, "In The Name of Her Majesty The Queen," as if they were part of a letter personally addressed to him.

The following morning found me standing on the bridge of the *Empire Melody* as second mate on a voyage to Benghazi. Since the captain spent most of his time in his cabin with a bottle, the responsibility for navigation and other routine shipboard activities fell on the first mate and me, which made for very long hours. Still, the wages were generous, the food was excellent, and I had a roomy cabin to myself. I was quite disappointed when the missing mate surfaced several voyages later and was given his old job back. Once again I was unemployed.

As often in my life, however, seeming bad luck turned out to be good, for had I sailed one more time on my alcoholic tanker I would not have been around when an opening came up on an Atid ship named after its company. Two days after leaving the *Empire Melody*, I was an officer on the *Atid*.

It was not exactly a sailor's dream. In fact, my first glimpse of its ancient hulk left me uncertain whether to laugh or cry. The *Atid* was an old Danube river boat revamped as a semi-seaworthy coaster with a tiny deckhouse and bridge, sailors' quarters underneath the forecastle, and officers' cabins so tiny that there was barely room for my small trunk. But what did it matter if there wasn't room in my bunk to stretch out my not especially long legs? I was a sailor on a Jewish ship at last!

The *Atid*'s crew was as varied as the Jewish People itself, a strange blend of old and new, discipline and anarchy, men of breeding and vagabonds. Its captain, a handsome man in his forties whose entire family had been wiped out by the Nazis, hailed from Hungary and had commanded a passenger steamer on the Black Sea. Although he often longed for this elegant vessel in a voice heavy with nostalgia while disparaging the reconditioned barge he sailed on now, he was a true professional who performed his job seriously and took proper care of his crew.

The first officer, a Polish Jew who refused to learn a word of Hebrew, was called by us *Pani* Stark, while our bo'sun was a small but muscular fellow from Salonika, a Greek city whose Jews had traditionally been port workers. We also had a third mate, the need for whom on such a tiny ship was a mystery to me until I realized that he was our liaison with the Haganah – a position whose importance I soon came to appreciate. To his credit, he pitched in as hard as the rest of us to keep the *Atid* afloat.

Our first voyage was to Tripoli, to which we carried a cargo of tiles packed in wooden crates lined with straw. Halfway we were caught in one of those brief but violent storms that are typical of the Mediterranean. The waves rose higher and higher until they took to crashing down on the deck with such force that two of the decrepit wooden hatches gave way and water began filling the hold. Soon there was a meter of it sloshing around below and causing the ship to grow sluggish and to nose down into the waves. Worse yet, some of the wooden crates were staved in and their straw began blocking the bilge pumps. No matter how furiously we pumped, the water in the hold kept rising dangerously.

There was nothing to do but send someone below who was a good enough swimmer to clear the bilge sumps. And although there was no time to ask the crew for swimming certificates, there did happen to be a new second mate aboard who had not yet proven his mettle...

I was in no position to decline, and together with Gavriel, a tough little lad and the youngest sailor on board, I lowered myself into the evil-smelling whirlpool and began diving in its murky depths. The water was sloshing madly, rushing back and forth with each roll of the ship, and we had to keep dodging flotsam from the broken crates while picking soggy clumps of straw from the pump openings. It was one of the foulest things I have ever had to do in my life, but once the pumps started working and the water receded, Gabi and I became instant heroes – and lasting friends.

★ ★ ★

Hundreds of thousands of homeless Jewish refugees were drifting around Europe with nowhere to go. Determined not to return to the countries that had butchered their families and finding the gates of America barred to them, they were clamoring to be admitted to Palestine – where the British, taking instructions from Ernest Bevin, the Labour government's anti-Semitic foreign minister in London, were refusing to let them in. In response, the Haganah had organized a network to smuggle Jews into Palestine behind British backs. Old ships were being purchased wherever possible, refurbished as much as money would allow, and sent to collect the illegal immigrants from the ports of Europe. Whenever such vessels were intercepted by the British navy, their passengers were taken to detention camps in Cyprus and impounded behind barbed wire.

From time to time, the *Atid* took part in these Haganah operations. She had a deep, two-meter-long tank in the forward part of the ship, which I first learned about from Gabi soon after our diving expedition. After showing it to me, he took me to the chart room and told me to regard the ship's General Arrangement Plan hanging on the bulkhead. When I saw nothing unusual, he said:

"Look in front of the hold. Wouldn't you say something was missing?"

Indeed, it was. The tank, which was intended to be filled with water when the *Atid* sailed in ballast and was accessible by a manhole in the hold, did not appear in the plan. Nothing in the drawing indicated its existence, and only an accurate measurement would have shown that the hold was two meters shorter than indicated.

"Well," I said, feeling a bit miffed that my superiors hadn't trusted me enough to let me in on the secret, "there's certainly no deep tank in these plans. It would make a nice hiding place, don't you think?"

"Possibly," Gabi grinned. There was no need to say more.

From Tripoli we sailed to Genoa, where we loaded a cargo of sanitary ware: washbasins, bathtubs, toilets, and the like. Shortly before sailing, I saw about a dozen men, led by our third mate, walk up the gangplank and disappear.

Although we weren't told what provisions had been made for putting these stowaways ashore, by the time we passed Cyprus our entire ship knew about them. By now we were approaching the coast of Palestine in darkness. I had taken the night watch and was beginning to see the lights of Tel Aviv reflected off the clouds when a British destroyer loomed suddenly out of the dark and started following us a short distance astern. Since it made no attempt to establish contact with the *Atid*, I didn't bother to wake the captain. I simply kept the ship on course while telling Gabi to make sure that the manhole cover was secured and hidden behind the highest possible pile of bathtubs.

Shortly before dawn, as soon as we entered Palestinian coastal waters, the destroyer's signal lamp sent a clear message: "Stop engines!" To impress on us that she intended to enforce it, she increased speed and was soon steaming abreast at a distance of some one hundred yards, her cannon pointed in our direction.

I sent an order to stop the engines over the ship's telegraph and alerted the captain, who quickly appeared on the bridge in his slippers and pajamas. After blinking sleepily toward the destroyer, he told me to "keep an eye on things" and went back down to get dressed.

The destroyer had already lowered a launch, which now came skimming toward us. Soon five heavily armed British sailors, commanded by a lieutenant, climbed aboard. "Sorry, old chap," said the lieutenant, a pimply young man who spoke an Oxford English. "I've got orders to search your ship."

I led him to the chart room so that he could study the General Arrangement Plan and went to fetch the manifests and bills-oflading, dumping the whole pile in front of him. Meanwhile, the deckhands had been told to open the hatches furthest from the bow so that the boarding party might inspect the hold.

All this time one of the British sailors was standing near the ship's telegraph with a loaded Sten gun pointed in my direction. Knowing it to be a weapon with the habit of sometimes going off uninvited, I went to my cabin and put on my old Dutch navy uniform with its campaign ribbons and two gold stripes. Returning to the bridge, I said crisply to the gun holder:

"At ease!"

The barrel of the Sten dropped as automatically as if I were a British commander.

My reappearance in the chart room had a similar effect on the lieutenant, who jumped up and nearly saluted me.

"Well, now," I addressed him in the most patronizing tone I could muster, "I trust you've seen what you wished to. Can I be of any further assistance to you?"

The poor fellow, who had been about to give his men orders to commence their search of the *Atid*, didn't know how to react. "Jolly kind of you," he said. "Jolly kind." He looked uncertainly about. "Quite right. I suppose that will be all, then." He turned to go, then apologetically turned back to me. "I'm frightfully sorry, old chap. It's a bloody nuisance, this. Don't really like it, you know. But one can't argue with the politicians, can one? Perhaps I'll just have a quick peek at your hold, if you don't mind."

He peered hurriedly into the hold, spoke briefly into a walkie-talkie, apologized again for the disturbance, lowered himself and his men into the launch, and chug-chugged back to the destroyer. Everything had gone so fast that when our captain returned to the bridge in his fancy dress clothes, the British warship was steaming away. Once again its signal lamp started flickering. The message this time was: "Bon Voyage."

The two of us stared at each other in our splendid uniforms and burst out laughing so loudly that I almost feared the British would hear us and come back.

Soon afterwards we dropped anchor off Tel Aviv port. It was a beautiful morning and bronzed youngsters in bathing suits were soon steering their *chassakes* – flat, kayak-shaped boats paddled by a long, double-bladed oar – in our direction. Several of these craft had pretty girls squatting on the prow. Pulling up alongside us, the boaters began chatting with our crew, Nothing seemed more natural than to invite them aboard for a cool drink, and a great deal of to-ing and fro-ing ensued, more newcomers clambering aboard while others rowed back to the shore. Nobody paid much attention to the fact that the same *chassake* that had arrived with a tanned young lady on the prow was returning with a pale young man. It didn't take long to unload all twelve of our illegal passengers, several of whom, I later learned, were high-ranking Zionist operatives from the DP camps.

★ ★ ★

Not that all our extra-curricular activities were so patriotic. There wasn't a crew member, from the captain down, who didn't make extra money by smuggling.

Most of our merchandise was bought in Egypt, where the locals had developed a major industry for the manufacture of fake American cigarettes. Though their quality was lousy, they looked impressive, and we bought hundreds of cartons and resold them in Italy at a nice profit. My already small cabin was so crowded with them that my throat ached from their sharp, dry smell.

Such contraband couldn't be hidden from the Italian customs officers, but fortunately, they didn't take their cut from us. They were reimbursed by the Italian black-marketeers who appeared at night on their sputtering three-wheeled motorbikes and left stacks of cigarettes at the customs post on their way out.

One couldn't amass savings from these transactions, which were carried out in bundles of well-thumbed lira notes that were useless outside of Italy. Consequently, while docked in Genoa, our regular Italian port of call, the entire crew of the *Atid* could be found every night at the Ragno d'Oro, the most expensive nightclub in town. Everyone, including myself, had his special girlfriend there, fiery and temperamental types who were ready to please. When we felt the need to stretch our legs a bit, we took the girls for excursions into the beautiful countryside outside of town.

Any liras left over from our bacchanalia were reinvested in merchandise sold in Tel Aviv. Everyone had his own line of trade. Our bo'sun, for example, dealt in fishing gear, while I specialized in imitation Leica cameras. The income from them went to buy more cigarettes in Port Said.

★ ★ ★

In some ways I felt more at home on the rickety *Atid* than on any other ship I had been on. What did it matter that the officers had to share the only available shower, or that in the absence of a proper winch even lifting the anchor was a major undertaking? We connected the anchor to the forward cargo winch by means of a system of pulleys and learned to lift it with that. Primitive? Perhaps. But it worked and we were all very pleased with ourselves.

After a while, though, boredom – always both my nemesis and good angel – began to set in. How long could I go on like this? I certainly didn't want to keep working for others, but where would I get the money to buy a ship of my own? Floating around the Mediterranean wasn't going to provide the answers.

I must have written some of my thoughts to my father, for in the spring of 1947 I received a letter from him. He had a new idea for me. During a recent trip to the United States he had run into a wealthy American Jew, Sam Derektor, who had bought a ship for which he didn't have any use. Since Sam was now interested in selling this vessel, I should return to Holland as quickly as possible in order to devise a plan of action.

It sounded exciting, but first I had to find out what kind of ship this American fellow had bought. After a good deal of back-and-forth correspondence, it emerged that we were talking about an old Hudson River day-tripper – that is, a coastal vessel not really equipped for the high seas. It had been acquired from the American War Surplus Board, which was selling just about everything from telephones and shoes to jeeps and complete warships – minus their armaments, of course.

Sam's vessel, which bore the proud name of the *Colonel Frederick C. Johnson*, was an old craft that had been requisitioned by the U.S. army after Pearl Harbor to ferry personnel around the coast. Short of returning her to the Hudson, I couldn't see how she could be used. An ocean steamer she wasn't. And yet neither was the *Atid*. That set me to thinking.

Under pressure from the American government, the British were now prepared to admit some 100,000 concentration camp survivors into Palestine. How to collect them and get them there, however, was the problem of the Jewish Agency.

I had a talk with Bar-Kochba Meirovitch. Jews-to-Palestine, I saw at once, interested him more than ships-for-oranges. There was a pressing need for second-hand passenger vessels that could make the short crossing from Genoa or Marseilles to Haifa, and since Zim's only ship, the *Kedmah*, was laid up in Singapore with turbine problems, the situation was especially urgent.

"Suppose I had a ship to transport immigrants." I asked. "Would the Agency give me a contract?"

"Definitely," answered Bar-Kochba. "The sooner, the better. We'll pay you $150 per head for as many passengers as you can bring to Haifa."

I asked him to put it in writing and he did.

Now I had a use for even a Hudson River boat!

★   ★   ★

I resigned my commission on the *Atid*, sailing with it one last time to Genoa, where I found myself with barely enough cash for a third-class rail ticket to Amsterdam.

My father seemed happy to see me. Never having believed in the Jewish merchant marine as a route to entrepreneurship, he envisioned a great future for me as the owner of the *Frederick C. Johnson.*

"I'm glad you feel that way, father," I said. "But where am I going to get the money to buy it with?"

"The money," mused my father, as if here were a new and unexpected aspect of the venture. "Of course, you have to understand, Hans, that right now I'm in the middle of trying to recover some of our lost property. When that happens I'll be only too glad – but at the moment – that is, strictly for the time being – well, perhaps I can manage your airfare to America. I'm sure Sam will be prepared to give you easy terms, and perhaps you'll find a partner over there. The States are full of rich Jews..."

I had really expected no more from him, and he did indeed come up with the airfare. A few days later I was on my way to New York, wondering during the long transatlantic flight why Mr. Sam had bought a ship that he didn't want and now wished to sell at a bargain price.

In New York, my sister Ellen invited me to stay with her – a fortunate development, as otherwise I would have been broke before I started. Previous experience had taught me that in New York you spent dollars as if they were gulden, except that each dollar was worth four gulden!

What does a Jew without money do when he wants to buy a ship from another Jew? He looks for more Jews to introduce him to other Jews who might help. Through Ellen I met a cousin who was active in Zionist causes, and through our cousin I obtained an appointment with Robert Szold, the older brother of Henrietta Szold, the famous founder of Hadassah. A prominent corporate attorney who was also director of the Palestine Economic Corporation, the old gentleman quickly put me at ease in his plush private office in a Wall Street tower and actually seemed interested in my intentions. Handing me his visiting card, he scribbled a name on the back of it. "Go see Elliot," he said. "He'll be in touch with me, and we'll see what we can do."

This led me to Elliot Glassberg, a bright young lawyer with excellent connections in Zionist circles. He knew all about Sam Derektor – a businessman with a speculative streak, I was told, who had bought not one but two old War Surplus Board excursion liners. The other was called the *President Warfield* and had already been sold for $50,000 to the Weston Trading Company, a Haganah front. Renamed the *Exodus*, she would be captured, with 4,000 illegal immigrants aboard, by the British in a pitched battle in Haifa Bay, and eventually became the subject of a best-selling novel and hit movie. At the time I met Elliot, the *President Warfield* was being interned in Portovenere, Italy (from where she was soon to escape with forged documents) after having stolen fuel in the Azores and left an unpaid bill of 30 million francs for ramming and damaging a French vessel in Marseilles. The American State Department, Elliot told me, was none too happy about Sam's transaction.

Sam's problem was that since the *Colonel Johnson* was being kept under close supervision to prevent further embarrassment, he was unable to get an export license for her. Nor, because of the exorbitant wage demands of the all-powerful American Seamen's Union, could he operate the ship under an American flag.

Armed with this useful knowledge, I decided to pay him a visit. Receiving me jovially in his 25th-floor office, he spread himself out in his easy chair, planted his feet on his desk, and suggested that we get right down to the details of the sale.

"Don't you think," I parried, "that it might be a good idea for me to see your ship first?"

This was easily arranged, and the next day I saw the *Colonel Johnson* at her pier. To my surprise, she was an extremely nice-looking vessel and apparently in a good state of repair, including a fresh coat of white paint. I liked her even better when I saw the inside: the roomy dormitories with plenty of showers and toilets, the large kitchens full of shiny utensils, and the many lifeboats and life rafts. There were even fire extinguishers all over the corridors, a bridge fully equipped with modern instruments and shiny compasses, an up-to-date radio room, and two dozen private passenger cabins. And when I spoke to the vessel's former chief engineer, he assured me that with a few spare parts, a supply of lubricants, and a few hundred tons of fuel the *Colonel Johnson* could be on her way. It needn't take more than a week.

Time was indeed of the essence, for it was now the summer of 1947 and the British were dropping hints that they might soon pull out of Palestine – or, in more diplomatic language, "return their mandate to the United Nations." Meanwhile they were making every effort to thwart the Haganah's efforts to defend the Jewish population against mounting Arab attacks. Sooner or later a full-scale war would break out and Palestine's Jews were desperate for more manpower.

Elliot and I got to work and suggested to Sam a scheme whereby he would establish a Panamanian company that would own the *Colonel Johnson*, with him as sole share-holder. We would also set up a second company to charter the ship from him for the purpose of transporting immigrants. My profits from it would be applied to purchasing Sam's shares of the Panamanian concern, and in due time I would become the *Colonel Johnson*'s sole owner.

Though Sam agreed in principle, the entire summer and autumn went by in countless negotiating sessions, complicated by the problem of the export license. Then, in late November, the United Nations voted to partition Palestine into an Arab and a Jewish state. Concluding that there was no longer any reason to keep the *Colonel Johnson* out of the Haganah's hands, the State Department approved the ship's transfer to foreign ownership. Elliot drew up the necessary documents and Sam cheerfully signed the lot.

By now, however, I was getting cold feet. I still had no money and had begun to doubt whether, at the age of twenty-five, I was ready for so much responsibility. Perhaps I shouldn't go it alone. And so I sent off a cable to Dr. Wydra, proposing that Zim and I buy the *Colonel Johnson* as partners.

I had played my cards badly. The next time I saw Sam, his attitude had changed completely. He received me curtly, and as soon as I broached the subject of the ship he declared:

"I'm sorry, but she's been sold."

I stared at him dumbfounded. "To whom?" I managed to whisper.

"To Ampal. Let's be realistic, Hans. I would have been a fool to turn down their offer."

I was too shocked to admit that I had no idea what he was talking about. I stormed out of his office and ran all the way to Elliot. "What kind of shipping company is Ampal?" I demanded.

"It's not a shipping company," explained Elliot. "It's the American fund-raising organization of the Histadrut."

To make a long story short, Dr. Wydra, delighted to learn that the *Colonel Johnson* was for sale, had gone and bought it behind my back for Zim. She became the second ship of Zim's fleet under the name of "Negba" and soon started ferrying immigrants to Palestine, just what I had intended to do.

Elliot was as indignant at such doubledealing as I was and threatened to sue if I wasn't compensated. In the end I was paid $15,000 for my pains, which enabled me to repay some debts, including the air fare that I owed my father. I had failed in my first attempt to own a ship, but I had learned a lesson in doing business. It was as ruthless as the rest of life. Your only dependable partner was yourself.

★　★　★

Sam Derektor had a wealthy brother who lived in White Plains, and one day during that summer of fruitless negotiations I was invited up there for a barbecue. There was a tennis court on the grounds and I was asked if I could play doubles.

"Sure," I said. I didn't know what doubles were – in fact, I had never hit a tennis ball in my life – but I had bluffed my way through enough situations in life to be confident that I could get through a game of tennis.

I couldn't have been more wrong. I hit so many balls into the sky that after a while it began to cloud over.

Playing across the net was Sam's brother's daughter, a young lady named Tinka, who was so amused by my ineptness that she took a fancy to me. We went out a few times, and it was in her Manhattan apartment, an East Side brownstone, that I met her roommate Molly.

Blond, slim Molly was more my type than dark Tinka. The daughter of a Presbyterian father and a Mormon mother, she had just graduated Bryn Mawr and was as fresh and innocent as a wild flower. As beautiful, too. She never wore make-up, and she had a directness and honesty that reminded me of Hannah Neubauer. In love with New York and stage-struck, she dreamed of a career in the theater. I hated New York but was in love with her.

As slow as my negotiations with Sam were, so my affair with Molly was rapid. It wasn't long before we decided to get married. Swept away by my rhapsodizing about the little white cottage that we would live in on the Carmel with the blue Mediterranean at our feet, she even agreed to come with me to Palestine. We booked passage on a ship to Holland, took the New York State-required Wasserman Test, and set a date to be wed by a justice of the peace at City Hall.

Just a few days before our wedding day, Molly backed out. Frightened by the failure of my business plans and by the uncertain prospect of a new life in a strange country, she gave in to pressure from her parents, who were against the match from the start. I had never felt so passionately about anyone, and coming on top of the *Colonel Johnson* debacle, I was left badly depressed. For a few weeks I hung around New York in a state of lethargy, hoping that Molly might change her mind and not knowing what to do next.

The one possibility to arise during this aimless period grew out of an encounter with a Haganah official. His name was Teddy Kollek, and he was much later to become renowned as the dynamic mayor of Jerusalem. At the time, however, he was in New York on a secret arms purchasing mission. Our paths had crossed in the course of my negotiations for the *Colonel Johnson*, and some time afterwards he approached me to ask if I would be ready to put my wartime experience at the service of a Jewish navy. I unhesitatingly said that I would, and Teddy told me that I could expect to hear from him. But when more weeks went by and there was nothing new from either him or Molly, I packed my bags and returned to the Netherlands.

★ ★ ★

A month or two later, in the spring of 1948, I was contacted by the Haganah. The message given me was a short one:

"Come at once."

Because the new State of Israel and the Arab countries were now at war, it was no longer possible to travel via Cairo. I flew to London and from there to Cyprus, where I was instructed to go to a small hotel near Nicosia. When I entered its lobby, the only person visible was a tall, blond fellow lounging at the bar. He didn't look at all Jewish, and I was surprised when he ambled over to me and introduced himself as a Jew from Chicago, a former U.S. Air Force pilot who was flying special transport assignments for the Israelis.

His fragile-looking machine took us safely to Haifa. There I was whisked to some wooden barracks and workshops, hidden amid a patch of pine trees on top of the Carmel, that served as the headquarters of the Israeli navy.

My next stop was to visit this navy's ships – all of which, it seemed, were currently in Haifa Port. Although my expectations were not great, I had quite a shock when I was taken to a faraway corner of the harbor, where two little vessels were forlornly anchored at a wharf.

"What are those?" I asked.

"The Israeli fleet," I was told.

They were both corvettes, escort vessels of the type I had so often admired on the Atlantic when, lurching and pitching amid the towering waves, they had pluckily accompanied our convoys.

Purchased from the Canadians and renamed the *Haganah* and the *Wedgewood*, they had seen service as immigrant transport vessels and were now supposed to be put in shape for combat in the shortest possible time.

I approached the first of them. There was no guard at the gangway. Nor was there a soul visible on deck. Neither could the limp, blue-and-white rag drooping from the mast have been called a flag. And just imagine a warship without cannon! There was not even an Oerlikon in sight – although on closer inspection I saw that the protective steel plating of the old machine gun emplacements was still in place.

Finally, at the entrance to the galley, I discovered the first sign of life in the form of a half-naked, potbellied fellow who was busy peeling potatoes. Asked by me where I could find the captain, he aimed a fat thumb at his own hairy chest. I left him to his spuds and tried imagining how the two corvettes could be rearmed.

Lo and behold, it didn't take long. From somewhere a few Swiss 20-mm Oerlikons turned up, and from somewhere else four World War I vintage French 10-mm cannon. Similar to the 4-inch guns on the *Nijkerk*, they unfortunately lacked proper swivels and couldn't be accurately aimed or controlled when a ship rolled. But meanwhile we were still in port, and as soon as they were installed I began training the first gun crews.

This, however, wasn't as simple as I had hoped. The sailors given me were gung-ho kibbutz boys, and they had the typical know-it-all Israeli mentality that goes all the way back to Mount Sinai, when the Jews told Moses: "We will do and we will listen." Why, in other words, listen to your instructor before first grabbing a gun and starting to shoot?

Discipline and teamwork did not come naturally to these types, no less than five of whom were required to operate the French cannon. Indeed, they were inclined to handle it with the lighthearted air of fireworks operators at a fair instead of working like the well-oiled mechanism that they were required to be in order to achieve the optimum firing rate of one shell per twenty seconds. Every movement and every grip had to be exercised until it became a reflex, turning these buccaneers into a team of robots.

"Goddamit!" I would shout like my old infantry sergeant in London. "That took thirty-four seconds. I want twenty, twenty, do you hear?! If you can't load and fire a shell every twenty seconds, you're dead! I don't give a damn if you have courage. I don't give a damn if you have enthusiasm. I want a shell in and out of that gun every twenty seconds!"

I drove them day in and day out. I pulled them out of their beds for drills in the middle of the night. "Don't think!" I screamed at them. "Machinery doesn't think. I want twenty seconds, not twenty-three!"

How unpopular I made myself I learned quite by chance when, not too many years ago, I moored my yacht in the small port of Acre north of Haifa. Alongside me was a fair-sized Israeli boat, whose skipper was a sun-tanned fellow in his fifties. He was surprised to find a Hebrew-speaking captain on a Dutch yacht, and it soon turned out that we shared a common past, for he too had served in the Israeli navy in its early years. In fact, in 1948 he had been a gunner on the *Haganah*, and he particularly remembered training with some Finnish Jew, a real bastard who had made his life miserable. "We used to call him the Goy," my new acquaintance confided, "because no Jew ever behaved like that."

"You know," I said, "I think I've heard of the fellow. If I remember correctly, though, he was Dutch, not Finnish."

"Dutch, Finnish, what does it matter?" came the answer. "Those Arctic types all have ice in their veins!"

Ice or not, I like to think that my Nordic pedantry paid off when, their course finished, my crews had their first combat experience with an ancient Egyptian cruiser near Gaza. The cruiser was covering the landing of a battalion of Egyptian troops that was supposed to break through Israeli lines toward Tel Aviv, and our corvettes were sent to engage it. Although I wasn't there with my stopwatch to make sure that my crews were firing at the prescribed rate of three shells per minute, they did hit the cruiser with several 10-mm rounds and forced her captain to retreat at full speed, leaving the exposed troops behind.

Before that, however, one of the cruiser's 12-pounders managed to hit one of our Oerlikon positions, seriously wounding a young gunner named Nehemia. Brought back to Haifa more dead than alive, he not only pulled through but lived to help launch me on my shipping career.

When the Israeli-Arab war ended in November 1948, I found myself at a crossroads. Basically, I had three choices. One was to remain in the Israeli navy and become a professional officer. A second was to go to work for either Atid or Zim, the two Israeli shipping companies in existence. A third was to go back to Holland.

In many ways, the last of these choices was the least attractive.

I loved Israel and I didn't want to leave it. I felt that I belonged there more than anywhere else. Socially, it was the ideal place for me. But economically, it was a nightmare.

The trouble was the country's socialist economy, which was in the iron grip of a bureaucracy ruled by the all-powerful Histadrut, for which "profit" was a dirty word and "entrepreneur" the equivalent of "parasite." The whole climate was anti-business. The chances of someone like me becoming an independent shipowner were nil. And when you came right down to it, I wasn't an organization man. If I couldn't run it, I didn't want it. I had put in my time in two navies and I had proved that I could be part of a machine, but at heart I was the same loner I had always been, the boy who had wanted to be like Klaus Stortenbecker.

Israel had given the Jewish People life, and for that I was grateful. But I feared that if I stayed it would stifle me.

I left.

Chapter Thirteen

Holland was not exactly waiting for me with open arms. The post-war period of reconstruction offered plenty of opportunities, but none of them was knocking on my door. I didn't know where to begin.

I went to London, where the Borchards, who had begun operating internationally again, now had their headquarters. I didn't bother to make an appointment. I walked in off the street, past an open-mouthed receptionist, and into the office of old Lucy Borchard. "My name is Hans Kahn," I said to her. "I don't want to take up your time. I just want to ask you one question. How do I become a Jewish shipowner?"

Mrs. Borchard didn't have a ready answer for that, but by the time I walked out we had established the beginning of a close business relationship that has lasted fifty years.

Not long after that, I was married and working as a shipping agent.

A shipping agent is part spy and part traveling salesman, and I was in Paris one day on the trail of some business when I dropped in on the Bienstocks. Visiting them was a relative of theirs, a young Dutch Jewish widow whose husband had been killed fighting in Israel's War of Independence. Her name was Cilly Lifschitz. She worked for the Israeli embassy in The Hague, and when I got back to Amsterdam she called me. We began spending time together, much of it in her place, where she cooked for me and did my laundry. I liked that. It made me realize how much I needed an anchorage; I had been for years like a ship without a home port. And I was also on the rebound from Molly, whom I had never quite gotten over. When Cilly suggested marriage, I agreed.

We were married in London because my father was against the match and in Holland there was a prehistoric law that you had to be practically as old as your grandfather before you could wed without parental consent. What Isidor Kahn most objected to in Cilly Lifschitz, it seemed, was that her parents were *Ostjuden*, benighted Jews from Eastern Europe, which made her unworthy of a superior *Westjude* like myself. It was unbelievable. The man had been in Bergen-Belsen and learned nothing.

Cilly and I celebrated our honeymoon in a London hotel before rather than after the wedding, in order to establish the required week's residence in England. The night before the ceremony I had an attack of doubt. I had already had too many women in my life to have any illusions about being monogamously disposed. "Look here," I said, "all this faithful stuff won't work for us." But the next day we went to Westminster Court anyway.

The fact that soon after Molly turned up in Paris, having decided to run away from her bourgeois family, didn't help get my marriage off to a smooth start. Neither did my neglecting, in my bewilderment at her sudden appearance, to tell her that I was no longer single. She ended up years later in New Delhi, the wife of an American diplomat, and even sent me a wedding invitation.

★ ★ ★

It's easy now to write about those years in a tone of wry detachment, but I was anything but wryly detached at the time. I was a tight knot of anger, ambition, frustration, and dreams. Anger, above all. It was constantly seething beneath the surface, waiting to erupt. Just let the world that had tried to kill me lay a finger on me!

My father was still staying in the Wittebrug, and one Yom Kippur, a day that both of us would once have spent in synagogue, I drove to see him. There was a circular driveway leading up to the hotel, and alongside it, a number of parking places. I left my car in one of them.

"Hey!"

I looked up to see a big policeman.

"You can't park there."

"Why not?"

"It's reserved for a minister."

"Well, that's quite all right, then," I said, putting the keys in my pocket and starting to walk to the hotel. "If it's good enough for a minister, it's good enough for me."

The policeman blocked my way. I tried walking around him. He grabbed me. Although he was so much taller than I that I practically had to leap into the air, I landed an uppercut on his jaw.

Even when he clamped a body lock on me, I fought so hard that he had to call for reinforcements. Two more cops drove up on a motorcycle with a sidecar, into which they threw me. I fought to climb out. The policeman I had punched jumped on top of me and sat on me all the way to the station house. He was even more uncomfortable than I was, because all the way I kept pinching his fat behind. The minute we got there, I told the desk sergeant that I wanted to file assault charges. "He had no right to touch me," I said. "The hotel is a private place. It was up to the doorman to ask me to move."

The sergeant wrote up a protocol saying I had attacked a policeman and asked me to sign it.

"I *counter*-attacked," I said.

He changed it, and I signed and was released on my own recognizance.

My father was distraught. "Hans," he wailed. "And on Yom Kippur!"

"It's a far better way to spend the day than asking a non-existent God for forgiveness, father," I said. "And now get me a lawyer, because I want to sue."

I didn't, of course. But the charges were dropped, and several months later, when the police balked about giving me a certificate of good conduct that I needed for a visa to Brazil, I went to the mayor and got him to overrule them.

★ ★ ★

Part of the tension in my life was due to the fact that I wasn't making spectacular progress. I had my small successes and my little failures, but after a year or two I still hadn't advanced beyond the ownership of a minuscule shipbroker's agency in Rotterdam that was in effect the refurbished kitchen of an accountant's office. Cilly and I were living in a tiny apartment in Scheveningen, and there were months when her embassy salary exceeded my brokerage earnings. We had to watch every penny, budgeting ourselves 700 gulden a month and keeping a ledger in which each expense was recorded. Rent was 85 gulden, and food averaged about 200. Every month there was an entry for "Savings," and every month it said zero. There was also a sum, too small for serious mischief, that each of us was allowed to spend privately without telling the other what it was for.

It was clear that I wasn't cut out to be an agent. The cajoling and toadying weren't for me. I couldn't stand being dependent on other people's plans and decisions. It was just another trap that life had set for me.

I began to look for a small ship that I could charter on my own and be at least the temporary boss of. The idea was to operate a regular line between Europe and Israel, which was then struggling against the Arab boycott. My first thought was to find a small coaster, the kind that in Holland was often a family business – the captain being the owner, the wife the mate, and the children the crew. Most of them sailed out of Groningen, and for a month or two I poked around there without anything coming of it. I had the distinct impression that no one was eager to entrust their vessel to a Jew.

Finally, I found a nice little ship called the *Koningshaven* that belonged to a firm in Rotterdam. The firm wanted 850 gulden a day to charter her, and the Borchards in London agreed to put up half of it. I scraped together the remaining half and was in business. One of my first cargoes was a complete circus that was going to Israel to perform. I had to move it lock-stock-and-barrel – horses, monkeys, bears, trapezes, everything. If there had been an elephant, or even a fat man, I might have gotten into heavy-lift shipping sooner.

The *Koningshaven* was a one-man operation. I lined up the cargoes, did the accounts, took care of the administration, even sailed with the ship. After half a year of this we were slightly in the red and decided not to go on with it, but the education I had received was worth my small losses.

I was thinking of what to do next when Cilly came home one day from the Israeli embassy and casually mentioned that a delegation of kibbutzniks had arrived in Holland to buy cows for the improvement of the Israeli breed.

I perked up my ears. "Where are they?"

"In Friesland."

That was a good three hours' drive away, but I was out of the house and into my old car in three minutes. A group of Israelis in the Dutch countryside was not a common sight in those days, and I was soon able to trace them to a hotel called The Golden Egg. "*Shalom, chaver!*" I said, spotting the first of them in the lobby. A Hebrew-speaking Dutchman was not a common sight in those days either, and we were soon engaged in conversation.

"How many cows are you planning to buy?"

"About sixty."

"That's quite a herd. How are you planning to get it back to Israel?"

They looked at each other. Quite obviously, they hadn't thought of it.

"Well," I said, "you can't walk them back. Suppose I were to ship them for you?"

"Would you?"

"I'd be glad to. It will cost you money, of course."

That was normally something a customer could be expected to understand, but with kibbutzniks you never knew.

"How much?"

"25,000 gulden."

They didn't bargain and I phoned Lucy Borchard from The Golden Egg and told her that I needed to charter a ship in a hurry. Not a whole boat – just the deck. I had sixty cows to put on it.

She sounded doubtful.

"Mrs. Borchard," I said, "if I can do bears and monkeys, I can do cows."

"Done!" said Lucy Borchard.

I went to a carpenter and ordered sixty wooden stalls for the deck. Then I found a veterinarian who was about to immigrate with a group of young Zionists to Israel and offered them all free passage if they would take care of the cows on the way. This time, I wasn't cleaning out the barn myself.

My total expenses for the trip were 20,000 gulden – a small profit, but my first as a charterer.

My next venture was "brokered" by Cilly too.

One evening she brought home a young Israeli who had just arrived in Holland. I rubbed my eyes when I saw him.

"Nehemia! I had given you up for dead."

It was the sailor from my gun crew who had been badly wounded by the Egyptian cruiser off Gaza. Wordlessly he took my hand and placed it against his chest. It felt as soft as a stomach. One side of his ribs was gone. "They also took out my spleen," he said laconically, "but on the whole they fixed me up nicely."

Nehemia had come to the Netherlands at the suggestion of his grandfather, the president of a large family-owned business in New York. This company was one of the largest international traders in animal hides purchased from slaughterhouses in Chicago and Argentina. After being cleaned, pickled, and neatly folded, they were sold throughout the world to be transformed into shoes, handbags, coats, leather upholstery, and whatever else. But this was no longer of any interest to Nehemia's family, which made its money solely from the sorting and selling of vast quantities of malodorous, wet, salted cattle skins.

"I'm here because we have a problem in Rotterdam," Nehemia told me. "That's where our main warehouse is. We've got a serious backlog of several thousand tons of hides waiting to be shipped, and no ships to transport them."

The reason, he explained, was that salted hides could not be carried by just any vessel. Not only did they smell bad, their salinity corroded the steel of ships' holds, which in turn left them stained with rust; the two elements did not get along. Hides, therefore, were transported in special compartments, small separate holds that were lined with wooden planking. And no ships having them were currently available. "My grandfather is at his wits' end and is sending my cousin Shimon here with full authority to... Are you listening, Hans?"

Of course I was listening. If I didn't seem to be, this was only because I was already thinking of a solution. Actually, it was a solution that anyone could have thought of – if only everyone wasn't so bloody stupid. *Hide-bound*, that was exactly the word for it! Without going into the details, I said to Nehemia:

"I'll move those hides for you immediately. Tell Cousin Shimon to contact me when he gets here."

Cousin Shimon turned out to be a pleasant fellow, small but crackling with energy. "All right," he wanted to know, "how are you going to do it?"

I wasn't giving away any free ideas. "First I want a contract," I told him.

To his credit, he didn't blink. He asked my price, which was considerably lower than the customary freight rate, pulled out a large notebook, tore out a page of it, and wrote:

"Hans Kahn, 5,000 tons of hides, Chicago to Rotterdam, within 3 months, $45 per ton."

We shook hands. "My secret," I now enlightened him, "is garbage bags."

My plan was simple and effective. I chartered a small Dutch vessel, the *Arizona*, to sail from Rotterdam to Chicago for the first 1,100 tons of hides. Then I purchased enough huge rolls of very wide black plastic sheeting – the same material, more or less, from which garbage bags are made – to line the ship's entire hold. This was not only far cheaper and quicker than building wood-lined compartments, it left more space for the hides.

But this was only half of it. Why sail an empty ship from Rotterdam to the United States? It had struck me for quite a while that, although a vast market for small European cars existed in the U.S., the cost of shipping them was disproportionately expensive: cars are a bulky cargo and could not be stacked on top of each other. Special car transporters such as exist today were a distant dream in those days.

The *Arizona*, it so happened, had a hold that was divided horizontally into two cargo decks, each just high enough for a European car. Getting in touch with the British Ford Company, I offered to come and pick up their cars at their factory on the Thames. I was told that I could take as many as I wanted – and at the same price Ford paid the scheduled liners.

The *Arizona* sailed from London to the Great Lakes, via the St. Lawrence Seaway, with a full hold of Fords and returned with a full hold of hides from Chicago. I cleared $50,000 on that first trip. That was more like it!

That was also the beginning of Hycar Lines. Chartering more ships, I started a regular liner service between Europe and Great Lake ports like Chicago, Milwaukee, Detroit, and Toronto. Many of the ships transported cars, but I kept my eyes open for new niches. And the wider I opened them, the more I saw how dumb the big carriers like Cunard and French Line were. They were totally stuck in their patterns of thought.

For instance: all the big boys were charging different prices for different items, taking more for the expensive things, like cheeses and wines, and less for the cheap bulk items like steel or fertilizer. Their reasoning was that, since the manufacturer's profit per unit was higher on cheese than on steel, the cheesemakers should pay more than the steelmakers. In effect, America's cheese eaters were subsidizing America's car makers – and everyone was going along with it.

"All right," I said. "From now on it's one price for everything!"

Naturally, my ships never saw another ingot of steel – but what did I care about steel when my holds were full of cheese? And whiskey. We transported so much Scotch that more than once the American stevedores got drunk just from inhaling the vapors when they unloaded. Within a few years Hycar was one of the biggest carriers plying between Europe and the American Middle West.

It was transporting items back from the Middle West that seriously got me to thinking about heavy-lift shipping. For example, when we moved a U.S.-made steel factory in hundreds of pieces to a shallow-water port in Greece, I couldn't help wondering whether there wasn't a more efficient way to do it. And there was also the case of Nikita Khrushchev. When the head of the Soviet Union toured America in 1959, eating hot dogs, pinching tomatoes, and doing a can-can to mock the vulgarity of Hollywood, he also visited some farms in Iowa, where he purchased an entire state-of-the-art dairy plant to take back to Russia. Only afterwards did it occur to anyone that there might be a problem shipping it. Even when disassembled it had parts too large to fit into the hold of a ship, or even to be stowed easily on deck.

Our Milwaukee agent heard about it and contacted me. "Can we do it?" he asked.

"Of course we can," I said – and sat down to figure out how.

As usual, the idea I came up with was a simple one. If the dairy plant was onloaded by shore derricks, I could remove the cranes from a cargo ship's deck, create a single, unobstructed stowage space large enough to accommodate the entire plant, and weld the cranes back when the voyage was over.

All I had to do now was find someone who would trust me to take apart and put together his vessel. There was a Danish ship owner I knew, a man called Lauritzen, who liked doing unusual things; I called him and got his permission. The captain of the ship was so agitated by the thought of his cranes being torched away that he all but lay down on the deck in the way of the workers, but another call to old Lauritzen took care of that problem too. Mr. Khrushchev received his dairy plant, the captain got his ship back with its cranes in place, and everyone was happy – except me. There *had* to be another way to do it!

By now I was a ship owner myself, having built the *Stellaprima* in 1956.

The *Stellaprima* was a small 1,200-ton vessel with a single hold and only one large hatch. (This was a concept I preferred to the common multi-hold ships, which had the advantage of permitting several shore gangs to load and unload simultaneously but the drawback of many compartments, each too small to accommodate large pieces of freight.) She was built in Germany for a million-and-a-half Deutschmarks, and I had to bluff my way to practically every one of them.

At the time I had only some 50,000 marks in cash, but there were banks that would loan you up to 60% of a new ship's value, and I went to the Netherlands Mortgage Company and asked them to finance me. I not only talked them into giving me the loan, I convinced them to grant me a commission of 5% on it for being the agent who brought me, the lender, to their doors!

That still left me 500,000 marks short, and I went to the Borchards in London and suggested taking them in as partners in return for half of that sum. They thought it over and agreed. What they didn't know was that I didn't have the other half.

I scrounged for it everywhere. I even went to an old ship chandler named Mr. Poons, who was lousy with money. "Look," I said to him, "you make a bigger percentage on any item that you sell to a ship than you do on the interest you get from a bank. And a ship is what I'm going to build. Lend me some money for it and you can be my exclusive supplier."

"Hmmmmm." Mr. Poons stroked his chin. He couldn't argue with my logic. "How much do you want?"

"50,000 Deutschmarks."

I got 30,000 at 3%.

I still didn't have enough. But I have always been a lucky bastard.

I don't know how he managed it, but my father once again had a chauffeur and a car – this time, a big Chevy with American license plates. One day, as he was cruising around Germany with it, he saw a truck that said: "Johannes Fritzen & Co. of Emden."

"Stop that truck," my father ordered his chauffeur. In his days as a Berlin banker, it seemed, he had financed the whole town of Emden – one of whose leading businessmen, Johannes Fritzen, had been not only a ship owner but a Freemason who was friendly with many Jews.

The chauffeur got the truck to pull over and my father asked its driver whether old Johannes Fritzen was still alive.

"Indeed he is," said the driver. "He lives in Leer."

My father, who had not been going anywhere in particular, told the chauffeur to take him to Leer. There he found the old man and his son Herbert, who had spent the war as an elevator man in a German naval base because the Third Reich didn't trust him to bear arms. They were bigger ship owners than ever, and my father told them about my problem and convinced them to meet me.

"That's very kind of you," I said to him. "But I have no intention of meeting them. I'd rob a bank before I'd ask a German for a cent."

"Hans, there are good Germans too," my father said.

"That may be," I replied. "But I've yet to meet one."

Nevertheless, I agreed to get together. The four of us went to a restaurant, and to my surprise I hit it off with the two men. We talked about this and that until I turned to Herbert Fritzen and said:

"Look, you people are building one bulk carrier after another. All I want is one little ship. Can't you help me?"

"We'd be glad to," Herbert said. It was as easy as that.

They lent me the rest of the money and I built the *Stellaprima*. She later worked for Hycar for most of the year, and when the Great Lakes froze over in winter, carried cargoes for Borchard Lines to Israel and back. One of the first of these was a shipload of oranges. I wished my Uncle Nehemia had been alive to see it.

★ ★ ★

My oldest son Rafi was born in 1960, and that same year I left Cilly. Our marriage hadn't worked out.

My marriage to my second wife, Caroline, lasted longer. We had two more boys, Michael in 1963, and Benjamin in 1965.

Jumbo was born in 1968. Its first ship, the *Stellanova*, was built that year and more ships were steadily added.

Even today, though, it's not a large company. Compared to really big firms like Sealand or Nedlloyd, it's a pygmy. People sometimes ask me how, in an economic world dominated by giants, I have managed to survive. The answer is, in the same way that I got to England during the war: by trusting my intuitions and learning to think a step ahead. You have to anticipate what others will do before they know themselves. You have to become them to think like them.

And people don't think alike. An American mind isn't like an English mind, and neither is like a Japanese one. I wear a different mask for each of them. If you saw me negotiating a deal over martinis in New York and over a saki in Tokyo, you would think I was two different people.

It's not just a question of mimicry. I can slap backs and put on an American accent if I have to, but that isn't the point. On the contrary: it's a question of deliberately staying slightly out of tune while putting yourself on the same wave length. If you try coming across to an American like an American, you'll simply sound like a phony to him. It doesn't matter what you're like on the outside; you have to play to the hidden thing he vibrates to. With Americans, that's power. They're the biggest power lovers in the world. When you're dealing with them you have to convey in a frank way: "I know that you're powerful, far more than I am – but my power is that I can be of use to you."

The Japanese are entirely different. They're totally ethnocentric. I never try to tell them anything. What I'm constantly beaming to them is: "Look, I'm just a poor stupid European. You have to tell me what to do." I'll never make a suggestion to them unless I can make it sound like their own idea.

It took me a while to understand the Japanese. They don't like to give work to foreigners and for a long time I couldn't break into their market.

My first real success came in the early 1970s. I was in Japan on my first visit, and I was traveling with another Western businessman on one of those bullet trains from Kyoto to Tokyo. We had planned to take the nine o'clock train, and arriving early we bought tickets – Coach 13, Seats 41 and 42. We had just finished purchasing them when a train pulled into the station. It was a cold, rainy day, and we were only too glad to take our seats in our empty car.

After a while the conductor came along and asked to see our tickets. He looked at them and shook his head.

"No good."

"What's wrong?" I asked. "Doesn't this train go to Tokyo?"

"Yes, yes. Tokyo."

"Isn't this Car 13?"

"Yes, yes. Car 13."

"Then what's the matter?"

"This Train 38. You Train 39."

"But this train is empty."

"Yes, yes. You wait 39."

We got off in the cold rain and watched the empty 8:30 train pull out of the station.

"Hmmmm," I thought. "This is interesting."

It was even more interesting in Tokyo. I had a room on the 14th floor of the best hotel in town, and I decided to stay an extra day. When I went to inform the reception desk, I was told by the clerk: "Sorry, your room is taken for tonight. We'll have to move you to another room."

I had no objection, and I packed all my bags and waited for the bellboy to come and take them. He did – to an identical room on the 13th floor! It had never occurred to the clerk that he could have given the new arrivals the 13th floor and let me stay on the 14th. No, those people had been booked for the 14th, and the 14th they would get.

That gave me an idea.

I canceled another appointment and went back that same day to a company I had been talking to about shipping a large turn-key project to an Arab country. The negotiations hadn't gotten very far, partly because I was a Dutch round-eye, and partly because the Japanese and the Arabs didn't have a contract yet and all kinds of details about the shipment were still vague. Obviously, no shipping company was going to sign with the Japanese until the Japanese signed with the Arabs. But I had learned something.

"I'll tell you what," I said. "I can give you a fixed price for the job right now. Absolutely final – there won't be the slightest change in it."

It was an unheard-of offer.

"Thank you very much, very much," said the Japanese. "But you don't understand. We have no sales contract with the purchaser yet."

"I understand perfectly," I said. "And you will want to calculate everything in advance, transportation too. Why don't I give you a 'subject-to-sale' contract? If the deal falls through, we'll tear it up."

"Eh? Ai ai! Very nice, very nice!"

I got the contract. In the end, I had to leave a ship idle for three weeks in Indonesia in order to execute it, but I had understood how their minds worked. They wanted certainty. Well, I would give it to them.

Being small isn't always a disadvantage. That's something you can see easily at sea. When a yacht like the *Ophira* and a huge freighter are on a collision course, it's the yacht that turns to avoid it. This isn't just because it has more reason to fear an accident. It also has far greater maneuverability. It can change course swiftly, while the freighter takes three miles just to stop. Big freighters can't carry out quick decisions. All they're really good at is plowing straight ahead through the water.

Big corporations are the same. On the fine points you can always outmaneuver them. I first realized that back in the days when I was running Hycar. One day, when I was flying into Detroit, I found myself sitting on the plane next to a fellow Dutchman. We got to talking and I asked him what his business was.

"I represent a Dutch firm," he said. "We make tractors."

What? He was coming to Detroit, the capital of the world's largest motor industry, to sell tractors made in Holland?

Yes, indeed. And he did it very successfully. His company made highly specialized machines for very specific tasks in small batches – production lines of no more than a few hundred vehicles. "Detroit isn't interested in such small stuff," he said. "It couldn't gear up for it efficiently even if it were. You'd have a hundred engineers, executives, and assembly line workers sweating to turn out each tractor."

It's the same with heavy-lift ships. Sure, the big boys could build them if they wanted to. But they don't want to because it's too much trouble to run them. The market is too small. There are too many complications and split-second decisions. If you're operating big container ships, each job is the same. Floating mass production, that's all it really is. With heavy-lifts, each job is different. Jumbo is a totally customer-oriented company. It has to be.

★ ★ ★

The only thing you can't outguess in my business is the sea. I don't really feel like talking about the *Gabriella*. I didn't plan to include her in this book. But it wouldn't have been right to leave her out.

I remember the year because it was the year of my son Michael's bar-mitzvah. We celebrated it in the King David Hotel in Jerusalem, opposite the walls of the old walled city. That makes it 1976.

The *Gabriella* was one of our early heavy-lift ships, a B-class vessel. She had transported a shipment of locomotives from St. John, New Brunswick to Algiers and was returning empty to pick up another consignment, when she ran into a bad storm near the Bay of Fundy. There's no way of describing an Atlantic storm to someone who hasn't been in one. It's one of the most terrifying things you can imagine.

At some point the *Gabriella* began to pitch so badly that the A-frame that had been used to secure her stabilizer while unloading in Algiers broke lose in the empty hold and punctured the inner bulkhead of the double-plated hull, causing 300 tons of ballast water to pour into the hold. In no time the ship was listing at thirty degrees. In a storm like that, this was more than enough to capsize her on a moment's notice.

The *Gabriella*'s captain issued a Mayday call, and a Norwegian freighter that was in the vicinity arrived and stood by at a distance of some 200 meters, the closest it could safely approach.

The *Gabriella*'s captain decided to abandon ship. There was no question of using the lifeboats; they would have been utterly useless in such a sea. But the *Gabriella* had two rubber dinghies of the kind that inflate automatically and these were now lowered into the water.

It's horrendous even to picture it, that ship thrown about on the waves like a marble on a seesaw while fourteen men and a woman tried descending from her onto two wildly tossing bits of rubber. Two men leaped for the first dinghy, missed it, and disappeared in the water. The remaining thirteen, including the captain, somehow managed to make it into the second dinghy.

Those two men in the water were as good as dead the minute they hit it. There was a thousand-to-one chance of finding them in those waves, and the water temperature was 6 degrees centigrade. You can't survive for more than ten minutes in that before you die of hypothermia.

And the dinghies weren't weather-proof.

If that Norwegian captain –

It's hard for me to talk about it even now.

If that Norwegian captain had had any bloody sense, he would have done the hard but right thing. He would have written those two men off and rescued the dinghy. But he didn't. He spent hours maneuvering back and forth in the storm, looking for those two corpses while more and more water filled the dinghy and the thirteen people in it began to die too. They shouted and waved at him – I suppose he thought they were cheering him on. By the time he got around to picking them up, only two of them were still alive, the captain and the second mate. Both were fat men, and that's what saved them. The captain lost a finger. The mate nearly died. He arrived in the hospital with a body temperature of 30 degrees.

I first learned all this from a cable that came to the hotel. The fate of the *Gabriella* wasn't clear yet, but the thirteen deaths were. I had to decide what to do: set out for St. John at once, or go on with my son's celebration. I would put a total damper on the bar-mitzvah by leaving, but if I stayed I would have to turn a switch in my mind and simply pretend that nothing had happened.

Lo hametim yehallelu yah, velo kol yordei dumah.

The Hebrew words came to me suddenly across a gap of forty years. They were from the Hallel, the Prayer of Praise, recited in synagogue on Jewish holidays.

The dead do not praise God, nor do those who descend into the silent abyss.

And I was still among the living.

I stayed and celebrated my son's bar-mitzvah.

When I arrived in St. John, the *Gabriella* was there waiting for me. There was even still life on her – her mascot Whiskey, who came barking down the gangplank when I boarded. By a cruel miracle, she had stayed afloat and been towed into port. Everyone would have kept alive by remaining on her. But of course her captain had no way of knowing that. Once I had heard his entire story, I had no doubt that he had made the correct decision. As soon as it became clear that the *Gabriella* wasn't going under, he had asked to be put back on her so that he could bring her into port.

But the captain of the freighter turned out to be not such a damn fool after all. He had the presence of mind to keep the *Gabriella*'s captain on his own ship and have his First Officer bring her in so as to increase his salvage claim.

The First Officer did a brilliant job – I had no complaints about him. I even gave him a golden watch as a token of my gratitude when I went aboard the freighter. It had a fancy bar and drinks were served by Chinese waiters. The Norwegian captain was there too. I didn't tell him he was responsible for the deaths of eleven people. If I had gotten started, there's no knowing where it might have ended.

I ignored him and got stinking drunk.

Chapter Fourteen

When Jani and I sail the *Ophira* by ourselves, he does the dog watch and I take the 4-to-8 shift. The sea is the one place where I don't mind rising early.

Even in my deepest sleep, I feel the boat. If a sail begins to luff, or if we're running on the motor and it coughs, I know it immediately without waking up. If it's nothing serious, I go on sleeping. Jani will take care of it. He's been with me for seventeen years, ever since I told the head of Jumbo's Crewing Department:

"Find me the best all-around deckhand on our ships and ask him if he'd like to crew for me."

Before going to bed, he hands me a cup of hot chocolate and shows me our position on the chart. We're in the Gulf of Aden, about a hundred miles out from Djibouti. There we'll pick up my son Benjamin, who is coming from Australia, and proceed to Eilat. Benjamin is a marine biologist, and we plan to do some diving in the Red Sea. There are some uninhabited coral islands off the coast of Sudan that I'm eager to explore.

I check the compass course and the global positioner, and glance at the instrument panel, the barometer, and the radar screen. Then I step out on deck for a look at the sails.

They sometimes remind me, the mainsail and big genoa, of horses in harness. They're our two basic working sails, and in the darkness they paw and snuffle as if they knew me, the genoa nervously twitching and drooping its clue, the mainsail stamping sulkily because the wind has gotten slightly behind it. I study the port tack that we're on, take the *Ophira* a few degrees off the wind, and adjust the sails with the pneumatic buttons of the hydraulic winches. They fill and stop grumbling, and I feel the *Ophira* pick up speed. The dial by her helm shows that she's gained half a knot.

It's a partly cloudy night, with only a slight milkiness on the eastern horizon behind us to indicate the approaching day. Between the clouds I can see the Dipper and Draco coiled overhead. Once, when Jumbo was already up and running, I went back to school to get a degree in astronomy. I felt that I was using only ten percent of my brain and that the rest needed exercise. In the end I had to give it up after two years at Leiden University, which is something I still regret.

There are lights to port, where a big tanker is headed for the Persian Gulf. Otherwise the sea is empty. Nothing but the slap of the waves and a warm tropical December breeze in my face.

And all the time in the world to think.

I couldn't be a more happy man. The further I get from civilization, the better I like it. The minute you tie up to a bloody pier you've got people, rats, and cockroaches.

Dawn breaks with a huge sky, colored with great drifts of dappled cloud as in a van Ruysdael landscape.

You get to see such skies only in Holland and at sea, and the Holland I love is as generous as its skies. I like to think of it as the Holland of de Ruyter, the great 17th-century Dutch admiral who sailed his fleet boldly up the Thames and took the British by surprise in London. He wasn't fighting for territory or possessions but for a principle that the Dutch always stood for: open seas and open ports. Let a man be free to follow his star!

The Dutch are just about the only European people who never expelled the Jews, or barred them, or treated them as pariahs, or dealt with them violently. I've often wondered why the two peoples have gotten along, because they're not at all alike in many ways. The Dutch are phlegmatic; the Jews are nervous and high-strung. The common denominator is their distrust of authority. They're both constantly questioning it. That's why they've gone well together, like white cheese and pepper.

The great questioners are my favorites. Call them my heroes. Abraham. Moses. Michelangelo. Rembrandt. Spinoza. Newton. Einstein. Four of them Jewish and two of them Dutch. Not a bad percentage.

There is something special about us Jews. We are the world's askers, its idol-breakers. I'm convinced the world needs us, even if the world doesn't think so. Where would Europe be without us? What are Christianity and Islam but watered-down Judaism for the masses?

Our problem is that we're good at theory and incompetent at its application. We're better at seeing to the far end of the universe than what's under our noses – especially if there are people there who want to murder us.

Thinking of the Holocaust still infuriates me. I'm not a Holocaust historian. I don't know how many tens or hundreds of thousands of Jews might have saved themselves if they had behaved differently instead of lining up to go to their deaths. Even those who went into hiding often made too passive a choice. The whole world goes on pilgrimage to the Anne Frank House on the Prinsengracht, but in 1945, when the war against the Nazis ended, I was alive and Anne was dead. She was only a few years younger than I. If she and her parents had taken their fate in their hands, instead of waiting helplessly like mice in a hole for the trap to spring on them, she might have survived.

That's why Israel has been so important to me. It's the place where Jewish helplessness stopped. Without it, I don't know what I would have done. Perhaps I would have killed someone, like the German sailor who stopped me as I was walking down the gangway of the *Atid* in Tripoli and asked, *"Hast du eine Zigarette für mich, Kamerad?"* It was the word *Kamerad* that did it.

Or like the time a neighbor of ours in Noordwijk, where I was living with Caroline, swore at my sons for kicking a football into his yard. "You rotten little Jewboys!" he shouted. I told Caroline I was going to burn his house down. She knew I might do it and convinced me to go to the police instead – who explained very nicely that since my boys were minors, their testimony in a defamation trial would not be acceptable.

My rages frightened Caroline. She wanted me to go to a psychiatrist. But I knew that no psychiatrist was going to persuade me that Hitler was a figment of my imagination.

Israel helped more than a psychiatrist. It kept me a Jew. If not for it, I would have been ashamed to be one.

I'll be glad to be back there in a few days. Several years ago I built a house in Caesarea, near where my oldest son Rafi lives with his wife and child. I spend as much time in it as I can. If home is anywhere for me on land, it's there.

The sun is well above the horizon. It's going to be a hot day. It's already warm enough to strip to my shorts and do my exercises.

In my bedroom in Amsterdam I have an exercise bicycle. It helps keep a 74-year-old man in shape. But stretching and bending in the prow of the *Ophira* is much better. Anyone looking at me might think me an old sun-worshiper, holding my arms up to the sky and bowing again and again.

I check the sails one more time, make another little adjustment, and go humming happily to the galley to slice myself a mango for my breakfast. *Yah-yah-yah-yah-yah-yah-yah...* it's a bit like one of those Hasidic chants that I learned in the *shtieblakh* of the Nieuwe Kerkstraat.

By now Jani is up and about, and after marking our position and filling out the log I turn the watch over to him and settle down with a book by Stephen Hawking in the double-curved teak love seat behind the helm.

Books about science are what I like to read most. Even if I am the author of the Kahn Rule, I don't have the mathematics for the technical stuff in the physics journals, but for a layman I'm pretty good. Good enough, in fact, to know there's something wrong when Hawking says, writing of current theories about the basic subatomic building blocks from which all matter is made:

"In particular, there is a largest such theory, the so-called $N=28$ extended supergravity. This contains 1 graviton, 8 3/2 spin particles called gravetinos, 28 spin-1 particles, 56 spin-1/2 particles, and 70 particles of spin zero. And even large as these numbers are, they are not large enough to account for all the particles that we seem to observe."

Phhhtttthhhschsch!

That's a Bronx cheer for Mr. Hawking.

What inelegance! I don't believe a word of it. All those particles spinning irreducibly around like little dervishes are pure polytheism. No Jewish God would have created such a messy universe. There's got to be a simpler principle of construction, something like what Spinoza had in mind when he wrote, "There cannot be two or more substances, but only one possessing the same nature or attribute."

It's a pity Spinoza wasn't born a few centuries later. Or even ten years later, so that he could have read Newton's *Principia*. If he had, he would have realized that what he called God is the system of universal natural law. I once started writing a book about that. It's in a safe right now, but perhaps I'll finish it some day.

There's a ratcheting sound behind me. I know without turning that it's Jani, paying out the fishing line from the rod attached to the taffrail. With a little luck we'll catch something for supper, although you never know. Sometimes you go three or four days without a bite and sometimes there are three or four of them in an hour. After catching the first fish, I put the rod away. I'd rather have fish in the ocean than in my freezer.

I return to my book. Ah, that's much better! He now believes, Mr. Hawking, that there may be "discontinuous space-time quanta" – in other words, that once you cut space and time up into small enough units, you may arrive at infinitesimal quantities that cannot be divided any further.

You'll find that theory in the safe with my Spinoza book. I wrote it down thirty years ago. I always thought it the only way to resolve Zeno's paradox, the ancient riddle that states that an arrow can never reach its target, since before it does it must travel half the way, before it travels half the way it must travel a quarter of the way, and so on. Time and space quanta are like the stones you cross a stream on – without them, you could never get to the other side.

I'm glad that Hawking has gotten around to agreeing with me. That calls for a cigar!

Going to the cabin for one, I see two messages on the telex machine. One is from my German-born wife Lilo, who lives in our house near Geneva, where Jumbo has its main financial office. The other is from our Rotterdam office and includes the latest schedule of our ships. I look it over, type a few comments on my computer, and telex them back.

The wind is almost dead astern now, a nice breeze of fifteen knots, but we'll have to shift to a starboard tack to stay on course.

Even with all the hydraulics jibing isn't easy on the *Ophira*, because to keep the big mast from toppling in a sudden gust it has a backstay that has to be moved. I work the mainsheet and the traveler while Jani unties the stay from the starboard winch and moves it to port so that we can bring the boom around.

Then it's time for lunch and a nap.

★ ★ ★

I'm awoken by a light whirring, and at the same time I hear Jani dash from the cabin to the stern.

There's a fish on the line.

By the time I join him at the taffrail, he's already reeling it in. My eyes follow the angle of the line to a faint gleam beneath the surface of the water some fifty meters behind us.

"Dorado!" says Jani.

He reels, gives some slack as the rod bends like a bow, reels again. Slowly the outline of the fish grows clearer, as if riding the underside of a wave. Then, tugged by the hook, it breaches the water with its head. At the end of the barely visible line, it seems to be racing toward us of its own free will as though gamely trying to catch up with us.

They're not big fighters, dorados. Not like tunas, which will give you a real battle. This one only bucks a little at the end, as the shortening line yanks it upward. Then it's out of the water, wriggling by the side of the boat. I smash its head hard with the winch handle, splattering the *Ophira*'s hull with blood, and Jani hauls it still flopping onto the deck, removes the hook from its jaw, runs a rope through its gills, and hangs it back over the side to finish bleeding while he hoses off the deck and hull and goes to the galley for his knife.

"Ten kilo!" he says.

I watch the life seep out of the fish. For a short while it's a nosegay of colors, sky-blue on top with pink and golden-green flecks and white in the belly with pink and blue. Then, quick as a fading rainbow, it turns a dull green-gold, its big mouth open in a last protest.

I look to see if any sharks have been attracted by the blood. There's no sign of them in the neighborhood.

I like sharks. Any diver can tell you that, apart from the tigers and the great whites, they aren't very dangerous as long as they don't smell blood. Why tangle with a diver in a bulky suit when there are plenty of more inviting fish around?

The only time to worry is when they start circling. That's a sign that they've taken an interest in you and that you had better keep an eye on them. Most of all, you musn't turn your back on them. They like to attack from the rear – very human of them! Sometimes they'll make a pass at you just to see what you're made of. They'll come at you very fast and veer off at the last second and brush by you. You have to stand your ground and hope that they don't cut you, because their skin is quite abrasive even if it looks smooth and shiny.

I like to swim with them, although not as much as Benjamin, who thinks nothing of jumping off a boat into a whole school of them.

Jani returns with his knife and a bucket, hauls the dorado back on deck, and begins cleaning it. When he's through cutting it into steaks, we'll have to move the mainsail again because the wind is shifting back to starboard.

There's an Arab dhow off to port and a container ship crossing our bow. Even at a distance you can see how huge it is. Those bloody stupid box carriers just keep getting bigger and bigger! First they carried two thousand boxes, then three thousand, now it's six thousand – each of them weighing up to twenty tons. Some of the big boys are now three hundred meters long, the length of three football fields.

That's the force of competition. It's more economical to carry two thousand boxes than one thousand and three thousand than two thousand. But it only works if there aren't too many ships doing it. There's already a surplus of tonnage, and more and more of it is being built all the time. They'll cut each other's throats and lose billions, and in the end there will be only a few big firms left. The big ships will call at fewer and fewer ports; everywhere else will be serviced by feeder lines. There'll be a slaughter. The middle-sized companies will be dead.

That suits me fine. The more the big boys invest in their boxes, the better we'll do.

Sometimes I worry what will happen to Jumbo after me. It will go on running smoothly, I have no doubt, but without new ideas it will stagnate. Someone young and ambitious may come along and push it aside.

Well, so be it. That's life.

Still, if a young man walked into my office today as I did into the Borchards' and asked how he could become a ship owner, I'd probably shake my head. There aren't many opportunities left in the field. I'd tell him to look elsewhere. There are always niches for a smart entrepreneur who believes in himself – just look at Bill Gates. For instance, I'd suggest he think about... but no, I wouldn't. Why give away free ideas? The one I almost mentioned just now is a pet notion of mine that I've been turning over in my head for years. Perhaps one day my son Michael will do something with it.

You don't make money by thinking about money. That's something most people don't understand. You make money by thinking about ideas. If you have a new concept, the money will come by itself.

And ideas are something I've been good at. My problem is feelings, not thoughts. I've never been good at getting out of emotional tangles.

Perhaps this is why I've had three marriages. You can't communicate with a woman through ideas. Sometimes I think that a man's brain is closer to a male chimpanzee's than to a female's of his own species. I suppose that's the reason I've gotten along better with my sons than with their mothers. They're stubborn, like me, each in his own way.

But my marriage to Lilo has been different. At first it seemed crazy that I had gone and fallen in love with a German woman. What a joke for life to play on me! For a long time I went about telling people that she was Danish, because I couldn't bring myself to admit the truth to them.

I don't do that any more. And since I'm living with her, I've become calmer. I may still be quick to lose my temper, but I haven't had one of my old, blind rages for years.

Jani is finished with the fish. He takes the bucket of dorado steaks to the galley and together we move the mainsail.

I settle back into my seat with Stephen Hawking, and Jani brings me a big tumbler of chilled Dutch *jenever* and a plate with thin slices of carrot. That's my regular sundowner.

I suppose you could call Jani my Man Friday and me his Robinson Crusoe, but in Indonesia I would be known as his *tuan*. That's a kind of feudal lord who commands absolute devotion from his vassal and has absolute responsibility for him in return. If you've served your *tuan* faithfully and are in trouble or in need, the *tuan* is expected to take care of you. Jani expects no less from me, and I've never let him down.

He's totally attuned to me. Often I feel him watching me, straining to make out my needs and desires – and as soon as he senses that I am satisfied and no longer require him, he goes off into a Jani-world of his own that I have not the slightest access to. He would no more think of sharing it with me than I would think of talking to him about gravetinos.

He's a crackerjack helmsman, navigator, mechanic, cook. And yet though he's younger than I, he's quicker to tire under stress. He's stronger but has less stamina. When we're fighting a bad storm, I do longer watches than he does, because he needs the extra sleep more than I do.

We've been in some pretty rough weather together. I remember once when we were anchored in the rocky bay of a Greek island, south of the Peloponnesus. There was a very narrow entrance to it, facing south and flanked by rocks, and we had been told by the local fishermen that at that time of year the bad winds came only from the north. In the middle of the night, though, it began blowing like hell from the south and we started dragging our anchor toward shore. We couldn't head for the open sea because we couldn't see the entrance in the dark, and all night we kept drifting closer to shore and casting the anchor again and again. In the first light of dawn we saw that we were barely ten meters from the rocks. The wind was a good forty knots by then and getting stronger.

We began to head out of the bay. The wind was so fierce that we had to use the sails together with the motor to make any headway against it. We had to tack every fifty meters or so while zigzagging toward the entrance, wearing harnesses to keep from going overboard, and each time we tacked the boat lost momentum and the wind pushed us back again. It was more tiring than the worst storm in the open sea. Jani was on the verge of collapse by the time we were out of the bay, and I wasn't in much better shape myself.

Even after that, it took us a whole day to make Cape Sounion. The Mediterranean is a bastard of a sea. It sloshes around like water in a tub and makes very steep, close waves. You zoom to the top of them, like in one of those high-speed elevators, and crash right off the edge.

Storms exhilarate me. I become extra calm in them, the way I sometimes did in the war. My heartbeat slows to a crawl. I stop feeling entirely and become nothing but a thinking mind.

I don't mean to romanticize. In any storm there's a moment when you say: "What am I doing here? *Godverdomme*, I wish it would stop!" But if I could choose my own death, I would choose to die in a storm.

Not yet, though. I'm not ready for it. There's too much that I haven't figured out. I need another fifty years.

The question of government, for instance. I've been wrestling with that for a long time. I hate to admit it, but some government is necessary. Not for social justice or morality – that's baloney. Society never did a thing for me. I believe only in individuals and in enlightened self-interest. The sole morality I know is, "Be good to your friends, do your best to harm your enemies, and always keep your word." I don't need government for that.

Governments are necessary for two things. One is to defend the sheep against the wolves. They're dumb, the sheep, but you can't just leave them defenseless. The other is to help transmit knowledge. If there weren't organized transmission of knowledge, civilization would collapse.

The less government, the better. I still haven't worked out the proportions. I'm thinking about it.

Jani brings me another *jenever*. There are four fingers of Dutch gin in each.

"I'll set up the Hannukkah candles," he says.

"How many tonight, Jani? Five?"

"Six, Mr. Kahn."

He knows better than I do. When we light Sabbath candles on the *Ophira*, Jani puts on a yarmulka and says "Amen" after I recite the blessing. He's an honorary Jew.

The sun is slowly dropping straight ahead of us. I watch it go down. There's hardly a cloud left of the great herd that rode through the sky this morning. Perhaps there'll be a green flash tonight.

That's something you see only in the tropics. You need an absolutely clear western horizon for it. It takes place immediately after the sun has set. The sun plunges into the sea, and right afterwards – pop! – there's a brilliant green incandescence.

The whole thing lasts a fraction of a second. There are people who say it's an optical illusion, the aftereffect on the retina of the intense orange of the sun. But that isn't true. It's a real color in the sky, caused by an upward refraction of the sun's rays through the water – as real, that is, as anything is real in this world.

Because what is reality? Each one of us creates it for himself. There is no absolute Truth.

There are questions. And I believe that for every question there is an answer. I suppose you could call that my religion.

I hand Jani my tumbler. "I'll have another," I say.

He brings it to me. He doesn't start to worry until the fourth.

The bottom rim of the sun touches the horizon. It won't be long now.

"Hans!"

For a moment I don't recognize the voice. Since I know I'm only imagining it, it can't do any harm to reply.

"How did you find me here?"

"It was the logical place to look," says Dr. Neubauer.

"It would have been more logical to look in Amsterdam."

"Not at all. You're easier to spot here. And going back to Amsterdam is too sad."

"I know. I know. I stay away from the old Jodenbuurt too. I live a few minutes' walk from it and do all I can to avoid it. But I did try to find you there once."

"You did?" Is he touched, or hurt that I didn't try harder?

"Yes. I went back to the old street. Nothing is the same. It's horrible. The Weesperstraat – they've ripped everything down, made a wide thoroughfare of it with modern buildings. And that old flour mill across the canal from us: gone too. I wasn't even sure about the house. I couldn't remember if it was number 22 or 24. They share one entrance and I stood looking at it and asking myself: When we walked to the staircase, did we go to the left or to the right? Did we go left or right? I couldn't remember."

"It was number 28, Hans."

"28!"

"Yes. But you're a busy man. You've had a full life. You can't be expected to remember such things."

"That's not so. I may not think of you often, but you're the only person... the one person who..."

"...You never stopped arguing with?"

"Why should I argue with you? I'm half again as old as you were when you died."

"The things I believed in didn't die."

"Yes, they did. They died with you and Yehoshua."

"Ah, Hans! The God of Israel is a living God."

"Do me a favor and don't talk bloody nonsense! We're not at your Friday night dinners any more. This whole business of a God who cares for our immortal souls.... *Phhhtttthhhschsch!*"

"A God who made the Universe."

"Nothing made the Universe. That's already positing something outside it. The Universe is by definition everything. Read Spinoza."

"As if I didn't know Spinoza as well as you do! Where does his Seventh Proposition that the essence of Substance necessitates existence come from, if not from Maimonides' Second Proof of God?"

"God is the Organizing Principle of Everything. He doesn't care about you or me."

"But you still care about Him. Come on, Hans. Those mystical, out-of-the-body experiences. Those Sabbath candles."

"*Mama mia!* Now I'm accused of mysticism! Look here, there's nothing mystical about it. It's a matter of total self-control. If I decide to lie down now and go to sleep, I'll be asleep in a minute. If I decide to wake in half-an-hour, I'll wake in half-an-hour. If I decide to separate my mind from my body, I'll be a mind without a body."

"Those visits with your grandson to the synagogue in Caesarea..."

"I want the boy to be a Jew, to know about his people's heritage."

"From the man who believes only in individuals! Who despises authority and governments but loves Israel!"

"All I've ever wanted for the Jews was for them to be an individual among the nations. To behave like one when they're threatened."

"Violently."

"Brutally! With as much force as it takes to keep from being threatened again."

"And compassion for others?"

"A handicap to survival."

"But you survived because of it. That French priest. That Canadian wing commander."

"I was an *Engelandvaarder*! Compassion is for the weak."

"I was weak."

"No. You were strong of intellect. I was in awe of you. Einstein would never have survived a concentration camp either. But the weak will kill you if they can. They'll drag you down like a drowning man when you try to save him."

"Like that Jew in the Pyrenees."

"Yes."

"Or that young couple on the Rijnstraat."

"Forget about them. That's something I don't want to talk about."

"I'm afraid you have to."

"Please. Can't we skip it?"

"You're crying, Hans. Tell me why you're crying."

"I was responsible for their deaths. I should never have helped them. It wasn't safe."

"They would have died anyway. You were like a person in a car with bad brakes who is asked to take a sick child to the hospital. You're not to blame if the car had an accident."

"With no brakes. None at all! Look, you can explain it this way... you can explain it that way... never mind. Helpless people are dangerous. I hate them!"

"But why do they make you so angry?"

"Because they disturb my complacency. They throw me into conflict with myself."

"Then that conflict is already inside you."

"Goddam it! You asked me a question. I gave you an answer. Don't explain it like a bloody psychiatrist."

"I was simply pursuing it."

"All right. I hate them because they bring out a part of me that I've tried to fight all my life. You know, this is ridiculous. You're not even real, and I'm baring myself to you as I've never done to anyone. Helping people makes me vulnerable."

"So does loving them."

"Love is bullshit."

"Of course. All those women. But your sons? Your wife?"

"That's purely biological... No, I'll tell you what it is. It's pure egotism. Here, let me think for a minute. All right. I have it. Love is the identification with another person to the point that that person's happiness is identical with your own. How's that for a definition?"

"Jani?"

"What Jani and I feel isn't love. It's symbiosis. That's more than love. That's two lives depending on each other."

"That little boy and girl on the Rijnstraat?"

"I already told you. I don't want to talk about them."

"I understand, Hans. I have to go now. I'm pleased to see that you're not quite the person you think you are."

"What is that supposed to mean?"

"I have to go now, Hans."

"Wait. Just a minute! Yehoshua..."

Is he still there?

"Please tell him..."

The top rim of the sun touches the horizon.

Then it's gone.

If it's going to happen, it will happen now.

But it doesn't. There's no green flash. Just an empty sea and a cloudless sky.

It doesn't matter. There will be lots more evenings like this to wait for it.

Glossary

Ack-Ack   Colloquial for anti-aircraft gunnery.

Aliyah Bet   Immigration 'B' i.e., "illegally" conducted immigration in contravention of British immigration restrictions.

Anschluss   The movement in both Germany and Austria to unite the two countries in a Greater Germany. The actual plebiscite took place on April 20, 1938. 99% of the population of both countries voted for Anschluss and the Nazi Party of the Fuhrer, Adolf Hitler.

Bergen-Belsen   A labour camp in north-west Germany. It was originally intended for political prisoners. As Germany retreated, more and more prisoners from other camps were evacuated here. The camp commandant, Joseph Kramer, was tried and executed in November 1945.

Chayes   Literally the Hebrew word for wild beasts, entered into Amsterdam slang as an allusive expression for persons behaving inhumanly.

Grüne Polizei   "Green Police" so-called because of their green uniforms: a para-military body whose task consisted mainly of the brutal enforcement of the oppressive measures taken by the occupiers.

Histadrut   (General Federation of Jewish Labour) Founded in Palestine in 1920. It was intended to be a general labour organization, in which all political parties could cooperate on labour, economic and cultural issues, but evolved into a socialist state within the state.

Ijmuiden A small Dutch port of the entrance to the North Sea Canal, leading to the port of Amsterdam.

Jewish Agency Established originally by the Zionist Organization, and later to assume quasi-governmental functions in the period of the Mandate. Now, inter alia, overseas Jewish immigration to Israel.

Jewish Council An institution invented by the Nazis, consisting of a body of prominent volunteer Jews, to whom the Nazis delegated the administration and to a certain extent even the execution of their anti-Jewish directives.

Jonkheer The lowest title of Dutch nobility corresponding approximately to squire.

Kristallnacht (Crystal-Night) During the night of 9/10 November 1938, 'spontaneous' anti-Jewish terror was launched throughout Germany. The official toll was 74 Jews killed or seriously injured, 20,000 arrested, 815 shops and 171 homes destroyed, 191 synagogues set on fire. The total damage was 25 million marks, of which over 5 million was for glass, hence the term *Crystal Night*.

Macher A Yiddishism, often used pejoratively, to indicate a boss, or someone who runs things.

Maquis French, literally the dense undergrowth of prickly bushes covering much of the island of Corsica. Used during World War II to denote the French underground resistance movement.

Mishpoche Family, in the wider sense.

Nehemia de Lieme Prominent Dutch Zionist of the early days of Zionism. Member of the executive of the World Zionist Movement during World War I.

Oerlikon A heavy machine gun of Swiss make, 20 mm bore, used extensively by Allied vessels as a primary anti-aircraft weapon.

Palestine The name the British gave the territory under their mandate to facilitate the establishment of a Jewish homeland.

Pukka Sahib British colonial slang from India denoting colonial VIP.

RAF British Royal Air Force

Razzia   Sudden raid or round-up organized by Nazi occupying forces to pick up and arrest any "suspect".

Revs   Propeller revolutions per minute.

Sabra   A native-born Israeli. The word means a cactus plant and the reference is to the image of someone prickly on the outside and sweet inside.

SD   Acronym for Sicherheitsdienst (Security Service), the operative arm of the Gestapo.

Sieg Heil (Hail Victory!)   A triumphant chant adopted by and for Nazis.

Sonar   A device to identify and locate underwater objects by producing high frequency sound bursts and analysing the resulting echo.

'Stalin Organ'   was more popularly known in the Red Army as a Katiusha (i.e. Little or Darling Katey).

Talmud   The collection of rabbinic writings, which include the Mishnah and the Gemara and, together with the Torah, constitute the basis of religious authority. The word stems from the Hebrew root for "to learn".

Todt Organisation   Named after Fritz Todt (1891-1942), head of construction for the Third Reich's Four-Year Plan and inspector-general of the road and highway system. Todt became Reich Minister for Munitions.

Torah   The word is used to refer to a scroll on which the first five books of the Hebrew scriptures are written and read in synagogue. It also refers to these first five books in any edition and, more broadly, the entire corpus of religious law and learning, written as well as oral.

Vichy France   Part of France that, after the French defeat in 1940, was originally not occupied by the German army and governed, instead, by a French government under General Petain. The border between occupied France and Vichy France was the so-called *Ligne de Demarcation*. In late summer, 1942, the Germans also occupied Vichy France, however, leaving the collaborationist French government in nominal control.

Völkischer Beobachter (Nationalist Observer)   Subscribing to this newspaper was a symbol of loyalty to the Nazi Party. It represented 'received truth'.

WAAF Acronym for Women's Auxiliary Air Force, a military organisation for young women volunteers, employed by the RAF in support functions.

Walkie-Talkie The first handheld wireless telephone.

Westerbork The Dutch transit camp for deportés.

Wren A member of the Women's Royal Naval Service, a military organization for young women volunteers, employed by the Royal Navy in support functions.

Yishuv (from the Hebrew root 'to sit'). The word has been adapted and readapted. It was used to refer (collectively) to the Jewish community of Palestine in its entirety.

Youth Aliyah A programme to resettle and train Jewish youth in Palestine. It saved tens of thousands of Jewish children from the Nazis, and continues to resettle Jewish youth in Israel and educate them.

Zero Type of Japanese fighter plane.

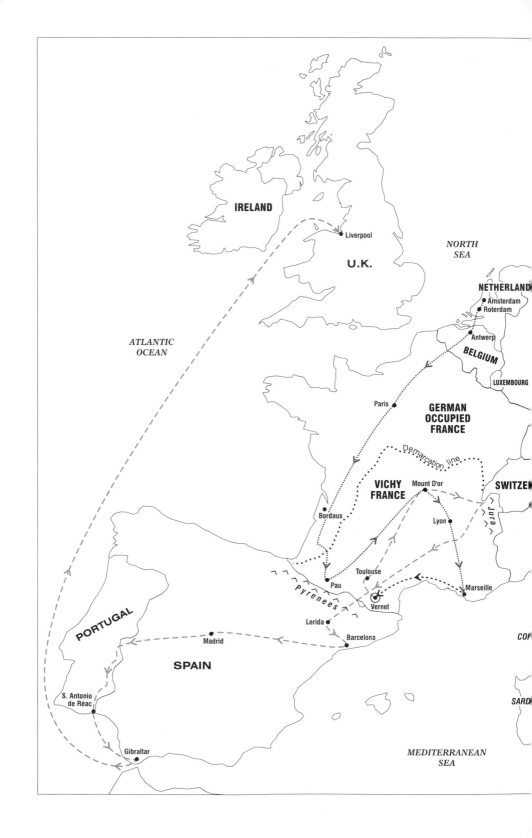